Elmar Kutsch

Barriers to Project Risk Management

Elmar Kutsch

Barriers to Project Risk Management

Processes, Techniques and Insights

VDM Verlag Dr. Müller

Imprint

Bibliographic information by the German National Library: The German National Library lists this publication at the German National Bibliography; detailed bibliographic information is available on the Internet at http://dnb.d-nb.de.

Cover image: www.purestockx.com

Publisher:
VDM Verlag Dr. Müller Aktiengesellschaft & Co. KG, Dudweiler Landstr. 125 a, 66123 Saarbrücken, Germany,
Phone +49 681 9100-698, Fax +49 681 9100-988,
Email: info@vdm-verlag.de

Produced in USA and UK by:
Lightning Source Inc., La Vergne, Tennessee, USA
Lightning Source UK Ltd., Milton Keynes, UK
BookSurge LLC, 5341 Dorchester Road, Suite 16, North Charleston, SC 29418, USA

ISBN: 978-3-639-06146-8

ACKNOWLEDGEMENTS

"O CAPTAIN! My Captain! Our fearful trip is done; The ship has weather'd every rack, the prize we sought is won; The port is near, the bells I hear, the people all exulting, While follow eyes the steady keel, the vessel grim and daring: But O heart! heart! heart! O the bleeding drops of red, Where on the deck my Captain lies, Fallen cold and dead."

Walt Whitman (1819–1892).

I wish to express my deep gratitude and appreciation to the following as without them the completion of this study would not have been possible.

My colleague Dr. Harvey Maylor, for being in the unfortunate position of dealing with my stubbornness. I thank him for his constructive comments, patient guidance and recommendations.

Dr. Kate Blackmon, for consistently pushing me to maintain my motivation and ambition, throughout both my up and down periods and for challenging my arguments to ensure the grounding in logic of this study.

The study could not have been completed without the many interviewees and respondents to the questionnaire who gave their precious time and provided valuable information. Special thanks to those who especially helped me to get to grips with statistics which is not my strongest area.

Finally, I wish to dedicate this study to my parents Irene and Leo Werner Kutsch and my brother Leo for their confidence, support, love and patience. I am grateful for the strength and love of my girlfriend Ivana, who has suffered due to the physical separation, and for not expecting too much of me through out my long periods of absence. I acknowledge the lost time while being apart from you all.

TABLE OF CONTENTS

Table of contents

LIST OF FIGURES

LIST OF TABLES

1. INTRODUCTION

A *project* is an undertaking to create "something that does not yet exist" (Young, 1998, p. 12), ideally with a defined scope that needs to be delivered within a defined time at an agreed cost (Buttrick, 1997). Projects may be considered to have failed when the expected scope, cost and time targets are not met. In particular *IT projects*, the provision of a service to implement IT systems and solutions, including a variety of hardware and software products (Howard, 2001), have a high rate of failure (McGrew & Bilotta, 2000; Whittaker, 1999); a third of all software projects in 1995 were terminated before completion and more than 50 percent of the projects cost approximately double the estimate (Whittaker, 1999).

According to practitioners surveyed by Whittaker (1999), IT project failure is most commonly attributed to a lack of top management involvement, a weak business case and inadequate risk management. The highest ranked factor for project failure (Whittaker, 1999) is *project risk management*, the systematic process of identifying, analysing, and responding to risks as project related events or conditions which are not definitely known and which have the potential of adverse consequences on a project objective (Project Management Institute, 2004). Despite well established and accepted project risk management processes such as PMI 2000, Prince 2 or PRAM, project managers commonly perceive these processes as not effective for managing project uncertainties (Pender, 2001; Whittaker, 1999).

1.1. Project outcomes and the role of project management

A project is a "vehicle of change" including a defined scope, which needs to be delivered in a defined time at an agreed cost (Buttrick, 1997, p. 20). Key features characterising a project are: a project is unique; each one will differ from every other in some respect, projects have specific objectives (or goals) to achieve, they require resources and have budgets, they have schedules and require the effort of people and measures of quality apply (Field & Keller, 1998). However, these common elements of a project are also included in routine operations except for one – uniqueness (Turner, 1993). In contrast to a "pure" operation, a project includes a certain degree of uniqueness and dissimilarity as Cicmil (1997, p. 392) noted: "In any project situation, there is always someone (the client, customer) who has a unique need (an idea) for something new, and some, often vague, expectations about tangible outcomes (the creation) of it...". As Figure 1.1 shows, pure project management, the application of knowledge, skills, tools, and techniques (Project Management Institute, 2004), is applied to a project, which includes 0% similarity, 100% dissimilarity to any previous project conducted and only one project unit is produced. This implies that in this extreme case no related historical information exists (Nylen, 1999). Associated with a dissimilar or unique project situation is the element of uncertainty and risk (Nylen, 1999; Turner, 1993), which forms the conceptual foundation of this study.

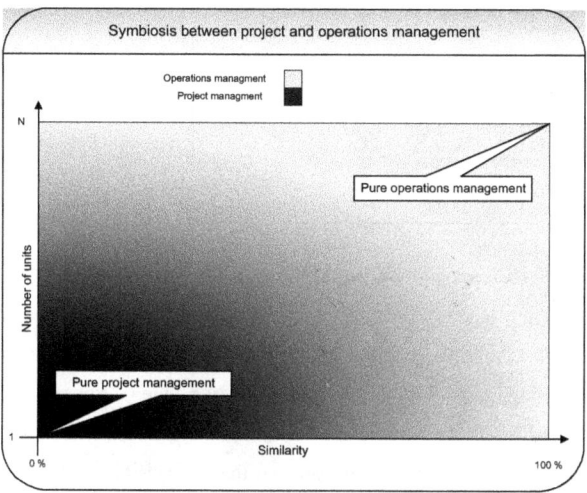

Figure 1.1: Symbiosis between project and operations management
(Adapted from Nylen, 1999, p. 125; Slack, Chambers, & Johnson, 2001)

Projects are often not completed on time and on budget (Kartam & Kartam, 2001). The result of one survey revealed that only twenty-six percent of all IT development projects are completed on time and budget (Hormozi, McMinn, & Nzeogwu, 2000). Another survey revealed that twenty-five percent of all software projects are cancelled right from the beginning and eighty percent run over their budgets.

Every two years, the Standish group publishes in their "Chaos" chronicles the outcome of IT projects. Figure 1.2 depicts the outcome of 30,000 IT projects in the United States. The project outcomes are measured by their completion on time, budget and scope.

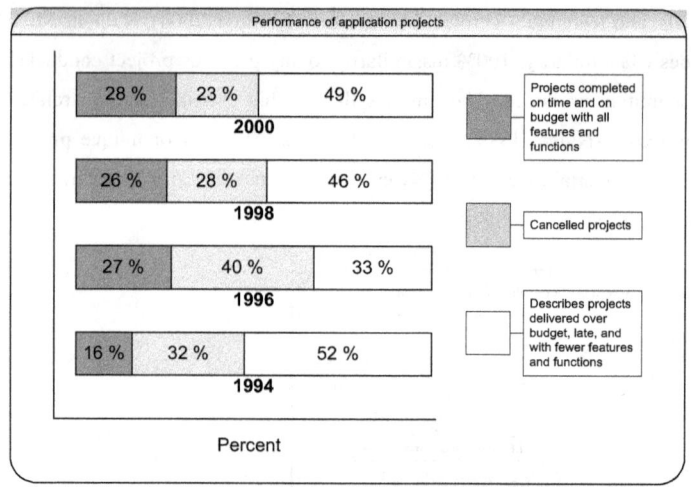

Figure 1.2: 30,000 application projects in the large, medium and small cross-industry U.S. companies tested by the Standish Group since 1994.
(PMnetwork, 2003, p. 18)

Overall, the "Chaos" study reveals that in 2000 more than seventy percent of all projects failed to meet budget, cost and scope targets. The TechRepublic Study by the Gartner Group paints a similar picture. In 2000, 1,275 North American IT specialists were asked about the outcome of internal IT projects. The analysis of the data showed that forty percent of all IT projects were considered to have failed. The projects considered to have failed by the Gartner Group were suspended on average after fourteen weeks and by this time on average $1,000,000 had already been invested.

Several organisations such as the KPMG, the Standish Group, and the Daily Telegraph have investigated possible reasons for project failure. In 1994, KPMG Management Consulting conducted a telephone survey including more than 1,200 British companies from different economic sectors. The most predominant reasons for project failure are shown in Table 1.1.

Reasons for project failure	Percentage[1]
Project objectives not adequately defined	51 %
Bad planning and estimation	49 %
The application of new technologies	45 %
Inadequate project management methods	42 %
Lack of experienced members in the project team	42 %
Wrong cast of project leader position	35 %
Inadequate software development methods	35 %
Over ambitious project objectives	34 %
Wrong casting of project team	34 %
Bad communication between project team members	32 %
Lack of knowledge about project problems at the upper management	30 %

Table 1.1: Reasons for project failure – KPMG survey
(KPMG Management Consulting, 1994)

The results from the IT Runaway study published by KPMG as shown in Table 1.2 shows significant overlapping with the results of the Standish Group:

Reasons for project failure	Percentage
Incomplete requirements	13.1 %
Lack of end-user involvement	12.4 %
Lack of resources	10.6 %
Unrealistic expectations	9.9 %
Lack of support through management	9.3 %
Changes in requirements and specifications	8.7 %
Lack of planning	8.1 %

Table 1.2: Reasons for project failure – Standish group survey
(The Standish Group International Inc., 1995)

Finally, a survey conducted by the Daily Telegraph also demonstrated that around 40% of all IT projects in Great Britain fail because of inadequately defined project objectives, lack of priorities, unclear responsibility of availability and quality of team members, the policy of the provider, changes during the project, culture of assignment of guilt, lack of support for the project manager and bad communication (KPMG Great Britain, 2001).

---

[1] Multiple answers were possible

The previously mentioned three studies about the reasons for project failure have been carried out by different organisations with methodologies which remain unknown to the author so criticism about their preciseness and accurateness is not possible. Nevertheless, although reasons for project failure as given in Table 1 and 2 are manifold, a picture emerges of typical project risks (Gaulke, 2002).

Project management has the purpose of "planning, organising and controlling activities so that the project is completed as successfully as possible in spite of all the risks" (Lock, 2000, p. 3). Standards in project management are various. Most dominant are the best practice standards of the Project Management Institute (PMI), the UK Government Centre for Information Systems and the British Standards Institution. Most of these institutions offer similar if not identical standards for project management. PMI offers a standard that is widely used and is considered to be a competency standard (Pender, 2001). The PMI standard "A Guide to the Project Management of Knowledge" (Project Management Institute, 2004) includes nine areas of project management knowledge:

Project integration management relates to the process of ensuring that various elements of the project such as project plans are coordinated. It includes tasks such as the documentation of the actions necessary to define, prepare, integrate, and coordinate all subsidiary plans into a project management plan.

Project scope management is primarily concerned with the definition and controls about what will or will not be included in the project. It relates to the planning, definition and verification of the scope of the project.

Project time management is composed of process stages which are claimed to ensure the timely completion of the project. It encompasses activity definition, activity sequencing, estimation of activity resource, estimation of activity duration, schedule development and schedule control.

Project cost management supports the project manager in completing a project within the approved budget including the three activities of cost estimating, budgeting and controlling.

Project quality management ensures the project's success in meeting quality targets focusing on quality planning and assurance, and quality control.

Project human resource management includes the processes such as human resource planning necessary to effectively use the individuals in the project. Individuals can be project stakeholders such as sponsors, partners, sub contractors and customers.

Project communications management provides processes to ensure effective communication in terms of establishing critical links among individuals that are important for project success.

Project risk management is a systematic process which includes the identification, analysis and response to project risks.

Project procurement management involves the processes of determining what to purchase or acquire and determining when and how.

Overall, nine key processes are suggested by PMI for ensuring[2] the successful completion of a project during the stages of initiating, planning, executing, controlling and closing the project. However, despite well-established project management processes, a substantial number of projects fail because of the risks such as those displayed in Table 1.1 and Table 1.2, leading to the practical problem of this research which is that project risk management appears to be inadequate. The resulting research problem and questions are introduced in the next section.

1.2. Personal motivations for this study

My work as an IT consultant in the field of project management in Germany gave me a chance to apply my theoretical knowledge about project risk management on practical IT projects.

However, having been prepared for project risk management in theory during my Master of Business Administration studies, I realised that dealing with project risks is rather confusing and frustrating for me and the entire project team.

This experience has left one question unanswered. Why did we not seem to be able to identify, analyse and respond to risks which substantially influenced the achievement of our objectives of scope, time and budget? It seemed that neither theory nor practical experience delivered a satisfying answer to that problem. To shed some light on this problem is the central motivation for this study.

---

[2] PMI and other organisations such as the Association of Project Management argue that their project management processes are generally accepted as best practice standards. That implies, that widespread consensus about the effectiveness of their processes.

1.3. Research problem and research questions

This study addresses the research problem of whether risk related interventions influence the effective application of project risk management by project managers in the context of IT projects. In order to shed light on the research problem in this study I will first describe the outcome of three general real-life examples which are the "Challenger" catastrophe, the attacks on the Twin Towers in New York or the Selby train crash in 2001. In all cases, risk management processes were carried out similar to the project risk management process described.

The first example is the Space Shuttle disaster in 1986 (see Example 1):

"On January 28, 1986, the space shuttle Challenger lifted off the launch pad at 11:38 a.m., beginning the flight of mission 51-L. Approximately 74 seconds into the flight, the Challenger was engulfed in an explosive burn and all communication and telemetry ceased. Seven brave crewmembers lost their lives. Following the accident, significant energy was expended trying to ascertain whether or not the accident had been predictable. Controversy arose from the desire to assign, or to avoid, blame."

Example 1: The Space Shuttle Challenger Disaster
(Kerzner, 2003, p. 231)

Prior to the launch of the space shuttle Challenger, a risk management process was applied. Threats were analysed and subjected to risk reduction as outlined in the NASA Hand Book. The threat of the erosion of O-rings that maintain the pressure in the two main booster rockets was already well documented because tests had been carried out at previous launches (Hauptmann & Iwaki, 1990). The night before the Challenger was due to lift off, temperatures dropped sharply. Faced by this environmental circumstance, management and engineers called in a meeting and debated whether to go ahead with the launch. The engineers objected to a launch because conclusive evidence of O-ring erosion under such extreme weather conditions was not available. One senior engineer being interviewed at the commission investigating the accident argued:

"There was never one comment in favour, as I have said, of launching by any engineer or other non-management person in the room before or after the caucus. I was not even asked to participate in giving any input to the final decision charts." (Kerzner, 2003, p. 263)

The NASA management decided to launch without the prior consensus of the engineers. Moreover, under the time pressure to decide whether or not to abort the launch, the management decided not to carry out further O-ring erosion tests, which would have included the condition of low temperature.

The commission investigating the cause of the Challenger disaster came to the conclusion that among other causes leading to the explosion of the Space Shuttle, the disagreement between technicians and management and the lack of knowledge about O-ring erosion under cold weather conditions was to be blamed. In hindsight, further tests would have revealed that the danger of launching under those weather conditions were unacceptable (Dalal, Fowlkes, & Hoadley, 1989). Kerzner (2003, p. 273) argued:

> "A careful analysis of the flight history of O-ring performance would have revealed the correlation of O-ring damage and low temperature. Neither NASA nor Thikol carried out such an analysis; consequently, they were unprepared to properly evaluate the risks of launching the 51-L mission in risk mediators more extreme than they had encountered before."

In drawing conclusions from the above, two problems can be identified which led to the Challenger catastrophe. In this situation, engineers explored worst-case scenarios but these were dismissed by the management as too far-fetched only for the engineers' initial assessment to be found to be close to the cause of destruction of the space shuttle (Beard, 2004; Wald & Broad, 2003). The disagreement between engineers and management and the lack of the managers' trust of the recommendations by the engineers not to proceed with the launch were driven by a lack of information. Hence, in this example, two factors appear to have intervened in optimal risk management and ultimately to have led to seven fatalities: the lack of agreement on whether the risk of O-ring erosion was valid and the problem of justifying the costs of carrying out further tests in order to increase confidence in the legitimacy of the estimation of the risk involved.

The second example relates to the terrorist attacks on the World Trade Center in 2001 (see Example 2).

8:45 a.m. (all times are EDT): A hijacked passenger jet, American Airlines Flight 11 out of Boston, Massachusetts, crashes into the north tower of the World Trade Center, tearing a gaping hole in the building and setting it afire.

9:03 a.m.: A second hijacked airliner, United Airlines Flight 175 from Boston, crashes into the south tower of the World Trade Center and explodes. Both buildings are burning.

9:43 a.m.: American Airlines Flight 77 crashes into the Pentagon, sending up a huge plume of smoke. Evacuation begins immediately.

10:05 a.m.: The south tower of the World Trade Center collapses, plummeting into the streets below. A massive cloud of dust and debris forms and slowly drifts away from the building.

10:10 a.m.: A portion of the Pentagon collapses.

10:10 a.m.: United Airlines Flight 93, also hijacked, crashes in Somerset County, Pennsylvania, southeast of Pittsburgh.

10:28 a.m.: The World Trade Center's north tower collapses from the top down as if it were being peeled apart, releasing a tremendous cloud of debris and smoke.

Example 2: September 11 attacks
(CNN, 2001)

The threat of terrorists using airplanes as weapons was not new. In 1999, a federal interagency intelligence report predicted that suicide bombers could crash aircrafts packed with high explosives into government buildings. Furthermore, the Federal Aviation Administration published a warning on their website that Bin Laden posed a threat to U.S. civil aviation. The president of the United States of America, George W. Bush also received a warning in July 2001 that an attack by Al Qaeda was imminent (CNN, 2001).

Although the threat was identified and the probability of the event actually occurring high, responses were not defined nor were actions taken to mitigate the threat. The reason for the failure to act is that these threats were not taken seriously (CNN, 2001). The administration came to the conclusion that risks from terrorism do not justify increased security only to learn one-day that a group of terrorists killed thousands of people (McGarity, 2002). Their lack of trust in the message that thousands of people may be killed because terrorists could use planes as weapons led to negligence and a lack of attention towards the already identified threats.

Hence, similar to the Challenger catastrophe, the problem of lack of trust in risks led to an unfortunate inattention towards risks and their mitigation. The risk management process started with identifying and analysing a threat, but stopped at this stage because individuals perceived those threats as not credible or legitimate so no response alternatives were sought, no response owner defined and ultimately no response action taken.

The last example is the Selby Train crash (see Example 3).

This is the sequence of events leading up to the collision on 28th February between Goole and Selby on the East Coast Line:

A Land Rover pulling a trailer loaded with a car veers off the M62 near the village of Great Heck and careers down an embankment before coming to rest on the rail line.

The Land Rover driver Gary Hart is able to get out of his vehicle and call police telling them that his car is on the tracks.

As he speaks to the operator he shouts that a train is coming and watches as it hits his car and trailer before coming off the tracks.

A North Yorkshire Police operator hears the Land Rover driver shout: "The train's coming" and then there was a bang.

The train involved was the 0445 Newcastle to London intercity 224 Great North eastern Railway electric express with about 100 people on board.

The GNER driver, who is thought to have been going at 125mph, spotted the vehicle on the track but was unable to stop in time.

After the impact, the passenger train remains upright until travelling through a set of points and subsequently colliding with a freight train travelling in the opposite direction at about 75mph.

Example 3: The tragic sequence
(BBC News, 2001)

A risk management process was applied by organisations such as GNER, the train operator. However, the threat of such a tragic sequence of events was unknown until it actually took place. In hindsight, the apparent lack of knowledge about the complexity of the threat and its occurrence led to the failure of the management of several organisations such as Railtrack and Freightliner Ltd. to prevent the risk from being identified in advance. Various events were interrelated and difficult, if not impossible, to predict in advance as a result of the infinite range of possible threats.

In all the three examples a risk management process was applied. However, due to problems such as lack of trust or lack of knowledge, the process with the goal of responding to the identified risks came to a premature halt with the ultimate consequence of a disastrous result. The evidence suggests that during the process of identifying, analysing and responding to risk, specific intervening factors constrained the risk management process with the ultimate consequence that risks materialised with adverse effects. In the first and second examples the key factor appeared to be lack of trust and in the third the lack of knowledge. Lack of knowledge as a reason for the failure of individuals to prevent the Selby Train Crash interfered with the process of monitoring the environment and collecting environmental data. The sequence of events of the train crash remained unknown until it actually happened because of all theoretically infinite possibilities. Hence, this threat was overlooked. Even if it had been identified in advance, this sequence of events would have been certainly perceived as being "incredible" with the likely result of risk actors not taking any actions to prevent such a sequence of uncertain events (Beard, 2004). "Incredible" implies that this sequence of interrelated multiple events leading to this tragic outcome would not have been perceived as worth managing in advance because the chance of such a sequence of events actually happening would have been perceived as incredibly low. Hence, the phase of interpreting the data would have given the false impression of such an event as unlikely to happen although in fact, it did happen. In hindsight, no sensible choice about the actual risk of such a train crash was made, as considerable uncertainty prevented decision makers from identifying the threat in the first place.

In contrast to the Selby Train Crash example, NASA was aware of the risk of O-ring erosion and similarly the US government had identified the threat of an imminent terrorist attack. However, the analysis stage of the threat was influenced by different and opposing perceptions of risk. However, in both the example of the Challenger catastrophe and the September 11 attacks a shared understanding was not achieved. Although the threats were identified, the collision of the perceptions of risk by technicians, civil servants and management resulted, with hindsight, in the definition of an unreasonable choice in the respect that actions should have been taken to prevent the risks already identified from occurring. Ambiguity in risk estimates and the consequent disagreements among decision makers influenced the stage of interpreting the threat. Opposing perceptions of risk by the management and technicians led to the fatal decision to go ahead with the launch of the space shuttle Challenger and in the case of the Twin Tower attacks in New York, to decide not to increase airport safety.

The evidence from the three scenarios gives a first insight into the type of problems and interventions managers face and how these interventions influence the effectiveness of individuals, group of individuals and organisations in managing risks and ultimately the outcome of three real scenarios. However, whereas in all three scenarios the outcome was the loss of human life, the outcomes of IT projects are very different.

In contrast to the examples above, this study addresses the research problem of whether interventions influence the effective application of project risk management by project managers in the research context of IT projects. Although much work has been done to date examining the reasons for project failure, little research has been carried out to ascertain why, despite well-established project risk management processes, IT project managers do not prevent risks from adversely influencing project outcomes. Therefore, five research questions have been defined.

First, in literature, project success and failure is often defined in terms of the project manager's ability to meet the time, cost and scope objectives. However, this view may be too narrow. Despite the strong tendency in project management literature to measure project outcomes in terms of meeting the scope, cost and time targets, recent evidence suggests that other factors of success also need to be taken into consideration. Hence in order to investigate whether risks influence the project outcome despite project risk management, the criteria for determining the project outcome should first be investigated:

1) How do IT project managers define project outcome (success and failure)?

Second, project risk management is one of nine key disciplines influencing the project outcome. Thus, the relationship between project outcome and project risk management needs to be researched:

2) Do IT project managers perceive that the use of project risk management processes contribute to the project outcome?

Once I have established whether project risk management influences the project outcome, I will investigate whether and to what extent project risk management influences the project outcome. A first step in answering this research question is to ask IT project managers whether a formal project risk management process was applied and if so how effectively they think they were able to apply the process:

3) Do IT project managers perceive the use of project risk management as effective in managing risks?

IT project managers may have difficulties in effectively managing risks; risks may adversely influence project outcome and to the extent to which project risk management enables the IT project manager to prevent risks from influencing the project outcome may shed some further light on how effective project managers are in managing risks:

4) Are IT project risks effectively managed?

As a result of intervening factors, IT project managers may perceive project risk management as ineffective. In addition, risks may not be effectively managed. For example, risks may be overlooked and thus adversely influence the project outcome.

5) Do IT project managers think that risk-related factors constrain the effective use of project risk management?

How these research questions are approached is described in the next section.

1.4. The research approach

1.4.1. Theoretical development phase

The theoretical development phase has the purpose of further developing the core concepts in this study and to create propositions for this study which I discuss in the literature review: the phenomenon of risk, the management of risk by project managers[3], risk related risk interventions and the project outcome. Through the literature review the phenomenon of risk,

---

[3] In this paper, for the purpose of clarity, it is assumed that the project manager is the main risk actor (individual who influences, applies and/or "owns" the risk process) as is often practised in reality. However, project management literature suggests that various stakeholders, which includes individuals and organisations, may be directly or indirectly involved in the

for example, is further developed and put into perspective. Logical relationships such as the relationship between the use of project management in terms of over- and underestimation of risk and the project outcome are proposed. Building upon previous research in areas such as psychology and statistics, I suggest a conceptual framework, a provisional combination of concepts supported by ideas from various authors (e.g.Akintoye & MacLead, 1997; Duncan, 1972; March & Shapira, 1987).

1.4.2. Empirical phase

The research problem is empirically investigated in the context of IT projects. Organisations delivering IT projects may include Computer Service Providers (CSP). Firms in this line of business include Unisys and IBM as stand-alone providers. In addition, many firms have this function provided as an in-house support function. Typical services that are provided by include "planning, operation, implementation and use of computer hardware, computer software and computer personnel" (Howard, 2001, p. 2). Examples of projects include "Roll Outs", the implementation of "User Help Desk" structures or "Outsourcing" projects. In 2001 in the UK, such services alone represented £20 billion in turnover for the stand-alone CSPs of which approximately 50% of this service volume was delivered through project work (Howard, 2001, p. 8). The strategic importance and costs involved in developing IT systems have raised the stakes associated with the project outcome (Keil, 1995).

In the research setting as described, I empirically investigate the research problem and research questions by using a grounded theory oriented research approach to explore concepts such as project risk management. The first phase of empirical research includes the use of grounded theory for exploring project managers' experiences in managing risk in IT projects. Semi-structured interviews are used to enable me to fully understand how IT project managers manage risk, what risk related interventions influenced their efforts to effectively and optimally manage risk and what influence these ultimately had on their achievement to meet project objectives they considered to be important. The data analysis follows an iterative process of proposing patterns from one case and checking these patterns with those in other cases. The process of proposing and checking comes to a conclusive end once new patterns cease to emerge and existing ones were confirmed to a certain extent.

---

process of managing risk. Key stakeholders include project managers, customers, performing organisations, project team members and sponsors; additionally, internally or externally, stakeholders such as owners, founders, contractors, team members and government agencies. Consequently, I will focus on the project manager as the main risk actor in this study.

Once I understand patterns that emerged about how, for example, which interventions led to sub optimal or ineffective project risk management, a survey to test these patterns on a wider population of project managers is conducted in order to further explain the relationships between the concepts explored. Overall, over 2.200 project managers who are members of the Project Management Institute (PMI) and the Association for Project Management receive an invitation to participate in the on-line survey. The data analysis includes descriptive as well as multivariate regression techniques.

1.5. Key findings and conclusions

The findings show that project risk management as one of the nine key disciplines identified by the Project Management Institute contributes to the outcome of IT projects. However, IT project managers encounter difficulties in managing project risk because of several risk related interventions such as denial, characterised by anxiety among stakeholders due to the identification and analysis of risk. These interventions tend to influence project risk management in such a way that project managers overlook risks that later materialise and result in an adverse effect on the project outcome. Hence, these risk interventions contribute to the inability of project managers to prevent risks from materialising and thus negatively influencing the achievement of the project objectives of scope, cost and time and other objectives IT project managers consider to be important such as team satisfaction.

This study contributes to our knowledge of managing risks as follows: first, it sheds light on how effectively project managers think they have applied project risk management and to what degree risks influenced the project outcome. Second, it increases the understanding of what kind of risk related interventions prevail in IT projects and how these risk interventions constrain IT project managers in effectively managing risk. These findings are important given the lack of current evidence about how optimal project risk management is applied. Through the management of such interventions, the use of project risk management may be improved. Third, the findings contradict some project management literature to measure project success too narrowly, that is to say, only in terms of meeting cost, scope and time. By extending the measurement of success beyond these traditional dimensions, further investigation into project outcomes may reveal a more accurate picture of the rate of success and failure of IT projects.

1.6. The structure of the study

In the second chapter of this study, I carry out a literature review, including a critical investigation of current evidence of why project risk management does not prevent project failure, including an investigation into the factors defining project success, the contribution of project risk management to project success and failure, and problems arising with project risk management. I develop each major concept in this study: project outcome, risk and uncertainty, project risk management and risk-related factors intervening with project risk management. The theoretical development of the literature reviewed includes the conceptual underpinning of each major concept, their relationships to each other (propositions) and conceptual definitions.

The third chapter includes methods and techniques to investigate the research questions. As a result of the current lack of evidence to answer the research questions, I suggest and justify the exploration of the major concepts as a first step. The second step in addressing the research questions includes the testing of the concepts explored on a wider population in order to increase the quality of the findings. From a theoretical perspective, I justify post-positivism as a valid philosophical view, taking the importance of the human factor and a subjective reality into account.

The findings and discussion of the exploratory and explanatory phases are presented in chapters four and five. In these chapters, I give an overview of the significant findings of the study. In addition, I consider the findings in the light of existing research introduced in the literature review.

Chapter six includes main conclusions, inferences, limitations, theoretical and practical implications of the findings as well as discussing suggestions for further research are discussed. I examine whether the findings answer the research questions, give recommendations for practitioners and discuss the limitations of the study. Following this, I give recommendations for further research. The study concludes with some final words.

2. LITERATURE REVIEW

The introduction provided a first indication that individuals, group of individuals and organisations encounter problems in effectively managing risks. In this chapter, I will explore literature about the project outcome, risk and uncertainty, on the effectiveness of project risk management and on reasons why project managers may not prevent risks from adversely influencing the project outcome.

The literature used in this review encompasses various approaches to the management of risk. As can be seen in Figure 2.1, approaches to risk have been classified into seven general categories. These approaches differ from one another in many respects regarding the basic problem areas, their major applications or their predominant methods. For instance, the psychological approach includes psychometrics as a main method while the toxicological and epidemiological approach emphasises experiments and surveys (Renn, 1992). In this study I will also look at other approaches to enlighten the investigation of the research problem. This chapter provides a first step in the investigation, by examining a wide range of publications.

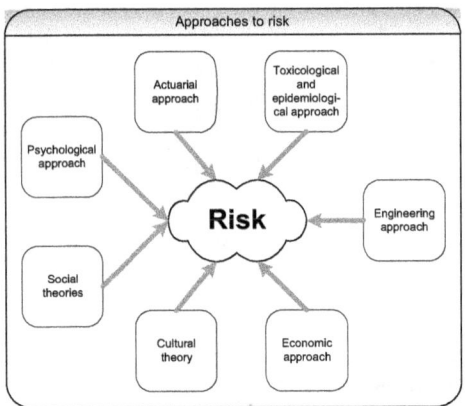

Figure 2.1: A systematic classification of approaches to risk
(Renn, 1992, p. 56)

In section 2.1 I review literature regarding the project outcome. In section 2.2, I critically discuss literature about risk and uncertainty. I distinguish between both concepts and investigate the nature and components of risk. In Section 2.3, I discuss project risk management and its structure, its underlying assumptions and also review research on its effectiveness. Section 2.4 offers an overview of the problems of project risk management. In section 0, I will provide an initial conceptualisation of all reviewed key concepts, their definitions and their relationships through the introduction of propositions. In section 2.6, I suggest a conceptual framework including all the key concepts discussed. In section 2.7, I summarise and conclude the literature review.

2.1. Project outcome

Project risks, as described in the introduction may prevent project managers from achieving their time, cost and scope objectives. The project outcomes of success and failure are often defined in terms of project managers meeting or not meeting time, cost and scope objectives. However, project management literature from various fields such as engineering shows that this view is too narrow. Hence, in order to investigate why IT project managers do not prevent risk from influencing the project outcome, the meaning of what project failure and success needs to be established.

The definition of project success or failure is important in the literature, not least because success and failure measures are widely used as dependent variables in many studies (e.g. Jiang, Klein, & Chen, 2001; Karlsen & Gottschalk, 2003, 2004). However, a review of project management literature provides no single interpretation of project failure or success. Often, project failure is generally defined in project management literature as the inability of project managers to meet specified project objectives of scope, time and budget (e.g. Burghardt, 1995; Buttrick, 1997; Young, 1998). The British Standards Institute's definition of project management embeds this notion of the pre-eminence of time, cost and quality/scope, by defining project management as the "planning, monitoring and control of all aspects of a project and the motivation of all those involved in it to achieve the project objectives on time and on the specified cost, quality and performance" (British Standards Institute, 2000, p. 10).

The criteria of cost, time and scope or quality are often referred to as the Iron Triangle (see Figure 2.2).

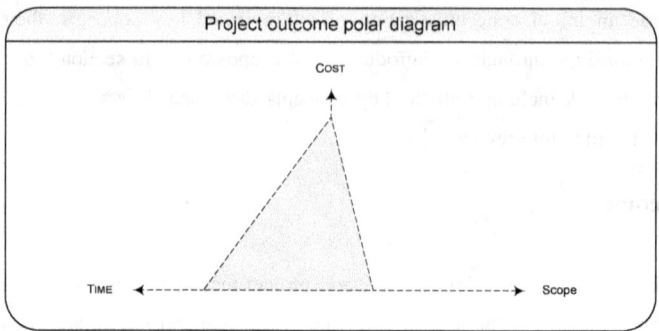

Figure 2.2: The iron triangle

Figure 2.2 shows that a project's criteria, product scope and quality grade, time-to-produce, and cost-to-complete are interconnected and cannot change without a corresponding, balancing change in one or more other criteria.

According to the traditional definition of project success in terms of scope, cost and time, the rate of failure of IT projects is immense (Hormozi et al., 2000; Kartam et al., 2001; Schmidt, Lyytinen, Keil, & Cule, 2001). However, this definition has attracted has attracted criticism from scholars (e.g. Gardiner & Stewart, 2000; Ghalayini & Noble, 1996; Lee-Kelley & Loong, 2003; Tukel & Rom, 2001). Atkinson (1999, p. 338), for example, argues:

> "To date, project management has had the success criteria focused upon the delivery stage, up to implementation. Reinforced by the very description we have continued to use to define the profession, the focus has been to judge whether the project was done right. Doing something right may result in a project which was implemented on time, within cost and to some quality parameters requested, but which is not used by the customers, not liked by the sponsors and does not seem to provide either improved effectiveness or efficiency for the organisation, is this successful project management?"

Other authors follow this criticism. Wateridge (1995) states that other success criteria such as the achievement of purpose or team satisfaction are neglected. One example of this is the Thames barrier project, the construction of a flood-protection scheme. Although the project had considerable time and cost overruns it was still considered a success because the contractors made a profit and the project achieved its purpose for the contractors (Morris & Hough, 1987).

The criticism of measuring project success and failure only when the criteria of scope, cost and time are met is underlined by various other researchers. Wateridge (1995, p. 171), for example, argues: "..., previous research mainly examines the views of industry projects managers and not sponsors or users of projects." He adds: "Project managers are putting too much emphasis on the time and budget aspects for judging project success at the expense of other criteria. (Wateridge, 1995, p. 171). Baccarini (1999, p. 29) goes further and ranks the criteria of time, cost and performance relative to other objectives: "The project management success criteria of time, cost and performance are subordinate to the higher success objectives of goal and purpose." Elkington (2002) concludes that the most important finding of his study was that the cost, time and scope criteria are not the most important criteria from a project manager's view. He suggests: "By far the most interesting fact is, that despite the success of the project as measured against benefits, time and cost, the manager of this project chose to state that only "some parts (were) successful" (Elkington et al., 2002, p. 55). To conclude, it appears that scope, cost and time measures are too simplistic to define project failure and success. Comprehensive criteria for measuring project failure have to reflect different interests; scope, cost and time targets may be important for the project owner or sponsor. However, from the point of view of the customer or the end-user they may be irrelevant. Hence, project outcome criteria often need to include other benchmarks. Some authors have taken the criticism mentioned above into account and suggested an extended range of success criteria. Morris and Hough (1987), for example, assess IT project success as follows:

- The project delivers its functionality.

- It is delivered to budget, on schedule, and to technical specification.

- It is commercially profitable for the contractor.

- It is terminated reasonably and effectively if it needs to be cancelled.

Pinto and Mantel (1990) suggest three main dimensions of project outcome: the implementation process, client or stakeholder satisfaction and the perceived value of the project. Evidence of project success and failure in literature can be categorised according to these three main dimensions (see Table 2.1):

Outcome dimensions	Authors
Implementation of the project; Project Efficiency	CCTA (1995); Powell and Klein (1996); Fleming and Koppelman (1996); Seddon (1997); Shenhar, Levy and Dvir (1997); Liu and Walker (1998); Atkinson (1999); Baccarini (1999); British Standards Institution (2000); Shenhar, Dvir, Levy and Maltz (2001); Stewart (2001); Hartman and Ashrafi (2002); Shenhar, Tishler, Dvir and Lipovetsky (2002); Elkington and Smalllman (2002); White and Fortune (2002); Project Management Institute (2004)
Stakeholder satisfaction; Impact on stakeholders	DeCotiis and Dyer (1979); Baker and Fisher (1988); Shenhar, Levy and Dvir (1997); Liu and Walker (1998); Atkinson (1999); Wateridge (1998); Lynn and Reilly (2000); Stewart (2001); Hartman and Ashrafi (Hartman et al., 2002); Shenhar, Dvir, Levy and Maltz (2001); Shenhar, Tishler, Dvir and Lipovetsky (2002)
Perceived value of the project; Business and direct success	Freeman and Beale (1992); Shenhar, Levy and Dvir (1997); Shenhar, Levy and Dvir (1997); Wateridge (1998); Atkinson (1999); Baccarini (1999); Lidow (1999); Ami (2000); Buchok (2000); Nade (2000); Shenhar, Dvir, Levy and Maltz (2001); White and Fortune (2002)

Table 2.1: Success factors
(adapted from Kendra & Taplin, 2004, p. 32)

The first success dimension of *implementation of the project* relates to project efficiency. This first dimension expresses the short term success of the project (Shenhar et al., 1997), and includes criteria such as meeting technical specifications, cost and time targets and other pre-stated project objectives. However, although the project may have been successfully implemented, a stakeholder may not be satisfied for instance, because the project provider has not established a good working relationship with the customer. Hence, the second dimension of *stakeholder satisfaction* should be taken into consideration. Key stakeholders in a project are the project manager, the customer, the organisation that carries out the work of the project, project team members and the owner or sponsor of the project providing the resources (Project Management Institute, 2004) and anyone else affected by the process or outcome. A key measurement of the impact on stakeholders dimension is the degree of satisfaction (e.g. Liu et al., 1998; Lynn et al., 2000). The third success dimension relates to the *perceived value of the project* or direct success of the project, the achievement of the purpose and benefits of the project. The achievement of the purpose addresses the direct impact of the project on the organisation; for example, the implementation of IT systems may be intended to save costs in an organisation. Measuring to what degree the project has achieved its purpose is also considered by many researchers to be important (e.g. Ami, 2000; Baccarini, 1999). The benefit to the owner or sponsor has also a direct impact on whether the project is considered a success or failure. The importance of meeting a project's scope, cost and time targets are often secondary; of primary concern are follow on contracts. Once the implementation of an IT system is accomplished, lucrative maintenance contracts to service the implemented IT system may follow.

The evidence from the current literature shows that determining project success and failure only by measuring the achievement of cost, scope and time objectives appears to be too narrow. As a consequence, the findings of the surveys about the rate of failure of IT projects introduced in chapter 1 may need to be considered with caution. A further problem is the definition of a set of outcome dimensions for the research context of this study – IT projects. The literature is not conclusive about what dimensions are indeed considered to be important by IT project managers. Various success factors are proposed, but no single set of success measures has yet been suggested for application in IT projects. The literature review on project success criteria leads to an expanded but incomplete view of how to define project success (see Figure 2.3).

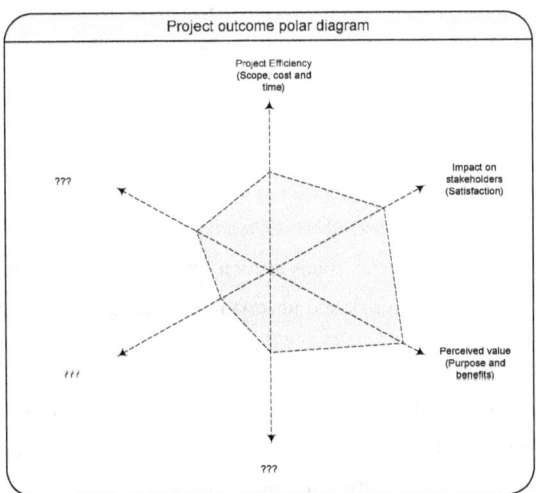

Figure 2.3: An expanded framework of project success

Cost, scope and time objectives are complemented by success criteria of stakeholder satisfactions and the business and direct success criteria. However, the existing evidence about project success dimensions, if empirically investigated, has been gathered mostly in areas different to the IT project environment. Two of the more prominent studies by Shenhar *et al.* (1997; 2002) include an investigation into a mix of industries such as construction, electronics and aerospace. Elkington and Smallman (2002) researched project risk management practices in the utilities sector. As a result, from the existing evidence reviewed it remains unclear whether the suggested success measures as displayed in Figure 2.3 are most important from the project manager's point of view, especially in IT projects. Hence, this study examines what factors are important for defining success and failure in the research context of IT projects from the point of view of the key player in IT projects – the project manager.

Moreover, the existing evidence about project success dimensions, if empirically investigated, has been gathered mostly in areas different to the IT project environment. Two of the more prominent studies by Shenhar *et al.* (1997; 2002) includes an investigation into a mix of industries such as construction, electronics and aerospace. Elkington and Smallman (2002) researched project risk management practices in the utilities sector. As a result from the existing evidence reviewed it remains unclear what success measures are most important from the project manager's point of view, especially in IT projects. Hence, this study examines what factors are important for defining success and failure in the research context of IT projects from the point of view of the key player in IT projects – the project manager.

2.2. Risk and uncertainty

Risks, as outlined in the introduction, have been argued to have adversely influenced the project outcome of a substantial number of IT projects. In this section I will review literature about the nature of risk and the distinction between risk and uncertainty, its components and dimensions.

Crockford (1986) suggests that any risk includes four components, which are threats, resources, consequences and modifying factors. A *threat* (a source of danger) may be, for example, environmental turbulence (i.e., constantly changing, highly uncertain and ambiguous), which could have adverse results on *resources*. Resources are components of a project such as budget, personnel and material (Burghardt, 1995) that could be affected by threats. The term *consequences* relates to the potential risk has to negatively influence on the project outcome (Project Management Institute, 2004).

In recent literature (e.g. Hillson, 2002, 2003), risk is characterised as encompassing both threats and opportunities. Hillson (2002, p. 235), argues: "Risk is an umbrella term, with two varieties: "opportunity" which is a risk with positive effects; "threat" which is a risk with negative effects." Although this definition may allow project risk management to also include the aspect of the management of opportunities, the traditional view of risk and its terminology predominantly focuses on risk as a chance of loss and not a chance of opportunity (e.g. Chambers English Dictionary, 1990; Gaulke, 2002).

Risk can lead to losses that range from the trivial to large (Crockford, 1986). Trivial losses present few problems unless their frequency leads to a threatening aggregation. One example, although not related to an IT project, is the Piper Alpha offshore installation accident in 1988. A minor problem with a faulty injection pump triggered a fatal sequence of events, which ultimately led to the death of eighty one persons (Waring & Glendon, 1998).

In this study, the consequences of risk impact on the project outcome of IT projects. *Modifying factors* that can also be defined a risk mitigation responses increase or decrease the likelihood of the threat becoming a reality or the probable consequence of such a reality. A project manager may modify or change risk by reducing the likelihood of a threat materialising or the severity of its consequences or both. This is the basis for the use of project risk management.

2.2.1. Two principal views of risk

In the literature, researchers principally take two different main views of risk. First, risk has been defined as a "quantifiable attribute of technologies and naturally materialising hazards" (Otway & Thomas, 1982, p. 70). From this perspective, project managers may objectively evaluate risk based on observed frequencies. This can be identified as the objective or statistical risk view (Bradbury, 1989). According to this view, risk has a "true" and objective value, however, within a certain degree of confidence and not with absolute certainty (Marks, Coleman, & Michael, 2003, p. 1405).

On the other hand, risk has been argued to be a product of social interaction, a continuous social construction and reconstruction (Dake, 1992; Jasanoff, 1993; Otway et al., 1982). From this viewpoint, project managers subjectively assess and respond to risk by relying on their own opinion and judgement (Raftery, 1994; The Royal Society, 1983).

However, dichotomising objective and subjective views of risk has been criticised by authors such as Otway and Thomas (1982) and Watson (1981) because of its undue simplicity (The Royal Society, 1983). Ritchie and Marshall (1993, p. 112) argued:

"This dismissal of a distinction is justified by the assertion that the introduction of some form of subjective probability assessment of the possible outcomes would be sufficient to overcome the need for any distinction."

Hence, it may be too simple to argue that objective risk analysis or risk assessment that includes estimating and evaluating risk consequences (Project Management Institute, 2004; Waring et al., 1998) can ever be totally free of all subjective opinion or judgement (Brehmer, 1987; Kasper, 1980; Lowrance, 1980; Otway, 1992; Short, 1989; The Royal Society, 1983). The viewpoint of Otway and Thomas (1982, p. 70) is very succinct:

"It is clear that truths do not exist independently of people, whether taken to be individuals, significant social groups in the general public, professional or political / industrial groups. It is people, and not independent facts, who constrain the way concepts are framed, questions posed, and research goals set. And it is people who design event and fault trees, close options, choose attribute sets, fund data collection, interpret and publish findings. Once the criterion of an absolute truth is abandoned, then surely no one can avoid the inference that people see the world differently and that these differences emerge from different experiences of differently constructed social worlds."

In contrast, according to Rosa (2003) subjective risk analysis or risk assessment may never entirely be free of any objective property of a threat:

"Can all risk be reduced to psychological categories? Are there no real risks outside those we find entering the mind? Even if we accept the psychological as a valid perspective, we can ask why, on the one hand, there is often considerable agreement over some risks (such as smoking), or, on the other hand, considerable disagreement about other risks (global warming)? Are these judgements, sometimes concurring, sometimes disagreeing, made solely on the basis of perceptions independent of evidence from the world? Unlikely." (Rosa, 2003, p. 69)

According to the concept of social amplification of risk (Kasperson et al., 1988) risk can not be viewed as objective (absolute) or subjective (socially determined) (e.g. Jaeger, Renn, Rosa, & Wehler, 2001; Kasperson et al., 1988; Pidgeon & Beattie, 1998; Renn, 1998). Risk can neither be concluded to be characterised as being purely constructed nor totally influenced by positivistic repetitive events of real "hazards" (Renn, Burns, Kasperson, Kasperson, & Slovic, 1992, p. 140). Risk lies between the extremes of pure objectivity and pure subjectivity; risk is a state of mind as well as an attribute of an objective entity (e.g. Dake, 1992; Holzheu & Wiedermann, 1993; Kirkwood, 1994; Smallman, 1996).

2.2.2. The concept of uncertainty

In the risk literature, some authors have distinguished between the concepts of risk and uncertainty (e.g. Head, 1967; Raftery, 1994; Remenyi & Heafield, 1996; Ritchie et al., 1993). A "risk-free" situation is one that can be anticipated in the future with absolute certainty. However, because there are very few examples of such situations, uncertainty is inherent in virtually every situation and generally accepted as an integral part of risk (Project Management Institute, 2004; Ritchie et al., 1993).

Uncertainty is defined by Leblebici and Salancik (1981, p. 578) as a "state arising from predicting outcomes from the actions taken to achieve them; the more one is able to predict outcomes, the less the uncertainty." The most common definitions concerning uncertainty to be found in the literature are:

- An inability to assign probabilities to the likelihood of future events (e.g. Ashill & Jobber, 1999, 2001; Duncan, 1972; Milliken, 1987)

- A lack of information about cause-effect relationships (e.g. Ashill et al., 1999, 2001; Duncan, 1972; Milliken, 1987)

- An inability to predict accurately what the outcomes of a decision might be (e.g. Ashill et al., 1999, 2001; Downey, Hellriegel, & Slocum, 1975; Duncan, 1972; Milliken, 1987)

Nevertheless, the term "uncertainty" remains "capacious" (Morgan & Henrion, 1990, p. 47) and various definitions can be found in the literature. The common element of these definitions is the condition of lack of information experienced by the project manager. This means that a project manager views an element of the project as not definitely known or certain. Such an element could be, for example, a project task that is not accurately predictable.

Ritchie and Marshall (1993, p. 112) argue that from a business risk view:

> "..., the state of mind that we term uncertainty can be viewed as arising from each person's imperfect knowledge concerning future events and, as such, it will influence the degree of confidence that the decision-maker has in the decision to be made."

Hence, I suggest uncertainty to be an attribute of the (project) manager's mental processes as well as an attribute of the physical project. Therefore, this study will consider uncertainty to be neither purely objective nor purely subjective (Ashill et al., 1999, 2001; Morgan et al., 1990).

In literature, the dimensions of the concept of uncertainty are various. Projects, for example, can be categorised into two uncertainty dimensions: goals and method related uncertainty. The former relates to "how well defined are the goals", the latter to "how well defined are the methods of achieving them" (Turner & Cochrane, 1993, p. 93). According to these two dimensions, four types of projects can be defined:

- Type-1 projects: for which the goals and methods of achieving the project are well defined

- Type-2 projects: for which the goals are well defined, but the methods are not

- Type-3 projects: for which the goals are not well defined, but the methods are

- Type-4 projects: for which neither the goals nor the methods are well defined.

Further concepts of uncertainty have been researched including those of Lawrence and Lorsch (1967) and Duncan (1972). These have attracted wide attention and have been used as a basis for further research (Aldrich, 1979; Buchko, 1994; Downey et al., 1975). Lawrence and Lorsch (1967) researched uncertainty that was related to a specific job in an organisation whereas Duncan (1972) examined environmental characteristics and their impact on the uncertainty experienced by decision takers. However, when Downey, Hellriegel and Slocum

(1975) investigated the conceptual and methodological adequacy of both researchers' uncertainty scales in a different research context (fifty-one division managers of a United States conglomerate) they determined that their findings contradict those of both Duncan (1972) and Lawrence and Lorsch (1967). They contradict Duncan in arguing that dynamism (stability of environmental factors) contributes to uncertainty to a greater extent than complexity (interrelatedness of environmental factors). Second, they criticise Lawrence and Lorsch for not meaningfully combining their scales of "clarity of information", "uncertainty of cause and effect relationships" and the "time span of definite feedback" to a total uncertainty score (Downey et al., 1975).

Although Downey *et al.* consider Duncan's conceptual framework to be useful, they argue that a key reason for the contradictory results was the inappropriate multidimensional conceptualisation of uncertainty (Buchko, 1994; Downey et al., 1975; Milliken, 1987; Tosi, Aldag, & Storey, 1973). Building on previous research, Milliken (1987) suggests three uncertainty dimensions that have drawn wide attention in uncertainty and project risk management literature (Ashill et al., 1999, 2001; Buchko, 1994; Ward & Chapman, 2002): state uncertainty, effect uncertainty and response uncertainty.

State uncertainty is likely to arise when initial estimates, for example regarding cost and quality, are not well specified or are perceived to lack certainty in their planning (Clawson, 1996; Valentine, 1991). Project managers will encounter state uncertainty when they perceive a project environment or component of the project management as being not fully understood or predictable.

Effect uncertainty describes the uncertainty that results when "rather than being confident that "given X, then Y", an individual is unable to derive a causal statement" (Milliken, 1987, p. 137). In IT projects, effect uncertainty may describe a project manager's lack of information about the impact of a future event on the project objectives. In a software development project, an example of effect uncertainty may be the unknown effect of a failure of a software modification on the project objectives (Jelassi & Dutta, 1993).

Response uncertainty describes the lack of knowledge a project manager has about his response alternatives and their possible consequences on the environment (Milliken, 1987). It is conceivable that a project manager might perceive response uncertainty although the effect of an event on project objectives is identified. For example, decisions about utilising a "patch programme" in a software project may be taken without predicting whether this is the most beneficial step or what consequence this response may have on project objectives such as time, cost and quality (Clawson, 1996, p. 7).

In their recent study, which synthesises among others early work by Duncan (1972), Lawrence and Lorsch (1967) and the revision of the uncertainty concept by Milliken (1987), Ashill and Jobber (1999) argue, that particular environmental and decision-maker characteristics to influence uncertainty are well established in literature.

2.2.3. Factors influencing uncertainty

In respect to *environmental characteristics*, despite major criticism of Duncan's research, his conceptual framework has been considered useful by various researchers (Ashill et al., 1999, 2001; Downey et al., 1975; Downey & Slocum, 1975; Milliken, 1987; Tung, 1979). Duncan (1972) identifies complexity and dynamism as sources of uncertainty variation. In the specific context of projects, Jaafari (2001, p. 93) defines a project as a "complex dynamic system". With reference to complexity, Morgan and Henrion (1990) find the following definition very useful:

> "Roughly, by a complex system I mean one made up of a large number of parts that have many interactions. …, in such systems the whole is more than the sum of the parts in the weak but important pragmatic sense that, given the properties of the parts and the laws of their interaction, it is not a trivial matter to infer the properties of the whole." (Simon, 1996, p. 184).

A complex system consists of many varied interrelated parts (Baccarini, 1996); it is characterised by differentiation and interdependency. Differentiation refers to the number of different inputs and outputs (Baccarini, 1996; Williams, 1999). Interdependence relates to the extent of engagement of organisational units where the actions of each unit influence the actions of other units (Andres & Zmud, 2002). In a project, these influences of differentiation and interdependency may impact on the project outcome as in the following example:

> "The Commercial System was certainly very impressive in scale: it operated in about two dozen different countries, contained more than a hundred electronic links between major BP commercial centres, and processed a few hundred thousand orders annually. Partly due to the complexity of the endeavour, the project had also experienced a

significant time and cost over-run – several times that originally estimated." (Jelassi et al., 1993, p. 1).

Downey (1975, p. 573) argues that a complex environment requires a "high degree of abstraction in order to produce manageable mappings". This implies that an increase in complexity may lead to higher perceived uncertainty due to the individual's inability to be able to identify the connection of related elements, for example tasks, to each other. Complexity is influenced by the size and uniqueness of a project. A project where previous knowledge from experience exists, is less complex than a purely unique project of the same size (Williams, 1999). Morgan and Henrion (1990) argue, that a complex construct need not imply many varied interrelated elements, although it usually does in practice.

Dynamism as a second environmental characteristic means "difficult-to-predict industry changes" (Palmer & Wiseman, 1999, p. 1045). Dynamism is identified as the degree to which individuals perceive environmental factors as static or dynamic (Downey et al., 1975; Duncan, 1972). Jafaari (2001, p. 93) explains that a project is dynamic in the sense that it "is subject to the shifting forces and constant changes due to external factors, changing objectives…". Frederickson and Mitchell (1984) determine that the likelihood of identifying critical elements such as project tasks decreases as the environment becomes more volatile. Nevertheless, Downey (1975) raises the question of whether there is a correlation between volatility of environment and uncertainty, and criticises Duncan's failure to address this issue. Milliken (1987) argues, that there is no correlation at all. It is not the rate of change which leads to the creation of uncertainty; it is the unpredictability of change. If all changes were predicable, whether the rate of change were high or low, there would be actually no uncertainty, at least no state uncertainty. Hence, dynamism may not have an influence on uncertainty at all. However, Bourgeois and Eisenhardt (1988, p. 816) explains that because of a high rate of change and more importantly, taking into account Milliken's criticism, because of sharp and discontinuous change, information for improving predictability is "often inaccurate, unavailable, or obsolete". As a result, taking these considerations into account the dimension of dynamism can be expected to be a driving force for uncertainty.

In addition to environmental characteristics, *decision-maker characteristics* are suggested to influence perceived uncertainty (Aldrich, 1979; Dermer, 1973; Downey et al., 1975). Although there are many individual characteristics to choose from prior research, Ashill and Jobber (1999) suggest that the three following individual characteristics hold much promise from the standpoint of explaining causal conditions of uncertainty: experience, tolerance of ambiguity and locus of control.

An individual's *experience* refers to the sum of relevant information gained through previous work (Daft & Weick, 1984; Downey et al., 1975). It is suggested, the less relevant historical data is available, the less the individual is able to rely on his repertoire of existing knowledge (Ashill et al., 1999, 2001; Daft et al., 1984; Downey et al., 1975). Projects are pioneering work, indicating a lack of relevant historical information (Jelassi et al., 1993). In this context, the term "pioneering" implies that a project is new and unique and that experience has not been gained by the project manager. Therefore, it is suggested that lack of experience will lead to higher perceived uncertainty (Ashill et al., 1999, 2001; Daft et al., 1984; Downey et al., 1975).

The second decision-maker characteristic is *tolerance of ambiguity*. This concept relates to an individual's desire to understand his environment (e.g. Dermer, 1973; Dollinger, 1984; Feldman & March, 1981; Furnham & Ribchester, 1995; March, 1981; Schere, 1982). It implies that decision-makers may avoid ambiguous situations and their motivation to deal with ambiguity is low (Bobbitt & Ford, 1980). The level tolerance towards ambiguity can be differentiated by the amount of environmental scanning (e.g. Ashill et al., 1999; Dermer, 1973; Dollinger, 1984). That is to say, to what extent individuals examine their environment in order to keep abreast with changes. In a project situation, this may to the amount of reporting between project participants (Young, 1998).

The amount of control which an individual has over is life is described as *locus of control* (e.g. Anderson & Schneier, 1978; Govindrajan, 1989; Miller & Jean-Marie, 1986). In a project, this may be the extent of control a project manager has over internal and external factors. If managers perceive their environment as less controllable, it might increase their level of perceived uncertainty (Ashill et al., 1999), because they attribute uncertainty to factors outside their control (Ford & Hegarty, 1984). Lack of control might arise through disagreements or the lack of consensus, which influences uncertainty (Morgan et al., 1990).

Environmental and decision-maker related conditions to influence uncertainty are shown in Figure 2.4. Elements A and B (e.g. project tasks) and their relationship to each other are uncertain, because of the influence of complexity, dynamism, degree of experience, tolerance of ambiguity and locus of control. Many interrelated elements, changes in these elements, lack of experience, low tolerance of ambiguity and lack of control over these elements are expected to lead to the phenomenon of "lack of sufficient information to predict accurately" (Milliken, 1987, p. 136). These environmental and decision-maker risk conditions increase the potential of adverse uncertain events, which might threaten the success of a project.

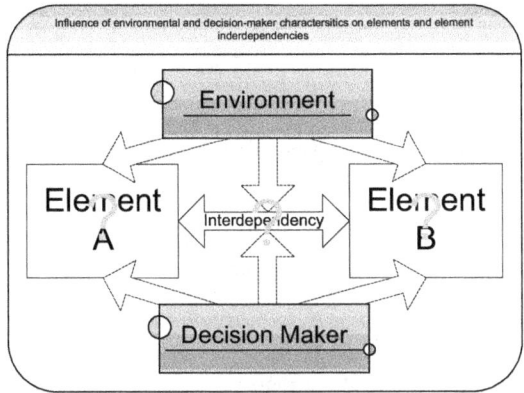

Figure 2.4: Influence of environmental and decision-maker characteristics on elements and element interdependencies

As a synthesis of the above discussion, Ritchie and Marshall (1993, p. 189) offers from a business risk management perspective a mathematical function for the product of risk and uncertainty – perceived risk. Risk is considered as the sum of both the level of perceived uncertainty and the level of extant risk:

$$\text{Risk}_{\text{perceived}} = \text{Uncertainty}_{\text{perceived}} + \text{Risk}_{\text{extant}}$$

This function is useful, as it considers the specific view of risk addressed in this study and includes the fundamental concept of uncertainty. Based on the prior discussion about risk and uncertainty, the following distinction can be made (see Table 2.2):

Risk (extant)	Measurable uncertainty	Foreseeable uncertainty	Lower state, effect and/or response uncertainty
Uncertainty (perceived)	Immeasurable uncertainty	Unforeseeable uncertainty	Higher state, effect and/or response uncertainty

Table 2.2: Distinction between extant risk and perceived uncertainty

The epistemic view of uncertainty characterises situations in which probabilities are measurable whereas the ontological/aleatory view emphasises immeasurable probabilities (Dequech, 2004). Davidson (1996, p. 479, 482) refers to epistemic uncertainty as a reality in which "the future path of the economy and the future conditional consequences of all possible choices are predetermined" and in contrast to an aleatory reality as one in which "the future can be permanently changed in nature and substance by the actions of individuals, groups … and/or governments, often in ways not completely foreseeable by the creators of change." On the one hand, epistemic uncertainty addresses the question of whether uncertainty is a result of people's limited ability to accurately predict the future using historical data. On the other hand, aleatory uncertainty questions whether uncertainty is created by a future that permanently changes. Fishburn (1994) argues that once epistemic uncertainty is reduced, only aleatory uncertainty or immeasurable uncertainty remains. Indeed, it is conceivable that during the process of reducing the level of uncertainty (state, effect, response uncertainty) through the identification of a threat, the analysis of its probability and its effects on the project objectives, and the evaluation of response alternatives and their consequences, previously unknown threats and consequences become exposed and consequently lead to a higher degree of extant risk perceived by a project manager.

In technical terms, risk means that a person does not know what will ultimately happen, but knows the odds that uncertainty will materialise. Uncertainty implies that a person does not even know the odds that the event will materialise (Adams, 1995; Williams, 1995). According to Millikens' dimensions of uncertainty, "not known" implies that a project manager is not able to attach probabilities, to identify a cause-effect relationship nor to accurately predict response outcomes (Downey et al., 1975; Duncan, 1972; Lawrence et al., 1967; Milliken, 1987; Runde, 1998). Extant risk can be defined as measurable uncertainty (Ekenberg, Boman, & Linnerooth-Bayer, 2001; Ritchie et al., 1993). *Measurable uncertainty* or in the words of Royer (2000) "recognisable risk" includes known and predicted probable effects of and responses to identified future states. "Measurable" implies that all threats and likely consequences can be well specified, that means, precise, clear and not vague (Morgan et al., 1990). In contrast to measurable uncertainty, Raftery (1994) argues that *immeasurable uncertainty* includes an unknown factor that is either more or less likely to materialise than the known measured uncertainty. Hence, immeasurable uncertainty (perceived uncertainty) includes higher state, effect and/or response uncertainty than measured uncertainty (extant risk); measured uncertainty includes a higher perception of certainty that project managers have in their estimates relating to the state, effects and responses in a project.

In conclusion, perceived risk can be influenced by measurable and immeasurable uncertainty, or in other words the accumulation of the perceived unknown and the perceived exposure to likely known threats, effects and adverse consequences. Risk and uncertainty are defined in this study as an entity which is neither purely subjective nor objective. In addition, due to the criticism in recent risk literature the concepts of risk and uncertainty should be considered to be a multidimensional concept including the dimensions of state, effect and response. However, despite the usefulness of the different uncertainty concepts for this study, the difference between (extant) risk and (perceived) uncertainty is solely the degree of perceived personal knowledge about the probable future state of the project, the effects of that state on the project outcome and the response of the project manager to reduce the probability or impact of such a future state. However promising this distinction may be, it is not one of substance, because it does not allow a clear, precise and unambiguous classification of what constitutes "known" and "unknown" uncertainty (Moore, 1983; Raftery, 1994; Ritchie et al., 1993). Therefore, in this study the terms risk and uncertainty will be used interchangeably.

2.3. Project risk management

Risks may potentially endanger the ability of the project manager to meet the predefined project objectives of scope, time and cost; tasks may take longer than planned, consequently negatively influencing the project manager's fulfilment of the project objectives (Project Management Institute, 2004). As a result of this potential to adversely influence a project's performance, the Project Management Institute, in its *Guide to the Project Management Body of Knowledge* (Project Management Institute, 2004), which according to Pender (2001) represents best practice in the area of project management, acknowledges the management of risk as one of its nine key areas of knowledge as shown in chapter 1.

2.3.1. Best practice project risk management processes

In order to avert adverse influences of risk on the project outcome, the project manager may apply a project risk management process. The basic structures of "best practice" project risk management processes in IT-project management such as those established by the British Standards Institution (British Standards Institution, 2000), The UK Government Centre for Information Systems (CCTA - The UK Government Centre for Information Systems, 1995) or the U.K. Association for Project Management (Chapman, 1997; Chapman & Ward, 2000) are similar (Gaulke, 2002). Regardless of the number of phases and definition of phases used the processes have one activity in common, one which deals with "planning actions that will be implemented in order to reduce the exposure to risk" (Ben-David & Raz, 2001, p. 14).

Best practice project risk management processes can be deconstructed into four major stages: planning, identification, analysis, and response. Firstly, a project manager can apply risk management *planning* to define which activities should be taken to approach project uncertainties. Secondly, risk *identification* allows project managers to single out uncertainties that may affect the project objectives. Thirdly, by using risk *analysis* a project manager evaluates quantitatively or qualitatively the likely consequences of uncertainties as well as the likelihood that uncertainties will become real (Raftery, 1994, p. 6). Fourthly, risk *response* enables the project manager to keep track of defined risks, to identify new risks during the project and to develop procedures and techniques to avoid, transfer and mitigate risks. The avoidance of risks implies adapting the project management plan so that risks can be isolated. The transfer of risk involves a shift of the impact of risk on to a third party whereas mitigation involves the reduction of the likelihood of a risk occurring or its impact on the project outcome. Finally, project managers may also choose to accept the risk (Project Management Institute, 2004).

2.3.2. Fundamental assumptions of project risk management

The basic project risk management process relates to models of decision making under uncertainty. Although the literature offers various models describing the process of decision making under uncertainty (Cowan, 1986; Daft et al., 1984; Kiesler & Sproull, 1982; Lyles & Mitroff, 1980), those models are similar in their process structure although they include different labels for the process stages (Milliken, 1990). Adapting Weick's (2001) model, Milliken (1990) suggests three basic activities in her study (see Figure 2.5): managers scan the environment to collect data (reduce state uncertainty), they analyse the environmental data (reduce effect uncertainty) and consequently take actions (reduce response uncertainty).

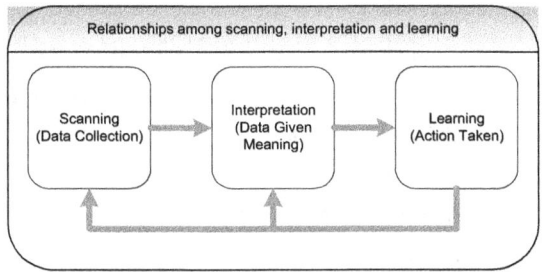

Figure 2.5: Relationships between scanning, interpretation and learning
(Weick, 2001, p. 244)

In relation to project risk management, the sequence of scanning, interpreting and learning is similar, if not identical, to the structure of the project risk management process which project managers use to reduce uncertainty (see Table 2.3). The phase of risk identification relates to the scanning of the environment and the reduction of state uncertainty, risk analysis equates to interpretation of environmental data in order reduce effect uncertainty and risk response relates to learning in order to reduce response uncertainty.

How decision makers notice and interpret issues and events in their environment (Milliken, 1990; Weick, 2001).	Purpose (Milliken, 1990)	Major steps in project risk management	PMI risk management process (Project Management Institute, 2004)	CCTA risk management process (CCTA - The UK Government Centre for Information Systems, 1995)	PRAM risk management process (Chapman, 1997)
		Planning	Risk Management Planning	Context	Focus / Define
Scanning	Perception of an environmental change – reduction of state uncertainty	**Identification**	Risk Identification	Risk Identification	Identify / Structure
Interpretation	Perception of a change's likely effect or significance – reduction of effect uncertainty	**Analysis**	Risk Analysis	Risk Analysis / Risk Evaluation	Estimate / Evaluate
Responding	Perceived knowledge of response options and their likely effectiveness – reduction of response uncertainty	**Response**	Risk Response Planning / Risk (Monitoring and) Control	Risk Treatment	Plan / Ownership / Manage

Table 2.3: Overview of main project risk management processes

The result of risk processes such as those defined by the PMI (Project Management Institute, 2004) and CCTA (CCTA - The UK Government Centre for Information Systems, 1995) is a decision based on the expected utility of different choices (Ekenberg et al., 2001; Kahneman & Tversky, 1979; Pender, 2001). Expected utility is "a weighted average of the utilities of all the possible outcomes that could flow from a particular decision, where higher-probability outcomes count more than lower-probability outcomes in calculating the average" (Borge, 2001, p. 21); the utility of decision making choices are weighted by their probabilities and outcomes (Arrow, 1983; Borge, 2001; Kahneman et al., 1979). Consider the following simplified example shown in Figure 2.6.

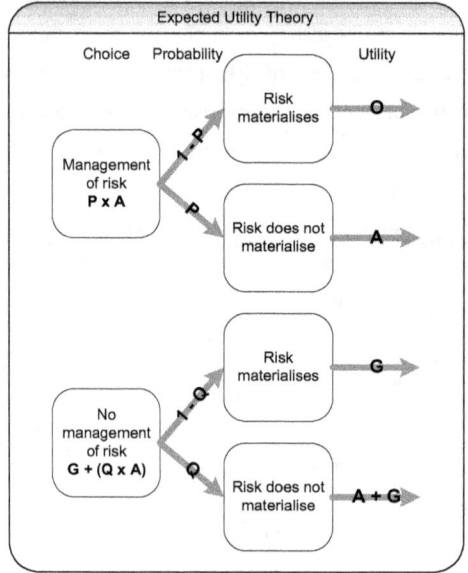

Figure 2.6: Expected utility theory.
The expected utility of taking risk response actions is $((1 - P) + 0) + (P \times A) = P \times A$. The expected utility of not taking risk response actions is $((1 - Q) \times G) + (A + G)) = G + (Q \times A)$.
(Pitz, 1992, p. 291)

According to Figure 2.6, four scenarios may unfold:

1. Project manager proactively executes risk response actions and risks materialise

2. Project manager proactively executes risk response actions and risks do not materialise

3. Project manager does not proactively execute risk response actions and risks materialise

4. Project manager does not proactively execute risk response actions and risks do not materialise

The probability of avoiding risks in a project through the execution of risk response actions is P and without risk actions Q, with P larger than Q and 1 - Q larger than 1 - P. The utility of avoiding risks (relative to the cost of materialised risk) is A and the utility of no actions (relative to the cost of those actions) is G while A is assumed to be greater than G. The utility of scenario 1 is presumably the worst and is therefore set at 0.

The utility of scenarios 1 and 3 depends on the cost of risk materialising and adversely affecting the project outcome. In contrast, the utility of scenarios 1 and 2 depends on the cost of executing actions and the commitment of scarce project resources such as time and money. Therefore, the decision by the project manager to take actions or not depends on the utility of avoiding the materialisation of uncertainty (benefit) while committing resources (cost), and on the relative magnitude of the objective or subjective probabilities.

Expected utility theory (EUT) has generally been accepted in risk literature as a model of rational choice for taking risky decisions (Anand, 1993; Borge, 2001; Jaeger et al., 2001; Kahneman et al., 1979) and is considered a very fruitful framework for decision-making under uncertainty (Einhorn & Hogarth, 1986). Rationality can be defined as "agreeable to reason; not absurd, preposterous, extravagant, foolish, fanciful, or the like; intelligent, sensible" (Simon, 1978, p. 2). According to EUT, rationality by actors includes the following claims:

• Rational actors can choose between different possible actions, each of which may lead to one or several possible outcomes. Actions as well as outcomes may differ in kind and scale;

• Rational actors assign (objective or subjective) probabilities to various outcomes;

• Rational actors can order possible actions according to their preferences. Preferences for actions involve some degree of risk aversion for specific choice situations;

• Rational actors try to choose an action, which is optimal according to their preferences (Jaeger et al., 2001, p. 52).

An important rational claim of EUT is the state of "perfect" knowledge possessed by risk actors (Jaeger et al., 2001):

- A clear and unambiguous identification of the problem, its constituent elements and its causes;

- Perfect information about all the relevant variables in terms of both quantity and quality;

- A well-developed model of the problem which incorporates all the variables likely to influence the decision outcome and a perfect understanding of the manner and scale of interaction;

- An exhaustive list of all possible solutions;

- An unambiguous statement of the objectives which is specific, quantifiable and internally consistent;

- Perfect knowledge of the future consequences of each possible solution and their implications for the project;

- The availability of all the resources and sufficiency of reliability in all the structures and systems necessary for the successful implementation of the chosen solution;

- The presence of perfectly rational and experienced decision-makers with unlimited analytical and cognitive abilities (Ritchie et al., 1993, p. 129).

Furthermore, in the context of project risk management, according to the Project Management Institute (Project Management Institute, 2004), the Government Centre of Information Systems (CCTA - The UK Government Centre for Information Systems, 1995) and according to the British Standard in project risk management (British Standards Institution, 2000), the preferences of risk actors should only relate to the *proactive* response to risk with adverse consequences on project objectives *of time, cost and quality*.

Under the consideration of the rational assumptions of EUT which inexplicitly build the foundation of best practice standards such as one promoted by PMI, an optimum or in other words a possible very best result of project risk management can be assumed. Based on the assumptions of EUT, the set of project risk management stages as suggested by the Project

Management Institute or the U.K. Government Centre for Information Systems should enable a project manager to minimise the adverse influence of project risks on the project outcome. Project risk management presents itself as a norm to be followed by project managers, a standard which once applied should lead to the effective minimisation of risk (Pender, 2001). Optimal implies in the context of this study that first, the project risk manager perceives the use of project risk management as effective. Second, from their point of view, risks are effectively identified, analysed and responded to with the ultimate result that the adverse influence of risks on the project outcome is minimised.

Various sources underline the supposed effectiveness of the basic project risk management process of identifying, analysing and responding to risk (e.g. Boehm, 1991; Elkington et al., 2002; Fairley, 1994; Williams & Walker, 1997). However, whether project risk management is actually considered by managers to be effective has been given little attention. In June 1998, Raz and Michael (2001) investigated whether project managers in the software and high-tech sectors in Israel perceive project risk management as an important activity (see Table 2.4).

Question: To what extent does the Risk Management process contribute to the following?		Mean	Standard deviation
1.	Overall project success	3.94	0.57
2.	Meeting project schedule	3.76	0.74
3.	Meeting project budget	3.58	0.78
4.	Meeting planned objectives	3.74	0.70
5.	Achieving customer satisfaction	3.36	0.93
6.	Success of other projects in your organisation	2.89	0.99
7.	Risk Management Contribution Index (average of the scores over the six items)	3.55	0.51

Table 2.4: Descriptive statistics for the risk management contribution questions
Likert scale 0 Very Low – 5 Very High
(Raz et al., 2001, p. 14)

Table 2.3 shows that project managers in the Israeli high tech sector think that in the project risk management contributes highly to the overall project success emphasising the importance of this project management discipline.

In 1999, (Burchett, Tummala Rao, & Leung, 1999) carried out research in the electrical supply industry. They researched the perceived benefits of formal project risk management. The findings are displayed in Figure 2.7:

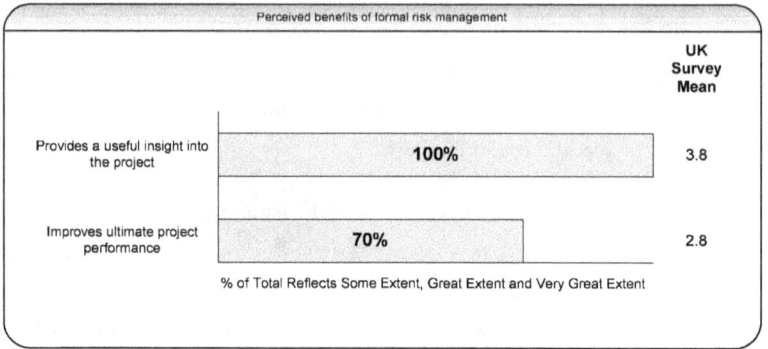

Figure 2.7: Perceived benefits of formal risk management in electrical supply projects[4]
(Burchett et al., 1999, p. 88)

According to Table 2.4 and Figure 2.7, project managers perceive the contribution of project risk management to the overall project success as significant. The findings of the survey show that project risk management among other key disciplines in project management is considered to play a significant role in ensuring project success. However, taking the considerable rate of failure into account, project managers also blame inadequate project risk management for not preventing project failure.

In 1997, KPMG launched another survey including a sample of 1,450 chief executives in organisations across Canada for the purpose of shedding further light on why project management does not ensure project success. The survey revealed that the most common contributors to project failure in terms of not meeting budget and schedule overruns are a weak business case (lack of specification), lack of management support and in particular inadequate project risk management. Whittaker (1999, p. 29) argues: "(Inadequate) risk management remains the highest ranked factor contributing to project failure, ...". Other authors such as Johnston (1995) reinforce this view.

Overall, the amount of literature suggesting how project risk management should be applied far exceeds the evidence concerning actual perceived effectiveness of project risk

---

[4] Projects are transmission, generation and distribution projects within the electricity supply industry world-wide.

management. Few researchers have addressed whether project managers perceive the process stages of identification, analysis and response as effective.

Little research exists about the project manager's self-evaluation of the effectiveness of project risk management stages, especially in IT projects. Furthermore, most evidence appears to come from researchers focusing on non-IT industries such as construction. Hence, this study investigates how effective project risk management in IT projects is perceived from the project manager's point of view.

2.4. Problems with project risk management

Although EUT as a foundation of project risk management standards describes how a manager *should* make decisions, evidence shows that their actions often deviates from EUT (Bourgeois et al., 1988; Cooke & Slack, 1984; Einhorn et al., 1986; Hedge, 1987; Jaeger et al., 2001; Jennings & Wattam, 1994; March et al., 1987; Neumann & Politser, 1992; Simon, 1978; Tversky & Kahneman, 1974, 1992). Hoehn (1988, p. 1120) suggests: "The expected utility model describes how an agent with unbounded cognitive capacity makes decisions when confronted with imperfect information." However, Ritchie (1993, p. 190) argues:

> "We acknowledge that these essentially normative models of decision behaviour have the advantage of simplicity and the ability to quantify risk, but we follow the line adopted by some commentators that such models are inadequate in their failure to describe the practical processes of risk assessment in decision-making."

In the next sections I will discuss theoretical violations of EUT and how those violations reflect practical problems for project managers.

2.4.1. Violations of fundamental assumptions of project risk management

The deviation from choices according to EUT may derive from

- the uncertainty associated with taking any given action and whether or not negative outcomes will result,

- cognitive and emotional overload that results from awareness of risk in many, if not most, behaviours and

- the complex and varied dynamics associated with performing any given behaviour (Adler, Kegeles, & Genevro, 1992, p. 251).

Other authors, such as Yates and Stone (1992), emphasise that the norm of rationality according to expected utility theory can be troubling to make sense of risky choices under the consideration of uncertainty and collective decision making, that is to say if more than one actor in decision making is involved. The discrepancy between how project managers decide and how they should decide is summarised by March and Shapira (1987). They base their conclusions on the findings of two major studies about managerial perceptions of risk: the study by Shapira (1986) which is based on interviews with fifty executives from American and Israel, and on a study conducted by Mac Grimmon and Wehrung (1986) based on questionnaire responses from over six hundred executives in Canada and America. They concluded that there is strong evidence in their studies as well as in others (e.g. Fischhoff, Lichtenstein, Slovic, Derby, & Keeney, 1981) that individuals "do not trust, do not understand, or simply do not much use precise probability estimates" (March et al., 1987, p. 1411). Moreover they state that risks with a low probability are ignored and risks are compromised by a conflict of interest between the individual who produces the risk estimates and the individual that is affected by the risks.

Another problem relates to the view taken in this study that risk and uncertainty are not a pure objective entities, but include subjective judgement. The role of judgement in estimating probabilities has found some attention in literature. In particular, some scholars have researched whether certain factors influenced their effectiveness to accurately predict probabilities. In one of the most prominent studies, Tversky and Kahneman (1974) investigated the impact of individuals' experiences of an event on their estimation of similar future events. Those with a more recent experience tend to believe that the events will be more likely to happen again, therefore overestimating the probability of its occurring. Estrada (2000), for example, comes to the conclusion that investors investing in the European securities market underestimate the risk of stock returns. Other results indicate, that individuals overestimate low risks and underestimate high risks (Lichtenstein, Slovic, Fischhoff, Layman, & Combs, 1978). Misestimating risk and its probabilities has also been the subject of other studies. Wright and Ayton (1989) come to the conclusion that personal events which are thought to unfold in the near future are associated with an increased probability. Milburn (1978) focuses on non-personal events and argues that in the last four decades undesirable events are considered to be less likely to occur.

Regardless what reasons lay behind the misestimation of risk, few attempts have been made to investigate the accurateness of project managers' estimations of risk in the context of IT projects. Hence, an assessment of the effectiveness of project risk management in terms of the accuracy of IT project managers' estimations is considered to be worthwhile for this study.

2.4.2. Violations in practice

The deviations from EUT, in principal, may already indicate why project risk management is not as effective as it should be. In practice, one reason that project risk management does not lead to the response and prevention of risk is because project management is not applied so ultimately risks are not managed. Not applying project risk management may explain why risks are not addressed as outlined before as a major problem. According to an investigation of a Munich consultancy firm, in seventy percent of all projects, project risk management is entirely missing (Steeger, 2003).

However, when project risk management is applied, problems in its application also arise. Some researchers report that project managers have difficulties in analysing risks (e.g. Bryne & Cadman, 1984; Teo, Quah, Torrance, & Okoro, 1991). Wood and Ellis (2003) examined the use of risk management procedures in the UK construction industry. They underline the fact that project managers encounter problems in managing risk. Exemplary, one of his interviewees mentioned: "A lot of teams get hung up on the scoring – well, how much is a point on these ratings; how much is a point worth?" (Wood et al., 2003, p. 259).

A review of existing literature has revealed several problems with risk management (see Table 2.5).

Problems with project risk management	Authors
Problem of hindsight	Zmud (1980); Ward and Chapman (1991); Akintoye and MacLead (1997); Tummala Rao, Leung, Burchett and Leung (1997); Frosdick (1997); Burchett, Tummala Rao and Leung (Burchett et al., 1999); Lanza (2000); Pender (2001); Ramgopal (2003); Lyons and Skitmore (2004)
Problem of ownership	Hall (1975); Ward and Chapman (1991)
Problem of cost justification	Ward and Chapman (1991); Akintoye and MacLead (1997); Tummala Rao, Leung, Burchett and Leung (1997); Frosdick (1997); Burchett, Tummala Rao and Leung (1999); Royer (2000); Lanza (2000); McGrew and Bilotta (2000); Raz and Michael (2001); Dedolph (2003); Vogwell (2003); Lyons and Skitmore (2004)
Problem of lack of expertise	Ward and Chapman (1991); Akintoye and MacLead (1997); Whittaker (1999); Burchett, Tummala Rao and Leung (Burchett et al., 1999); McGrew and Bilotta (2000); Dedolph (2003); Lyons and Skitmore (2004)
Problem of arousal	Frosdick (1997); Royer (2000); Steeger (2003)
Problem of ambiguity in risk estimates	Hall (1975); Ward and Chapman (1991); Tummala Rao, Leung, Burchett and Leung (1997); Burchett, Tummala Rao and Leung (1999); Royer (2000); Vogwell (2003); Ramgopal (2003)

Table 2.5: Barriers to optimal and effective project risk management

The purpose of project risk management is to manage risk in advance, that is to say, to respond to risks that may have a future adverse impact on the project outcome. Risk management is reliant on hindsight as a predicator for future risks. The *problem of hindsight* relates to the degree of uncertainty that is inherited in a project (Young, 1998). In comparison to other project areas such as in construction, IT related projects appear to include a relatively high degree of uncertainty (Graham, 1999; Wirth, 1996). Whereas projects in the industries of pharmaceutical and notebook development as well as in earth moving resemble "variation" projects as displayed in Figure 2.8 with cost, time and performance levels varying randomly but within a predictable range, the development of a software service (Internet) defined as "chaos" projects may to a large extent invalidate any prediction (Meyer, Loch, & Pich, 2002).

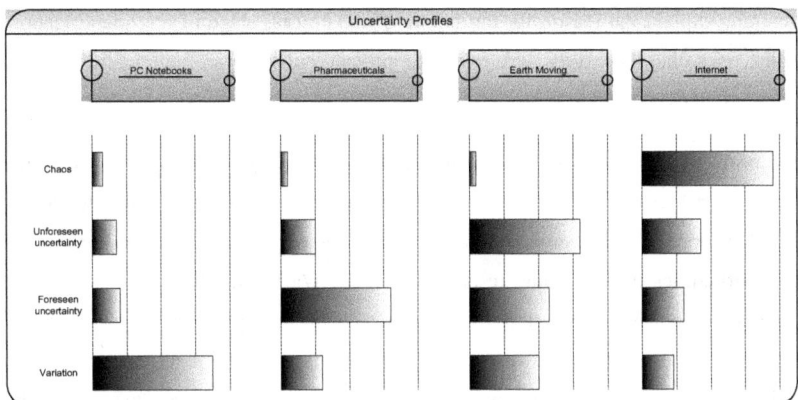

Figure 2.8: Uncertainty profiles
(Meyer et al., 2002, p. 96)

The problem arising through the lack of hindsight in projects is that project manager may not rely on the validity of probabilistic conclusions about future risk based upon historical data (Frosdick, 1997; Pender, 2001). In this respect Shakle (1952, p. 5) states:

"The theory of probability, in the form which has been given to it by mathematicians and actuaries, is adapted to discovering the tendencies of a given system under indefinitely repeated trials or experiments. In any set of such trials, each trial is, for the purpose of discovering such a tendency, given equal weight with all the others. No individual trial is considered to have any importance in itself for its own sake, and any tendency which may be inductively discovered or predicted a priori for the system, tells us nothing about any single individual trial which we may propose to make the future".

Frosdick (1997, p. 176) further adds:

"The techniques of risk estimation are largely quantitatively based and make claims to scientific objectivity, which are undermined on several fronts. There are question marks about the extent to which event and reliability data can itself be relied on for accuracy. In the absence of adequate data, the assignment of probabilities is a subjective process dependent on the assigner's own bias."

The degree of uncertainty implies that learning from past experience may not take place with the consequence that risks remain hidden until they materialise (Douglas & Wildavsky, 1982).

Hence, this may explain the reason for the failure of the process stage of risk identification, namely why risks that adversely influence the project outcome are not addressed and ultimately not proactively responded to.

The second problem of project risk management is the *problem of ownership*. As part of the process stage of risk response planning, risk owners are defined as those who should get involved in developing risk response actions. However, the perception of ownership of risks may lead to difficulties in developing responses to risks. Ward and Chapman (1991) argue that risk actors may not feel responsible for risks because they are perceived to be owned by someone else; no clear allocation of responsibility would mean that actually no risk owners are defined. The perception by risk actors that they are not the owner of a risk may caused by their reluctance to be blamed in case the response fails to help mitigating the risk (Hall, 1975). As a result, the risk process at this stage would break down with the result that no individual takes risk response actions.

A problem which has received much attention in risk management literature is the problem of *cost justification*. The application of project risk management requires the commitment of resources such as manpower. Time and money need to be invested to carry out the process of managing risks. However, the costs are often difficult to justify. The benefits of project risk management are not quantifiable in advance resources are committed to the identification, analysis and response to risks that are not certain to occur. The client owner or sponsor may not spend money and energy on a management process without knowing it has definite benefits (Lanza, 2000; Royer, 2000; Ward et al., 1991). Raz and Michael (2001, p. 14) mention: "One of the reasons we included this part is that we met many project managers who claimed that risk management was an unnecessary activity, and that the resources it required could be put to better use elsewhere in the project."

In consequence, during the phase of risk management planning stakeholders may decide not to implement project risk management at all or only to a very limited degree as Akintoye and MacLoad (1997, p. 37) state: "It is unsurprising that some of the respondents have identified project time constraints as one of the major reasons for not using risk analysis and management techniques". Therefore, the justification of time and ultimately costs involved in carrying out project risk management may pose a problem for project managers in effectively managing risk.

The *lack of expertise* relates to project managers' lack of skills and familiarity when carrying out risk management (Akintoye et al., 1997; Ward et al., 1991). Project managers may not know how to use statistical tests and or because of their lack of skills may not apply risk management process in the way suggested in best practice standards.

The next problem encountered in project risk management is the problem of *arousal*. The number of risks that could possibly influence the project outcome is infinite. The process of project risk management enables the project manager to expose these risks and to manage them. However, the exposure may also create anxiety, and negative thoughts may be suppressed (Frosdick, 1997). In an extreme case, the exposure to risk may result in the cancellation of the project because stakeholders take new risks into account and decide not to go ahead with the project which is now perceived as too risky (Royer, 2000). As a result, project managers may limit the degree to which they identify new risks; risks, although legitimate are then suppressed during the risk identification phase and ultimately not optimally managed.

The last problem bearing on project risk management that is salient in project risk management literature is the *problem of ambiguity* of risk estimates. Due to the lack of statistical data for predicting future risks, project managers often rely on subjective estimates (Ramgopal, 2003). However, other stakeholders may not believe in the credibility of these risk estimates and may not trust them. Hence, during the phase of risk identification and risk analysis, stakeholders may disagree over whether risks are "real" and what risks are considered to be untrue with the result that some risks which actually materialise will not be included in the process of risk response planning and risk monitoring and control but actually materialise.

In recent years, two studies investigating the problems similar to those discussed before have attracted attention. In 2002, Lyons and Skitmore (2004) investigated factors limiting the implementation of risk management in Australian construction projects. Table 2.6 shows the results of this study.

Frequency of items preventing implementation of risk management	
	Weighted average score (1 – low, 5 – high)
Lack of time[5]	3.0
Lack of familiarity with the techniques[6]	2.9
Lack of dedicated resources[7]	2.9
Lack of expertise with techniques[8]	2.8
Lack of information[9]	2.7
Difficulties in seeing the benefits[10]	2.6
Human / organisational resistance[11]	2.5
Lack of accepted industry model for analysis[12]	2.3

Table 2.6: Items preventing risk management in the construction industry
(Lyons et al., 2004, p. 54)

According to Table 2.6, the most dominant factor for constraining the effectiveness of project risk management is the lack of time, with a moderately high average. The lack of time and the lack of dedicated resources indicate a problem of cost-justification. Similar findings about the barriers of using risk management in three Hong Kong industries were found in a further prominent study (Tummala Rao et al., 1997).

---

[5] relates to the problem of cost justification
[6] relates to the problem of lack of expertise
[7] relates to the problem of cost justification
[8] relates to the problem of lack of expertise
[9] relates to the problem of hindsight
[10] relates to the problem of cost justification
[11] no categorisation possible
[12] relates to the problem of lack of expertise

	% of total reflecting agree to strongly agree		
	Building services industry[13]	Transportation industry[14]	Electricity supply industry[15]
Difficulty in obtaining input estimates and assessment of their probabilities[16]	78	75	77
Time involvement[17]	78	47	85
Difficulty in understanding and interpreting outcomes of risk management process[18]	62	44	62
Managers can not agree on quantification of uncertainty/subjective probability assessment[19]	46	72	76
Cost-justification of risk management process techniques[20]	58	31	58
Difficulty in determining trade-off between risk and return[21]	-	-	65

Table 2.7: Summary of the inherent problems encountered
(Tummala Rao et al., 1997, p. 310)

As can be seen in Table 2.7, the findings of this study reveal a similar picture. In two out of three industries, the lack of time was the major influence of constraining the use of risk management.

PMBOK guide style best practice project management standards as introduced in chapter 1 and promoted by organisations such as PMI or APM appear to be self-evidently correct. In this respect, Williams (2004, p. 2) argues:

"Project management as set out in this work is presented as a set of procedures that are self-evidently correct: following these procedures will produce effectively managed projects; project failure is indicative of inadequate attention to the project management procedures."

Assumptions of project risk management include as previously mentioned rationality, knowledge of probable future states, frictionless transactions, random events and repeatability of events (Pender, 2001). However, in principal, random events and repeatability of events can be rejected due to the theoretically unique nature of projects. Furthermore, these assumptions appear to be in conflict with the problems which have been identified in Table 2.5. In particular, the assumption of the knowledge of probable future states conflicts with the

---

[13] refers to current practice in preparing building services cost estimates
[14] refers to current practice in capital budgeting
[15] refers to current practice in project selection
[16] relates to the problem of hindsight
[17] relates to the problem of cost justification
[18] relates to the problem of ambiguity in risk estimates
[19] relates to the problem of ambiguity in risk estimates
[20] relates to the problem of cost justification

lack of hindsight. Frictionless transactions and rationality are not compatible with the problem of ownership, cost justification, arousal and ambiguity in risk estimates. Therefore, under the consideration of these contradictions, the idea of self-evidently correct project management standards is bound not to be fully effective.

2.5. Propositions

Although some evidence exists to answer the research problem of whether interventions influence the IT project manager in effectively managing risks, most of the evidence is descriptive and relies on assumptions rather than on empirical findings; hence these findings lack theoretical relevance. The empirical studies as reviewed above by Lysons and Rummala (2004) and Tummala *et al.* (1997) are first conducted in research contexts of construction, transportation and electricity supply projects but not in the specific context of IT projects. Second, although they investigated the impact of some problems bearing on project risk management such as the problem of hindsight, they failed to look at others such as the problem of arousal or the problem of ownership. In consequence, because of the lack of current evidence about which factors influence project risk management and to what degree they constrain the effective use of project risk management, the definition of hypotheses at this stage appears to be inadequate. Indeed, factors influencing project risk management need first to be explored before any statement regarding their existence and their relationship with project risk management and the project outcome can be made.

This section discusses the conceptual underpinnings of the key concepts of risk, project risk management, risk mediators and the project outcome. The first key concept is project risk management. According to the Project Management Institute, project risk management is defined as the systematic process of identifying, analysing, and responding to risk. Project risk management as outlined in standards such as the Project Management Body of Knowledge (Project Management Institute, 2004) is one of nine key disciplines ensuring that the project outcome is achieved, namely that the project manager is able to meet project related objectives such as time, cost and scope and as discussed in the literature review further outcome dimensions that will be explored. This leads to the first proposition:

Proposition 1: IT project managers will perceive that the use of project risk management contributes to the project outcome.

[21] relates to the problem of cost justification

Project risk management standards have traditionally relied on the expected utility theorem (Pender, 2001). The choice of whether to execute actions predominately involves statistically assessing threats and includes cost-benefit analysis (Glendon, 1987; Renn, 1992). That is to say it proposes a choice between risks based on the likelihood of their occurrence and the impact of threats. Project risk management offers an optimal and rational process that enables project managers to minimise the influence of risk on the project outcome. Under the assumed "perfect" conditions of EUT, the process of identifying, analysing risks and responding to risk should theoretically lead to the prevention of risks adversely influencing the project outcome.

Risk as a second key concept in this study is an ambiguous term because many meanings and definitions exist in different research traditions such as technology, statistics, psychology and economics (Otway et al., 1982). In the project management literature, a variety of definitions also exist (e.g. British Standards Institution, 2000; Grey, 1995; Keller & Keller, 1998; MacCrimmon et al., 1986; Maylor, 1999; Young, 1998). Whereas Keller and Keller (1998, p. 67) define risk narrowly as a "chance of adverse consequences or loss occurring", Buttrick (1997, p. 4) describes risk as a "potential threat or occurrence which may prevent you from achieving your defined business goals. It may affect timescale, cost, quality, or benefits." More broadly, Raftery (1994, p. 5) defines risk as follows: "Risk and uncertainty characterise situations where the *actual* outcome for a particular event or activity is likely to deviate from the estimate or forecast value". In the context of project management, a working synthesis may be along the following lines: Project risk can be defined as anything that causes the actual project outcomes to adversely deviate from their estimated value.

In principal, project managers should be able to prevent risks from materialising as is claimed by best practice project risk management standards. That is to say, they should perceive project risk management as effective:

Proposition 2: IT project managers will perceive the use of project risk management as effective for managing risks.

As discussed and defined in the literature review, the concept of risk is neither purely objective nor subjective; project managers manage perceived risks. Project managers identify, analyse and respond to risk in advance. However, the risk may or may not occur as predicted. Pablo (1999, p. 102) and Jemison (1987, p. 1088) argue risk is an *ex ante* construct (perceived risk), which leads to an actual *ex post* outcome (actual risk). Therefore, as Ritchie (1993) suggests, perceived risk can be lower or greater than the actual risk.

Project managers may attach greater risk to a project than the project actually inherits or they may predict greater effect uncertainty than actually exists. In the process of project risk management, project managers may misestimate risks, their *ex ante* estimation about risk may be lower or higher that the *ex post* outcome of risks (actual influence of risk on the project outcome).

The degree of misestimating risk or uncertainty, that is to say the divergence between *ex ante* estimated and *ex post* materialised risk can be determined by its degree of over- and underestimation. Bearing Milliken's recommendation to distinguish between three types of uncertainty in mind, underestimation of risk (*ex ante* estimated risk < *ex post* outcome of risk) by the project manager implies, that

- either uncertainties with probable negative effects have not been identified but actually materialised, **and/or** probabilities have been assessed as lower than their actual value (underestimation of state uncertainty)

- and/or consequences of identified uncertainties have been assessed as lower than their actual value (underestimation of effect uncertainty),

- and/or responses have a lesser impact than predicted (underestimation of response uncertainty).

Overestimation of risk (*ex ante* estimated risk > *ex post* outcome of risk) by the project manager means that

- uncertainties have been identified but not actually materialised **and/or** probabilities have been assessed as higher than their actual value (overestimation of state uncertainty),

- and/or consequences of identified uncertainties have been assessed as higher than their actual value (overestimation of effect uncertainty),

- and/or responses have a bigger impact than predicted (overestimation of response uncertainty).

Figure 2.9 displays the result of such a mismatch between perceived and actual risk. As can be seen, aspects such as risk perception by risk actors in a turbulent environment (i.e., constantly changing and ambiguous) are likely to lead to a mismatch between an anticipated world and a world as it actually turns out. Uncertainties become reality and may be perceived as surprises by project managers, as they may have been unaware of these uncertainties beforehand.

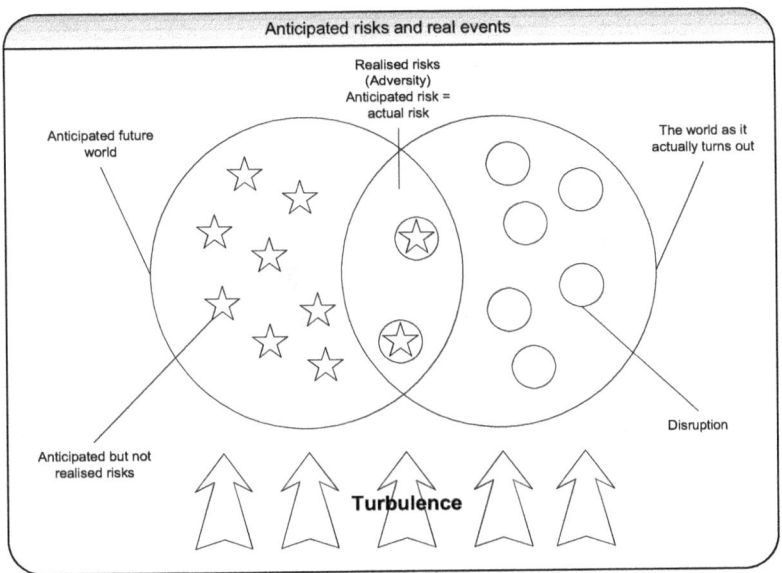

Figure 2.9: Anticipated risks and real events
(Adapted from Floricel & Miller, 2001, p. 447)

The consequence of this mismatch between anticipated risk and actual risk may adversely influence the project outcome and lead to the dismissal of the value of project risk management by risk actors; they may perceive it as ineffective. If project managers underestimate risks, they may regard project risk management as ineffective because it does not prevent uncertainties with an adverse consequences on time, cost and scope materialising; if they overestimate risk, they may also dismiss the value of project risk management since they spend time and budget on assessing uncertainties which have not materialised or with lower adverse consequences than estimated (McGrew et al., 2000). However, under the assumed optimal conditions according to EUT, project managers will not misestimate risks with the ultimate consequence that risks will not adversely influence the project outcome:

Proposition 3: IT project managers will perceive that project risks were not over- or underestimated.

Proposition 3 appears to be similar to proposition 2. However, they are not identical. Proposition 2 poses a statement about the perceived effectiveness of project managers in relation to their actions. In contrast, proposition 3 includes a statement about effectiveness perceived by project managers regarding the outcome of their actions. Those propositions may not reveal the same result. Project managers may under- and overestimate risk. However, taking expectations into account, they may still perceive their actions as effective or good enough.

As indicated in the literature review, certain problems tend to influence the use of project risk management. For the purpose of clarity, I define these problems or interventions as "risk mediators"; risk-related factors interfering with the orderly management of project risk by project managers. As outlined in the literature review, risk mediators may impose a barrier for project managers to effectively minimise the adverse impact of project risk on the project outcome:

Proposition 4: IT project managers will perceive that risk mediators constrain the effective minimisation of risk by IT project managers.

Based on existing literature, it appears that the norm established by EUT does not reflect of how project managers actually manage risks. Fundamental claims of EUT are violated by risk mediators that have found some attention in the literature. However, whereas in principal the existence of some risk mediators is well established in general risk literature (e.g. Morgan et al., 1990), the consequences of risk mediators in the context of project management have not received much attention. Although various researchers have evaluated the impact of decision maker-related aspects such as ambiguity on the rational choice of decision makers in risk disciplines such as psychology (Kahneman et al., 1979; MacCrimmon et al., 1986; March et al., 1987; Tversky et al., 1974, 1992), the consequences of such risk mediators on the choices made by project managers regarding the management of project risk in IT projects are inadequately researched.

2.6. Conceptual framework

Figure 2.10 presents a conceptual framework that consolidates and interrelates the theory and research results that have been previously evaluated. The conceptual framework of this study as displayed in Figure 2.10 links concepts selected from the literature and previous research I have discussed in this and previous chapter and is considered to be "an impetus for the formulation of theory" (Ambery, 2003, p. 4). In this conceptual framework I define the focus of the research and propose provisional relationships between the key concepts. Included in the model are concepts which have not yet been adequately researched in the field of project management, but which could potentially make significant contributions to the understanding of what risk related factors may restrict a project manager in optimally and effectively managing risks in IT projects.

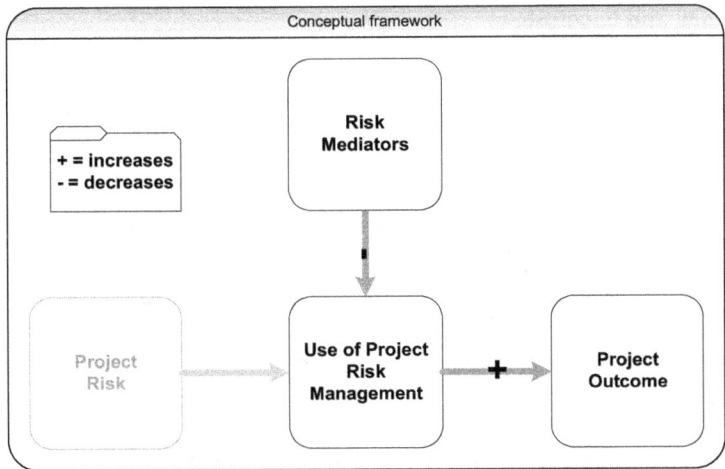

Figure 2.10: Provisional conceptual framework[22]

Through the review of the literature, several risk mediators have been identified which appear to limit project managers in successfully managing risks. Current empirical evidence suggests that despite rules and regulations, risk mediators such as the problem of cost justification appear to play a dominant role in constraining the effect of best practice project risk

---

[22] The aim of this study is not to investigate the concept of risk itself in terms of the degree of risk or what types of risk a project manager perceives or actually materialise. Under the assumption, that risks are inherent in a project and that IT projects fail because of risks, the existence of risk is taken for granted. This study investigates the outcome of project risk management; whether IT project managers perceive project risk management as effective and are able to "optimise the match between perceived risk and actual risk at the time of choosing between alternatives"; why and to what extent project managers fail to misinterpret risk and to prevent risks from adversely influencing the project outcome, characterised by the project manager's ability to meet pre-defined project objectives such as time and cost.

management standards. Navare (2003) points out: "What is clear is that risk management procedures alone do not prevent failure; behaviour can undo what was thought to be tightly controlled." Williams (1995, p. 24) addresses the issue of risk perceptions: "Risk analysis and management can only be good as the perception and quantification of risk by the project team, and it is at this point that the credibility of risk analysis often falls down". Moreover, Pender (1999, p. 80) states,

> "probability theory assumes future states are known and definable, however uncertainty and ignorance are inevitable on projects. Especially with regard to human actions, the future is fundamentally unknowable."

The objective of this study is to investigate the influence of risk mediators on project risk management and ultimately on the project outcome of IT projects.

2.7. Summary and conclusions

In the literature review, project outcome, project risk, the role of project risk management in contributing to project success and failure as well as problems constraining the use of project risk management have been evaluated. In this chapter, a provisional conceptual framework synthesising research on project risk management, project risks, risk mediators and project outcome is also presented.

Regarding the concept of project outcome, the literature review shows that success and failure tend not to be confined to scope, cost and time. Hence, I will research which project outcome criteria project managers consider to be important.

The various standards in project risk management assume optimal conditions, so that project risk management can be effectively applied. No mismatch between perceived risk and actual risk should occur. As a result, risks should to not adversely influence the project outcome. However, the norm of project risk management is questionable as existing evidence indicates that risk mediators interfere with the normative process of managing risks. The assumptions grounded in expected utility theory are heavily criticised by researchers and often argued to be violated.

Reasons for the ongoing failure of project managers to prevent risks from adversely influencing the project outcome in IT projects may be attributed to the consistent difficulties due to specific risk mediators that bear on the application of project risk management. Project risk management as defined by various organisations such as PMI or CCTA is a normative, rationalist set of process stages. However, in the research context of IT projects, reasons why managers do not minimise the influence of risks in particular have gained little attention in the field of project management. Existing research lacks empirical evidence and is often descriptive. Keil, Cule, Lyytinena and Schmidt (1998, p. 77) argue:

> "Since the 1970's, both academics and practitioners have written about risks associated with managing software projects. ...Unfortunately, much of what has been written on risk is based either on anecdotal evidence or on studies limited to a narrow portion of development".

In this study literature such as from the subject area of information systems (e.g. Keil, Mixon, Saarinen, & Tuunainen, 1995; White & Leifer, 1986) insufficiently answer the research problem of this study. Some evidence from industries such as construction about those risk related problems exist, but again, is overall insufficient to address the research problem in the research context of IT projects. As a result, this research will focus on the investigation into whether project risk management is effective from the IT project manager's point of view and whether and why specific risk mediators may constrain the effective response to risks in IT projects. The way the influence of risk mediators on the project outcome of IT projects is investigated will be introduced in the next chapter.

3. RESEARCH METHODS AND TECHNIQUES

In the previous chapter, I suggested three concepts to be investigated: risk mediators and their influence on project risk management and the project outcome. As discussed earlier, the influence of specific risk mediators on project risk management may lead to the perception by project managers that project risk management lacks effectiveness as well as to the over- and underestimation of risk by project managers and consequently to adverse impacts of risks on the project outcome.

In this chapter, I describe the methods and techniques I applied to investigate the research problem. In section 3.1, I introduce the two phases of the research; exploratory research at the beginning and explanatory at the end. I describe the phase of exploratory research to clarify my understanding of the influence of risk mediators on project risk management and the phase of explanatory research to test this understanding on a wider population of project managers. Section 3.2 includes a discussion of the chosen method for the exploratory research. In section 3.3, I evaluate the use of semi-structured interviews as the research technique in this phase. Concerning the explanatory phase of research, I discuss the suitability of a survey method for this study in section 3.4. As a research technique in section 3.5, a web-based questionnaire for data gathering from IT project managers and data analysis is offered to uncover patterns and to confirm these patterns. In section 3.6, I discuss the theoretical perspective for this research that lies behind the chosen methodology. In section 3.7, the ontology and epistemology inherent in the theoretical perspective is described. In section 3.8, I discuss the sampling process and in section 3.9, quality issues of the research such as validity and reliability are described. In section 3.10, I sum up the discussions about the research strategy for this study.

3.1. Research phases

This study was divided into two phases, exploratory research with the purpose of increasing the understanding of the research problem at the outset of the study and explanatory to confirm this understanding at the end (Miles & Huberman, 1994). Exploratory research is for clarifying "your understanding of a problem" (Saunders, Lewis, & Thornhill, 1997, p. 78). It involves the purpose of discovery (Robson, 2002). As the research problem in this study is little understood in risk management, especially in the project risk management literature, my rationale for an exploratory phase at the outset of the study was to "find out what is

59

happening" (Robson, 2002, p. 59), to gain a deep and rich insight into *what* risk mediators influence project risk management and *how* those risk mediators constrain or facilitate project risk management and ultimately the project outcome, and to generate patterns to be tested in the phase of explanatory research.

In contrast to exploratory research, explanatory studies seek to explain a situation or a problem (Robson, 2002). That is to say it identifies relationships between identified and explored concepts (Saunders et al., 1997; Scapens, 1990). The second phase of this study, explanatory research, investigated any patterns which developed during the first phase of research and also any new emergent patterns that remained undiscovered in the exploratory phase. This phase had the purpose of improving understanding of the research problem of this study gained during the exploratory phase. This means that after receiving a rich, detailed, deep and "complete" insight into the patterns of several cases, an informative, but inherently limited view was produced of the nature of the concepts in the proposed conceptual framework, and their relationships. As a result of the exploratory research, for example, I found out that some risk mediators appear to have an influence on project risk management. However, this influence could only be generalised to a maximum of eighteen analysed cases and therefore has limited predictive power. Hence, I showed that the explored concepts developed during the exploratory phase "fit together according to some rules" (Miles et al., 1994, p. 90) with the intention of obtaining evidence about these rules or patterns from a wider population of cases within the research setting of IT projects for the purpose of enhancing the generalisation of findings.

3.2. Research methods in the exploratory research phase

The purpose of the exploratory phase was to make sense of patterns related to the influence of risk mediators in the context of project risk management in IT projects. Although significant research has been conducted about risk in disciplines such as in psychology (Kahneman et al., 1979; Pablo, 1997, 1999; Sitkin & Weingart, 1995), data about risk mediators and their effect on project risk management in the particular context of project management are scarce. As the existing literature and existing theory identified in the literature review fail to sufficiently inform the research, the exploratory phase had the purpose of generating patterns to be tested in the second phase of the research which are grounded in the reality of project managers. This step prevents patterns being solely generated from literature and intuition (Turner, 1981) with the consequence that such patterns may have no relevance to what is actually happening in IT projects concerning project risk management. Hence, this phase included the element of discovery relying more on grounded theory.

Grounded theory was first developed by Glaser and Strauss (1967), who created a counterbalance to "logico-deductive methods" (Goulding, 1998; Partington, 2000; Smith & Biley, 1997).

> "A grounded theory is inductively derived from the process of study. The researcher does not begin with a hypothetical theory and then prove it. Rather, he begins by collecting the data in the field first; then he "starts analysing the data and generating a theory" (Backman & Kyngaes, 1999, p. 148).

The grounded theory "type of process of reflexivity" (Miller & Fredericks, 1999, p. 541) reflects the "constant interplay between proposing and checking" (Strauss & Corbin, 1990, p. 111), generating "provisional theory" (Miller et al., 1999, p. 543) utilising a variety of quantitative and qualitative methods. In this research, the labels of the concepts which emerged were rather fanciful at the beginning, vague and broadly defined. With the gradual gathering of additional data, I changed, changed again and adjusted these labels until they precisely fit the categorised data, in order to provide a valid and reliable but provisional theory to be tested in the second explanatory phase of the study.

This exploratory phase had a firm focus on grounded theory. On the one hand, it adopts two major techniques that are central to grounded theorising. First, it includes a comparative method or as previously described a process of reflexivity. Second, the other essential method to grounded theorising is the use of a theoretical sample rather than a representative sampling (see section 3.8) (Hammersley, 1989). On the other hand, not all the criteria to judge whether this study follows a pure grounded theory approach are fulfilled. In particular, some criteria defined by Corbin and Strauss (1990; 1990) regarding the research process and empirical grounding are violated. For example, grounded theory requires an exploration without any pre-determined or descriptive framework (Strauss et al., 1990). I had already established an *a priori* theory (conceptual framework) for this study before I carried out the fieldwork. Furthermore, the paradigm features of conditions, context, action/interaction (including strategies), and consequences have not been used as suggested. As a result, although no pure grounded theorising was carried out, the overall methodology that was applied as part of the exploratory research is grounded theory oriented. The resulting lack of explanatory power suggested by Corbin and Strauss (1990; 1990) was compensated for by the use of a subsequent explanatory phase of research.

By applying the two mentioned principles of grounded theory, my understanding of the research problem in the specific context of project risk management was framed and reframed as I analysed the data gained from project managers. A pattern in one case emerged, for example, showing that a specific risk mediator had a specific effect on project risk management. This pattern was reframed or confirmed by comparing it with each additional case. If an interview with a project manager revealed a new pattern, for instance, that one specific risk mediator did not lead to a specific project risk management action by a project manager as had happened in a previous case, then I asked "Why not?". I might have wrongly understood the first pattern or the second pattern might have included a different risk mediator. This iterative process of proposing and checking of patterns or as Bryman (2001) suggests the process of interpretation and theorising, although very time consuming, increased my understanding in order to answer the research questions.

A significant problem, which may arise through the use of exploratory research, is anecdotalism (Bryman, 2001). Arguably, this phase of research focuses on the qualitative analysis of subjective data. Hence, there is the risk that "we are left with interesting stories about what happened, of unknown truth and utility" (Miles et al., 1994). However, the analysis in this study not only provides a descriptive account of cases but also includes a stream of conclusion drawing and verification. Through the exploration of the influence of risk mediators on project risk management in more than one case, the ability to compare cases represents a "powerful conceptual mechanism" (Stake, 1995, p. 242), leading to the evaluation of similarities and differences between cases or groups of cases (Eisenhardt, 1989; Jick, 1979; Yin, 1994). One strategy for searching for patterns suggested by Eisenhardt (1989) is to select categories, then to categorise each case and to look for within group similarities and intergroup differences. In this study, the comparison between established categories included, for example, overestimation of risk versus underestimation of risk or success of a project versus failure of a project.

As a result, the phase of exploratory research already includes a certain degree of data reduction or in other words, leads to provisional theory or to the definition of hypotheses open to further testing in the explanatory phase of this research. Bryman (2001, p. 449) argues:

"Because of the tendency towards and unstructured, open-ended approach to data collection, qualitative research is often very helpful as a source of hypotheses or hunches that can be subsequently tested using a quantitative research strategy". Hence, although qualitative research facilitates quantitative research in this study, the problem of anecdotalism has already been addressed in this first phase of qualitative research.

3.3. Research techniques in the exploratory research phase

I study the research problem of whether and how risk mediators influence the effective application of project risk management by project managers and ultimately influence the project manager's ability to prevent risks from affecting the project outcome in the context of IT projects. The purpose of the initial exploratory phase of this study was to understand the "social reality" of project managers and how they have experienced risk mediators and their influence on project risk management. Hence, I required a research technique that allowed me first, to obtain a rich and detailed view of the social reality of multiple cases and to gain a deep insight into what is relevant from the respondent's point of view and second, to identify a range of different categories of intervening risk mediators and their consequences on project risk management. The number of cases was determined by the conceptual needs of the study. In this respect, Ashill and Jobber (2001), for example, explore Milliken's uncertainty dimensions in the context of marketing decision-making by conducting twenty in-depth interviews. They consider this technique to be suitable in order to gain an insight into how senior marketing executives interpret uncertainty in their environment. As a result, bearing in mind the purposes of this phase and the choice of techniques by other researchers such as Ashill and Jobber, I chose the research technique of interviews as being the most suitable to explore the research problem.

In addition to in-depth interviews, the general research literature (Burgess, 1984; Easterby-Smith, Thorpe, & Lowe, 1991; Saunders et al., 1997) distinguishes between two basic types of interviews: unstructured interviews and semi-structured interviews. Other authors have further differentiated between standardised and non-standardised interviews, although their definition slightly varies (e.g. Patton, 1990; Saunders et al., 1997). Structured interviews include questionnaires with standardised questions whereas unstructured and semi-structured interviews include an agenda of topics to be dealt with (Saunders et al., 1997).

Bryman (2001) argues a structured interview with standardised questions and a predetermined sequence may impose the researcher's view about managerial perceptions on the interviewee, leaving little space for the respondents own perspective. Hence, for the purpose of exploring the research questions, a semi-structured interview approach was initially considered as most appropriate for this study.

The use of semi-structured interviews enabled me to gather rich and detailed data about the social reality of IT project managers related, to their perceptions about risk, effectiveness of project risk management and project outcome. This technique allowed me gain an insight into what the respondent considered to be relevant. It provided me with the flexibility to adapt my questions to the specific social reality of the project manager in "real time" (during the interview), that means to the specific perceptions an IT project manager had, for example, about the management of risk, the effectiveness of project risk management and the project outcome of a particular IT project.

As can be seen in Appendix A, the semi-structured interview design included key questions about the background of the case, risk, perceived effectiveness of project risk management and about the outcome of the project. Some key questions to the project manager were asked as a starting point for discussions. These questions were open-ended questions to allow the respondent to answer however they wanted. Hence, the respondents could express their reality as they wished; they were able to give me new and "surprising" answers, for instance, about how and why they perceive project risk management as effective, which helped me to understand a pattern in a specific case and to compare these patterns with other cases.

In the initial stage, I carried out six pilot interviews to become accustomed to interviewing, which Robson (2002) describes as a complex social interaction. At the end of each pilot interview, the respondents gave feedback. It soon turned out that the interview approach was flawed and had to be changed. The questions used in the initial interviews were too closed and not flexible enough. Indeed, some questions were hypothetical and almost impossible for the respondents to answer. Furthermore due to technical problems, data was lost from two interviews. In consequence, the experience I gathered through the pilot stage was on the one hand important as it enabled me to change the whole approach of the interviews, to become more comfortable in interview situations, to increase flexibility and to be able to be more investigative and not only to adhere to pre-stated questions. On the other hand, the data gained through the pilot interviews was of a doubtful nature because no holistic view was gained. Therefore, theses data were not included in the data analysis.

After pilot interviewing, I conducted interviews with much greater flexibility. The questionnaire in Appendix A was merely used as a guideline. Questions emerged and were changed during the interview to explore developing concepts of intervening risk mediators and their impact on project risk management. As a result, in order to obtain a complete view about the IT project manager's reality, I gradually moved from a semi-structured to a rather unstructured interview approach.

The data in all interviews were recorded with a tape recorder with the consent of the interviewee. As Patton (1980, p. 247) argues, the "interactive nature" of an interview or the flow of interaction can be interrupted by taking notes. Bryman (2001) suggests that the interviewee may be distracted by having to concentrate on writing down notes. Although time consuming, the advantages of tape recording are considerable: it allows re-examination and a more thorough examination of the data by the researcher than is possible during the interview. Other researchers may access the taped and documented data to examine the interviewee's bias. They may also use the data in the light of new ideas (Heritage, 1984).

However, I did not only apply the technique of tape recording, but also used a specific checklist (see Appendix A). The rational behind this was to take notes of important issues in the interviews and to receive a broad, but immediate overview of project risk management in the projects under discussion. Note taking helped me to remain focused on some of the important information given by respondents. This allowed me to re-examine issues, for example, about project risk management and helped to summarise the case at the end of the interview and to check whether I had accurately interpreted the interview data.

3.4. Research methods in the explanatory research phase

During the exploratory phase of the study, patterns of risk mediators and their influence on project risk management and the project outcome within the "real-life" context of IT-projects emerged. However, as the exploration and partial confirmation of the concepts through conceptual saturation (Goulding, 1998), although satisfactory, was based on a relatively small number of cases due to time and cost constraints, the resulting confirmatory power was relatively low. For example, a specific pattern emerged based on the interview data that a project manager's denial of risk (see chapter 4) had an impact on the project outcome. The confirmation of this pattern was restricted the number of project managers I was able to interview as conducting interviews is a time consuming technique. Therefore, in order to generalise the findings from the exploratory phase to all other IT project managers, I applied a survey-related strategy. This strategy allowed me to increase the degree of external validity (see section 3.9).

3.5. Research techniques in the explanatory research phase

After the exploratory phase, I had a deeper understanding of *what* and *how* risk mediators influence the management of risk and the outcome of the project. This understanding was based on patterns that emerged through the analysis of the data from the semi-structured interviews. The purpose of the explanatory phase is to produce further evidence for the these patterns or explanations and to test grounded patterns that were gained through the phase of exploratory research on a wider population.

In risk and uncertainty research, the use of questionnaires to test provisional explanations (hypotheses) appears to be quite common; for example, Sitkin and Weingart (1995) used a questionnaire in order to measure the role of risk perceptions as a mediator in decision making, Milliken (1990) sent questionnaires to five hundred and eighty nine top-level administrators to test the environmental interpretation of different types of uncertainty, and Duncan (1972) used a questionnaire to study uncertainty as perceived by managers.

As can be seen in Table 3.1, in comparison to the research techniques of face-to-face interviews and telephone interviews, a self completion questionnaire has two distinct advantages that are considered important in this study – costs and distribution of sample.

Aspect of survey	Self-completion questionnaire	Face-to-face interview	Telephone interview
Resource factor			
Cost	Low[23]	High	Low / medium
Length of data collection period	Long	Medium / long	**Short**
Distribution of sample	**May be wide**	Must be clustered	**May be wide**
Questionnaire issues			
Length of questionnaire	Short	**May be long**	Medium
Complexity of questionnaire	Must be simple	**May be complex**	**May be complex**
Complexity of questions	Simple to moderate	**May be complex**	Short and simple
Control of question order	Poor	**Very good**	**Very good**
Use of open-ended questions	Poor	**Good**	Fair
Use of visual aids	Good	**Very good**	Not usually possible
Use of personal / family records	**Very good**	Good	Fair
Rapport	Fair	**Very good**	Good
Sensitive topics	**Good**	Fair	Fair / **good**
Data-quality issues			
Sampling frame bias	Usually low	**Low**	Low (with RDD[24])
Response rate	Difficult to get high	Medium / **very high**	Medium / high
Response bias	Medium	**Low**	**Low**
Control of response situation	Poor	**Good**	Fair
Quality of recorded response	Poor	**Good**	Fair

Table 3.1: Comparison of approaches to survey data collection
(Adapted from Czaja & Blai, 1996, p. 32)

The chosen technique of a self-completion questionnaire (in this study a self-completion web based questionnaire) is in comparison to other techniques such as interviews substantially cheaper to administer (Robson, 2002). It is used for the purpose of confirming or refuting patterns constructed during the exploratory phase on a wider scale than is possible through interviews. It may have been more convenient for the respondent because first, the set of questions was standardised and simple to answer and second, I did not need to be present when the project manager answered the questionnaire. However, the disadvantage of a structured questionnaire is that because of the absence of an interviewer to explain a question

---

[23] Entries in bold capitals indicate particularly the type of survey, which has an advantage for a particular aspect.
[24] Random Digit Dialling

which is not understood, the respondents may answer wrongly or decide not to answer the question. Checking the answers may be difficult and time consuming.

In order to tackle this potential problem, the first stage of surveying project managers included a pilot survey. The purpose of the pilot survey was to practise the technique of using a self-completion web based questionnaire in reality. The use of a pilot questionnaire may reveal technical problems as well as offering the opportunity to test the measuring instruments and whether people accept the procedure of a web-based survey (Sapsford, 1999).

Technical problems were not encountered during the trial. After the trial respondents had filled in the questionnaire, I contacted four of them by telephone enquiring whether the questionnaire was clearly structured and whether any problems had occurred in understanding the questions and response options. In addition, in order to increase the accuracy of the questionnaire, I asked the respondents how they had interpreted some of the response options; by cross checking it with other interpretations I was able to determine, whether questions and response options were similarly understood and interpreted by the respondents. The feedback led to a major revision of the structure of the questionnaire and minor corrections to the response options. With a revised questionnaire, the main survey was launched.

3.6. Theoretical perspective

In the previous section, I evaluated how a grounded theory-related method was used to replicate cases and how a survey method was used to generalise the findings gained through the grounded theory related method. In this section, I will show how this overall approach fits within a broader theoretical perspective.

Some literature about research has distinguished between two research perspectives: the positivist and social constructionist perspective (e.g. Bryman, 2001; Crotty, 1998; Easterby-Smith et al., 1991; Guba & Lincoln, 1994; Jankowicz, 1991; Manunta, 2000). A positivistic perspective implies that researchers rely on objective measurement methods, related to their basic belief that the world is external and objective, the researcher independent and science value-free (see Table 3.2). Habermas (1970) argues that the positivist paradigm is defined by its value freedom. The assumption of positivism is very often found in natural sciences, but is less convincing when the activities and behaviour of people are involved. In contrast, the social constructionist paradigm expresses the view that the world is socially constructed and therefore subjective, that the researcher is part of the observed and that science is driven by human interests (Easterby-Smith et al., 1991).

	Ontology	Epistemology	Methodology
Positivism	**Realist** – Reality exists "out there" and is driven by immutable natural laws and mechanisms. Knowledge of these entities, laws and mechanisms is conventionally summarised in the form of time and context free generalisations. Some of these generalisations take the form of cause-effect laws.	**Dualist / Objectivist** – it is possible and essential for the inquirer to adopt a distant, non-interactive posture. Values and other biasing are thereby automatically excluded from influencing outcomes.	**Experimental / Manipulative** – questions and / or hypotheses are stated in advance in prepositional form and subjected to empirical tests (falsification) under carefully controlled conditions.
Post-Positivism	**Critical realist** – reality exists but can never be fully apprehended. It is also driven by natural laws that can only be incompletely understood.	**Modified objectivist** – objectivity remains a regulatory ideal, but it can only be approximated, with special emphasis placed on external guardians such as the critical tradition and critical community.	**Modified experimental / Manipulative** – emphasises critical multiplism. Redresses imbalances by doing inquiry in more natural settings, using more qualitative methods, depending more on grounded theory, and reintroducing discovery into the inquiry process.
Critical Theory	**Critical realist** – as in the case of Post-Positivism.	**Subjectivist** – in the sense that values mediate inquiry.	**Dialogic, transformative** – eliminates false consciousness and energises and facilitates transformation.
Constructivism	**Relativist** – realities exist in the form of multiple mental constructions, socially and experimentally based, local and specific, dependent for their form and content on the persons who hold them.	**Subjectivist** – inquirer and inquired into are fused into a single (monistic) entity. Findings are literally the creation of the process of interaction between the two.	**Hermeneutic, dialectic** – individual are elicited and refined hermeneutically, and compared and contrasted dialectically, with the aim of generating one (or a few) constructions on which there is substantial consensus.

Table 3.2: Positivism and its challengers
(Manunta, 2000, p. 22)

As it involves human behaviour, the world of IT project managers cannot be reduced to a narrow technical, statistical, cost-benefit reality (Pidgeon et al., 1998; Slovic, 2003) and the criticism about the "less thoroughgoing versions of relativism found in some constructionist approaches on the other" (Robson, 2002, p. 42), so I consider the theoretical perspective of post-positivism in the context of project risk management to be most suitable, as it offers a basic belief system for this research perspective by acknowledging the assumption that a risk actor's reality is neither an objective entity of the physical world to be viewed through an extreme positivistic perspective, nor purely socially constructed to be viewed through an extreme constructionist perspective. The theoretical perspective chosen for this study underlines the duality of the project manager's reality regarding risk and uncertainty (see Figure 3.1).

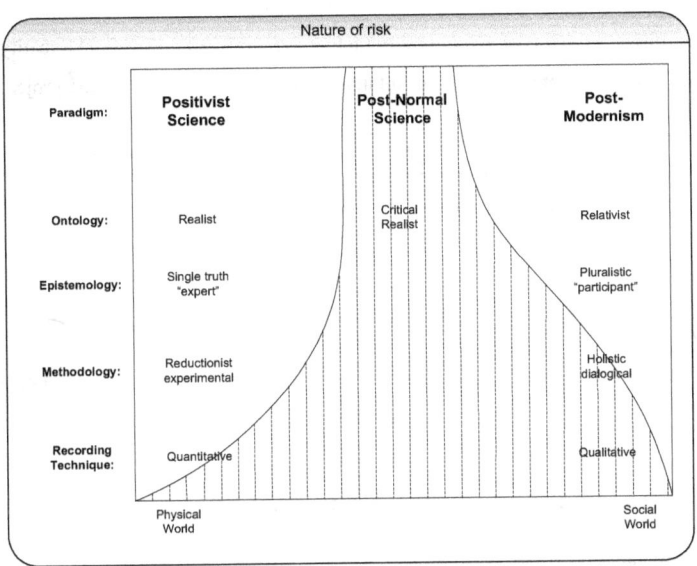

Figure 3.1: Analytical approaches to the study of the physical and social world
(Macgill & Siu, 2004, p. 320)

As can be seen in Figure 3.1, this study assumes a project manager's reality that lies between the two extremes of positivist science and post-modernism – post-positivism. Post-positivism broadly follows the tradition of positivism (Crotty, 1998), but has some distinctive features in terms of ontology and epistemology. These features will be described in the next section.

3.7. Ontology and epistemology

In the previous section, I have determined the research perspective of post-positivism as an appropriate theoretical perspective for this study to acknowledge a project manager's "reality". In this section, I will describe the ontology and epistemology inherent in the theoretical perspective with the purpose of describing whether my findings are subject to falsification or verification.

Inherent in the theoretical perspective of post-positivism is the "multi-level" ontology of realism (Bhaskar, 1975). This ontology includes two basic questions: Which knowledge is acceptable for this study? (Bryman, 2001) and "What is the nature of the knowable?" or "What is the nature of reality?" (Manunta, 2000, p. 20). As discussed, reality is determined as not purely objective, but is to a degree influenced by project managers' perceptions. Hence, as can be seen in Figure 3.2, my findings to the research problem may not actually reflect the empirical reality (empirical domain) or actual reality (actual domain), but may reflect a reality (real domain) which may predominately, but not totally, exist only in the mind of the project managers.

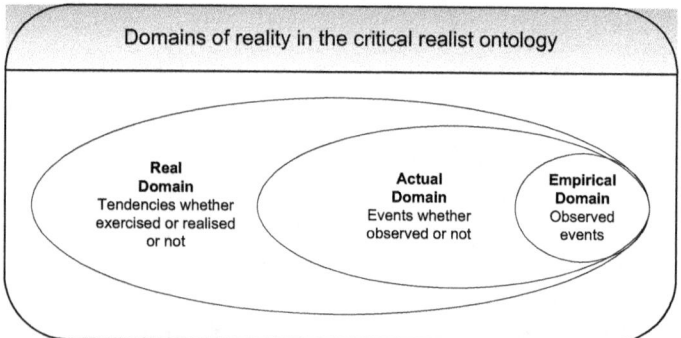

Figure 3.2: Critical realist ontology
(Partington, 2000, p. 98)

Therefore, despite the ideal of objectivity as an assumption of the post-positivistic epistemology (Manunta, 2000), I can only consider findings in this study as "probably true" (Guba et al., 1994, p. 109) and avoid any arrogance in viewing the findings in this study as "true". Justified true beliefs (Manunta, 2000) are generated, which are considered to be tendencies subject for falsification (Partington, 2000). Bhaskar (1975, p. 18) argues: "Roughly the theory advanced here is that statements of laws are tendency statements. Tendencies may be possessed unexercised, exercised unrealised, and realised unperceived by men; they may also be transformed."

Hence, in the context of the research problem of this study, the patterns about the intervening influence of risk mediators on the use of project risk management in the context of IT projects are "imperfectly apprehendable" (Guba et al., 1994, p. 110). As a result, my findings are not absolute or verified laws, but probable trends, that is to say they are neither unique nor absolutely secure and untouchable. Other researchers may attempt to conduct such a study in a different research context, at a different time or with different respondents and may come up with different findings. However, unless there is a methodological error, this does not mean that the findings in this study are not "credible". It means, that the failure to replicate the findings in another setting does not conclusively falsify the theory generated (Robson, 2002).

3.8. Sampling

The population from which I drew the sample in the exploratory and the explanatory phase consisted of a sample of IT project managers. Regarding the exploratory research, Miles and Huberman (1994) argues that qualitative researchers tend to choose their sample purposively rather than randomly. Whereas the chance of a case being chosen is equal in probability sampling, non-probability sampling includes a subjective judgement (Saunders et al., 1997).

During the exploratory phase, I emphasised non-probability sampling, because it is often more beneficial "to learn a lot from an atypical case than a little from a magnificently typical case" (Stake, 1995, p. 243). Eisenhardt (1989) recommends learning from between four and ten cases. However, as Goulding (1998) argues such figures are of arbitrary nature and do not represent an absolute guideline for a researcher. Hence, the sample size in the exploratory phase of this study was determined by conceptual saturation in order to allow me a "complete" insight into the research problem. The number of interviews was determined by the conceptual needs of the study.

In total, twenty-five project managers were interviewed by the researcher. The sample included interviews with project managers mostly employed at major CSPs such as EDS, Colt, T-Systems or PricewaterhouseCoopers. The interviews usually lasted between one and two hours. Most of the projects that were discussed were highly complex implementation projects that often lasted longer than eighteen months. The number of IT systems implemented in some cases reached the 10,000 mark. The implementation projects usually consisted of a planning phase, the actual implementation of the systems and the preparation of user help desk structures. Moreover, because of the volume and complexity of the projects, most often a variety of subcontractors were involved.

The sample of respondents for the survey stage was determined randomly using a cluster sample. Cluster sampling involves the division of the whole population, in this case the whole population of project managers, into units with similar characteristics (Robson, 2002). In the light of time and cost considerations, cluster sampling becomes important (Bryman, 2001). In this study, it allowed me to focus on one unit of IT project managers instead of having to access and to randomly select project managers from the entire UK population, incurring far greater time and cost for this research. However, the disadvantage of a multi cluster sample is sampling errors (Bryman, 2001). Biases might arise due to the undersampling of non-members of APM and PMI and the oversampling of those who are members of these organisations. For example, around 70% of all PMI members worldwide are PMP certified (Project Management Institute, 2005). This certification is similar to the APM's Continuing Professional Development (CPD) scheme. The prerequisite to join the PMP certification programme is a certain educational level and experience in the project environment. The participant further has to go through an examination process which is very much based on assessing and measuring project management knowledge. The foundation document for PMP project management training and education is A Guide to the Project Management Body of Knowledge (PMBOK® Guide) (Project Management Institute, 2004). As a consequence, the cluster sample chosen leads to probable biases in the educational and experience level. Furthermore, it is likely that the number of IT project managers who use the traditional project management process of PMI and APM are oversampled (see Figure 5.2). This may ultimately limit the extent to which the findings of this study can be generalised (see section 6.4).

The unit or cluster in the first pilot stage of the explanatory phase included two CSPs. The sample size for the pilot survey was about 70 and the population consisted of project managers in IT related projects who are employed for one particular CSP. The second cluster sample in the main stage of the survey was composed of 2,200 project managers who are members of the Project Management Institute Risk Management Specific Interest Group (RiskSig) and the specific risk interest group of the Association for Project Management. Slightly less than a third of these registered project managers, approximately 750 according to both organisations, are specialists in conducting IT projects and these were invited to take part in the survey.

Project managers who conducted IT projects were asked via e-mail (see Figure 3.3) to respond to the questionnaire, which was accessible through a web-link in the e-mail. In order to increase the response rate, the participants in the survey were also invited to take part in a prize draw.

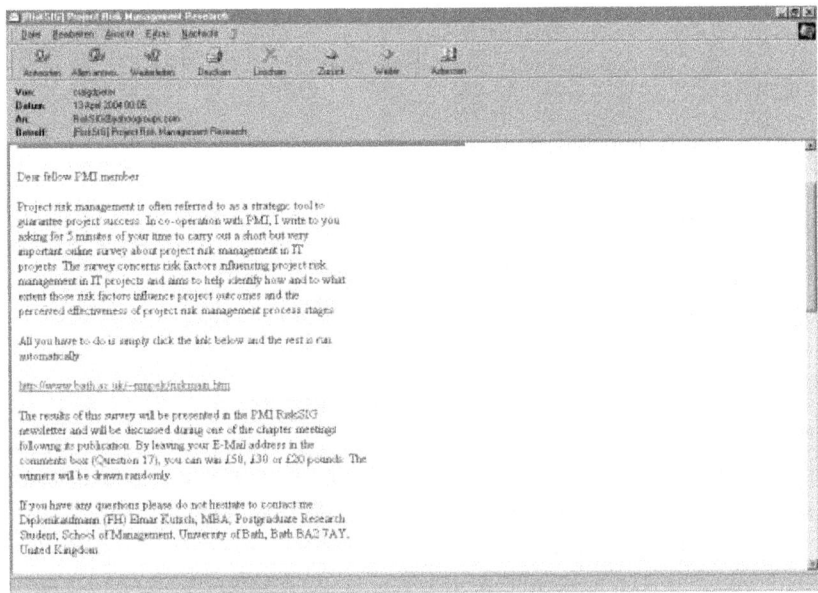

Figure 3.3: Covering letter for main survey

Overall, 102 respondents out of approximately the 2,200 contacted as outlined in chapter 4 answered the self-administered web-based questionnaire. Most of these IT project managers related their experiences with the management of project risk to Roll Out projects (see Figure 3.4). Roll Out projects include the implementation of computer systems. This implementation may include the installation of hard- and software and often the migration of data from an old to a new system.

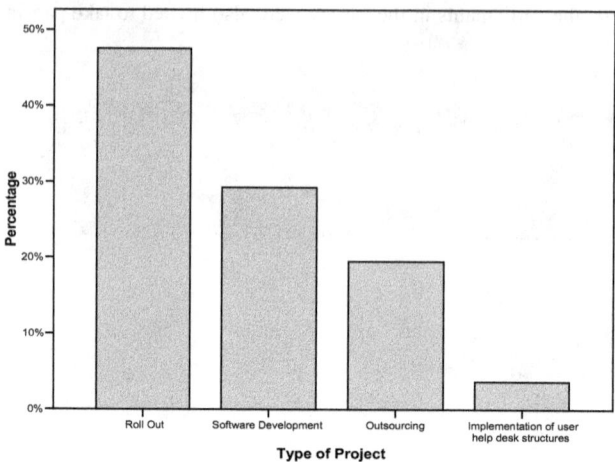

Figure 3.4: Types of project

The time frame of projects the respondents referred to varied (see Figure 3.5). More than a third of all respondents drew their experiences with project risk management from projects lasting between six and twelve months.

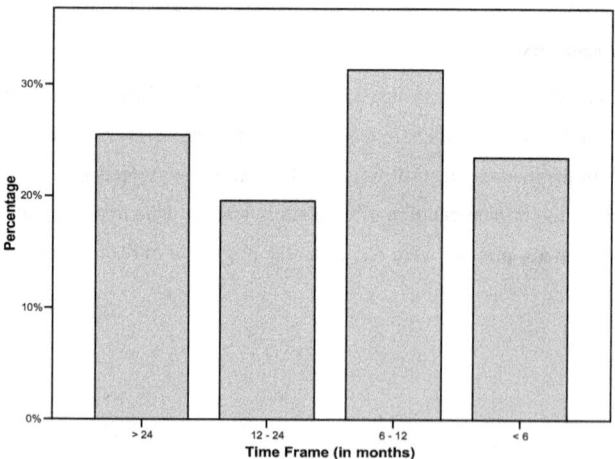

Figure 3.5: Time frame of projects

Regarding the project volume (see Figure 3.6), more than forty percent of the projects had a budget of over £1,000,000.

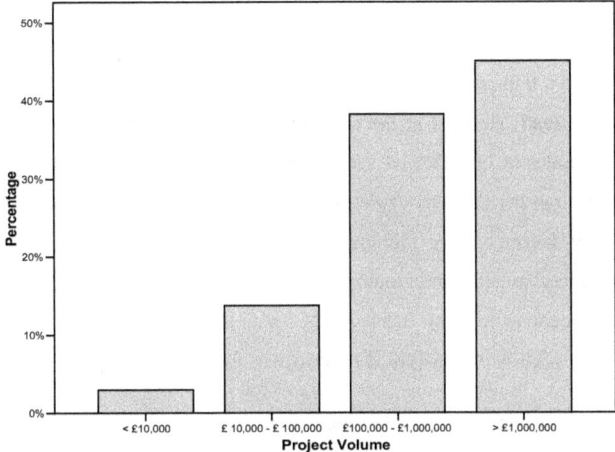

Figure 3.6: Project volume

Overall, considering only the project volume, at least £45,000,000 was at stake in the investigated cases.

3.9. Analysis of data

In the exploratory phase of the study, the number of interviews was increased until conceptual saturation was reached. Saturation according to Pandit (1996, p. 4) means "stable in the face of new data and rich in detail". Turner (1981, p. 235) suggests that saturation is achieved when a researcher "is fully aware of what is meant when any new phenomena encountered are classified into the category in question". Nevertheless, these requirements are ambiguous and do not accurately address the problem that "there is always something else to be found" (Marshall, 2002, p. 61) They give the researcher only a very broad objective about when to stop gathering data.

In this study, the arguably ambiguous conceptual saturation was reached after having conducted twenty-five interviews. In the last interviews, new data no longer illuminated the research problem, that is to say that I understood, for example, the concepts of risk mediators and new interviews neither increased the range of intervening risk mediators nor did they considerably help me to further understand each type of risk mediator and its impact on project risk management.

For the purpose of making sense of the qualitative data and for generating patterns to be tested the explanatory phase, I applied a template approach (Robson, 2002). Existing templates only related to the concepts I had already defined in the conceptual framework. These templates served as main codes or tree codes in QSR NVivo (Rouse & Dick, 1994). Within these tree codes, sub nodes emerged through the analysis of the data. Text segments were labelled and categorised as sub nodes by incrementally including sub notes under tree nodes. The characteristics of the main code changed continuously up to the stage where no data further illuminated the tree nodes (concept saturation). In accordance with the method put forward by Miles and Huberman (1994), the following analytical process was followed:

- Giving codes to the initial set of materials obtained from observations, interviews, documentary analysis, etc.;

- Adding comments, reflections, etc. (commonly referred to as "memos");

- Going through the materials trying to identify similar phrases, patterns, themes, relationships, sequences, differences between sub-groups, etc.;

- Taking these patterns, themes, etc. out of the field to help focus the next wave of data collection;

- Gradually elaborating a small set of generalisations that cover the consistencies discerned in the data (Miles et al., 1994, p. 9)

In order to follow through the process of analysing a vast amount of qualitative data, I used the software QSR NUDIST Vivo. This software enabled me to store the data in an organised way, gave me quick and easy access to the data and supported me in the process of coding the data.

In contrast to the exploratory research, the analysis of explanatory data included uni- and multivariate methods of analysis. The following steps were carried out:

- Descriptive statistics were provided, such as the mean score of each variable. In addition paired-sample T-Tests were carried out to determine a significant difference between the mean variables. Although this test is usually applied to compare mean scores of different sample or samples over time (George & Mallery, 2003; Walsh, 1990), in this study this test was used to determine significant differences between variables of the same sample.

- The next step preceding the factor analysis (see step 3) was to measure the linear relationships between the variables of each concept.

- The purpose of the factor analysis is the extraction of factors. In principal, two types of factor analysis can be carried out: exploratory factor analysis and confirmatory factor analysis. Whereas exploratory factor analysis aims to reveal the underlying structure of a large set of variables, explanatory factor analysis seeks to establish whether the number of factors confirm a set structure of variables which is expected for conceptual or theoretical reasons (e.g. Garson, 2005). However, the distinction between both methods and the merits of when to use which method appears not to be clear:
"In general proponents of confirmatory factor analysis believe that researchers need to have a strong theory underlying their measurement model analyzing data (Williams, 1995). Confirmatory factor analysis is often used in data analysis to examine the expected causal connections between variables. Supporters of exploratory factor analysis believe that explanatory factor analysis is over applied and used in inappropriate situations. Despite the rhetoric to the contrary, some researchers believe that confirmatory factor analysis is still being used with little theoretical foundation, ..." (Hurley et al., 1997, p. 667). Regarding this study, an *a priori* structure was already established. According to the concepts of project risk management, risk mediators and project outcome, a preconception already existed to allocate the subset of variables to these concepts. For example, based on the exploratory research and the literature review, the variables of cost, scope and time were hypothesised to belong to the concept of project outcome. As a consequence, a confirmatory factor analysis appeared more appropriate for this study. Having used a confirmatory factor analysis, depending on their factor loadings and on conceptual reasons, factors were retained or

dropped. As a result of the factor analysis, composite variables were generated that were used in the multiple regression analysis.

- Multiple regressions were used as a final step in the analysis of the explanatory research to define the relationship and in particular to determine the causality between composite variables.

In terms of quality, Easterby *et al.* (1991) strongly emphasise validity, reliability and generalisability in order to justify a chosen methodology. Jankowicz (1991, p. 83) describes a valid measure as being "accurate" and a reliable measure as being "precise". The test of internal *validity* relates to correctly establishing a causal relationship between variables; a relationship between variable X (e.g. perception of risk) and Y (e.g. project outcome) might be also influenced by an unknown variable Z (e.g. political influence) (Yin, 1994). In order to increase internal validity in this study, pattern matching (Eisenhardt, 1989; Miles et al., 1994; Yin, 1994) was applied. By using a pattern matching logic, I constantly checked patterns with my provisional patterns to determine an unequivocal relationship between variables. If a case failed to show a pattern, it led to a revision of the patterns. If it did show a pattern to a confirmation of the patterns. Further internal validity was generated through the explanatory phase by applying statistical tests such as multiple regressions.

External *validity* relates to the generalisation of findings. External validity is generated in this research because of the choice of more than one case. The similarity of cases within a group and differences between groups are likely to lead to a generalisation of findings in this study during the exploratory phase. Furthermore, the findings were tested on a wider population during the explanatory phase. However, the acknowledgement of the dilemma of critical realism described earlier implies that on the one hand, the findings I produced can not be used to anticipate *all* conceivable intervening risk mediators in *all* possible IT projects and their influence on the achievement of the project objectives. On the other hand, generalisation is not limited to a single case or to "it just depends" as this study has produced justified tendencies about *what* and *how* risk mediators influence project risk management.

To ensure internal *reliability*, which deals with the issue of whether a different researcher is able to produce the same findings in a different context, potential investigators must be able to follow the same procedure as used for this study in order to be able to do the same study over again. Yin (1994) suggests a case related protocol or a case related database. In this research, the process of applying research techniques and methods is documented. This documentation, as well as this study includes, for example, an overview of the respondents including addresses, field procedures such as how the interview was conducted and case questions. This means, the information documented is as follows: which project manager was interviewed, how long the interview took, whether there were any interruptions or unanticipated events, which questions were changed and why and which questions were added or modified during the interview.

External *reliability* is important in relation to multiple-item scales as part of the survey questionnaire (Bryman & Cramer, 2001). In this respect, the Cronbach's Alpha was calculated. As a rule of thumb, scales with a Cronbach alpha over 0.8 (Bryman et al., 2001) are internally consistent; however this may decrease to 0.5 in exploratory research (e.g. Hair, Anderson, Tatham, & Black, 1998).

3.10.   Summary

To sum up, two objectives for investigating the research problem can be identified. The first objective is the initial exploration of patterns and the second is to test these on a wider population. This means, to gain a deep and detailed insight into *what* and *how* risk mediators influence project risk management process and ultimately the project outcome to confirm the patterns for the population of IT project managers. Consequently, to achieve the two objectives of this research within a post-positivist paradigm, the methodology of grounded theory including the use of a semi-structured interview technique was most beneficial to gain rich data in order to explore the research problem. Supplemented by a cost and time-effective survey-based method composed of a web-based questionnaire, further confirmatory power on a wider population was gained in order to increase external validity of the study. Figure 3.7 displays an overview of the methods and techniques I used.

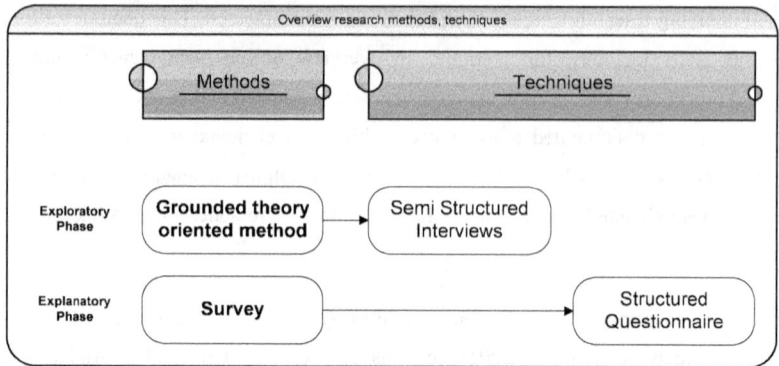

Figure 3.7: Overview of research methodology, research methods

The sample for both phases of research consisted of IT project managers. In the phase of exploratory research, 25 IT project managers were interviewed until conceptual saturation was achieved. Regarding the explanatory research, 102 IT project managers answered the questionnaire.

The analysis of the qualitative data gained through the interviews went through an analytical process of coding until certain patterns such as patterns about the influence of risk mediators on project risk management emerged. These patterns were used to develop measurement scales for the explanatory research. The results from this phase went through statistical analysis including tests such as factor analysis and regressions for the purpose to highlight relationships between the risk mediators, project risk management and the project outcome.

Concerning the quality of the findings, the issues of validity, reliability and generalisability were taken into account for both the exploratory and explanatory phases of research. In the next chapter, the findings of the exploratory research are discussed.

4. EXPLORATORY RESEARCH

This chapter describes the findings of the exploratory study which explores in detail project managers' perceptions about project risk management, risk mediators, the project outcome and the relationship between these three concepts. In the first phase of the research, I conducted interviews. The rationale behind the choice to use interviews was to understand from the point of view of the key player in an IT project, the project manager, whether and how risk mediators constrain the effective application of project risk management by project managers and ultimately influence the project manager's ability to prevent risks from influencing the project outcome in the context of IT projects. This includes an investigation into whether project managers applied project risk management, whether it contributed to the project outcome and whether they perceived project risk management as effective in managing risks. The study also includes an exploration into the outcome of project managers' actions and to what extent over- and underestimated risks influenced the project outcome.

The findings about the project outcome of all investigated cases are presented in section 4.1. Whether project managers perceived project risk management as a contributor to the project outcome will be presented in section 4.2.1. Section 4.2.2 will include the project manager's perception of whether each of the stages of project risk management stages is effective in managing risks. In section 4.2.3, I will provide findings about the outcome of project managers' actions to manage risks, that is to say, to what extent over- and underestimated risks influenced the project outcome. Section 4.3 will provide reasons (risk mediators) for the failure of project managers to prevent risks from materialising and adversely influencing the project outcome.

4.1. Project outcome

The project outcome as discussed in the literature review may include various criteria such as cost, scope and time or team satisfaction. However, the literature is inconclusive in that it does not clearly provide a single set of project outcome criteria for IT projects. Hence, in order to define what project outcome implies from the IT project manager's point of view, the respondents were asked whether and why they thought that the project outcome was a success. Table 4.1 displays an overview of the project outcomes. The data is ordered by the project outcome (success, failure, no clear categorisation possible). The categorisation of the project outcome into project success and failure is based on the evaluation of the interviewed project manager and is illustrated with excerpts from the transcripts.

Case	Project outcome	Illustration
Delta	Failure	"It was a failure because the project was postponed." (Interview ref. Delta)
Theta	Failure	"Internally, I would say very low morale, ..." (Interview ref. Theta)
Lambda	Failure	"I think it is a failure." (Interview ref. Lambda)
		"The project is to start again from fresh from now. There is probably a fair amount of expenditure and time from the authority to spend in the last eighteen month to get to this point. That is all being wasted and now we are going to start from fresh. Timescales were being pushed back." (Interview ref. Lambda)
Nu	Failure	"Up to that stage it was a roaring failure, absolutely." (Interview ref. Nu)
		"Eventually the goal life slipped after about six to eight weeks. The project was halted for about four weeks while the clients said to the consultants "go back with your costs, we are not happy with the costs for the next three months, go back to the drawing board, plan it out again and come back to us" and this had a knock on effect on the timelines. Timelines were pushed out to the following year which would have been April 2003. We continued on, the project team got back on site in December 2001 so we continued working on deliverables for April 2002. Then we went into a long contracted contractual stage throughout the summer of 2002. The team mobilised and round up again in December 2002 with an anticipated first goal life for April 2003. In December 2002, the project was cancelled." (Interview ref. Nu)
Zeta	Failure	"In the end, it was a failure." (Interview ref. Zeta)
Sigma	Success	"The scope galloped. You have heard of scope creep. The scope galloped all over the shop. As we got more and more into it, we realised that we are doing more and more things." (Interview ref. Sigma)
		"We also recorded ninety five per cent up time, we did not have any major problems with our software, hardware and network." (Interview ref. Sigma)
		"There was a huge in-house benefit that could be translated to other similar systems development projects and in fact many of the team have now gone and ended up either being managing or being in the sort of managing group of very large projects because of the expertise and knowledge they gained." (Interview ref. Sigma)
Alpha	Success	"The client's objectives were achieved, just not as planned. That's a big difference. We certainly achieved what the client wanted, but the input and the costs incurred were nothing like those originally planned. So from our point of view, it failed, but from the client's it went well and that's obviously the main difference." (Interview ref. Alpha)
Beta	Success	"Although the project was suspended, it was successful for us. Because of our pioneering position in this technical environment we have already received follow up orders." (Interview ref. Beta)
Iota	Success	"We maintained the relationship, we maintained the ongoing relationship, we covered our cost overruns, so it was still from my perspective a successful project even though we missed the time deadline." (Interview ref. Iota).
		"From my point of view the project was a major success. Like I said we maintained the relationship with the customer, we covered nine tenths of the costs, we contained a margin and we get additional business, probably now and currently we got another major Roll Out of technology which is ongoing and I am not the project manager for, because of the experience in the original roll out." (Interview ref. Iota)

Case	Project outcome	Illustration
Eta	Success	Not available
Kappa	Success	"It was definitely a success. I guess, also a measure of success is the learning experience, we as an organisation and the partner have come through and there was definitely some good learning that came out of it so I think this also a fundamental measure of success." (Interview ref. Kappa)
Gamma	Success	"The outcome was highly satisfactory for all the parties involved. For the customer, as well as the hardware supplier, this became a reference project. In the end, all the parties were highly satisfied." (Interview ref. Kappa)
Omicron	Success	"I thought it was a success." (Interview ref. Omicron) "Managing projects is about the three classic areas of cost, quality and time. You can not just sort of like disregard the cost and they said "It will cost whatever it takes". There was no cost element to success which is why I alluded to before about the having the current system running parallel to the new system and it was expensive. It did not matter." (Interview ref. Omicron)
Rho	Success	"From my point of view, I define it contractually in the sense from a (provider) perspective. We were contracted to provide support and resource to deliver something by a set time and we came within the estimates of cost that we would be slightly within the estimates of cost that we said would be required to deliver that. So for me that was successful." (Interview ref. Rho)
Xi	No clear categorisation	"We had several weeks slippage. I said it was quite a success. Yes, we were largely on budget, on target, we certainly delivered exactly was required in terms of the working environment, the systems and the operational business infrastructure but the business case was flawed." (Interview ref. Xi)"A qualified success. The business was launched two months later than the original plan. The delay was caused by a risk that we had correctly identified, that was totally outside our control and we knew about it and we actively managed it and we kept the launch date within a week." (Interview ref. Xi)
Epsilon	No clear categorisation	"There was a hold-up. Despite that, it's astonishing in view of the difficulties we had that we managed to carry out a complete roll-out of all the desktops and notebooks, though perhaps not to the level of quality the client expected. Overall though, it has to be said that this was probably a financial disaster for M+S." (Interview ref. Epsilon)
Mu	No clear categorisation	It was a partial success. (Interview ref. Mu) "A very expensive court case, millions of pounds of additional costs, ultimately four years delays of finalising the project and the organisation, the new organisation never fully worked, it never delivered its full promise as expected from in it." (Interview ref. Mu)
Pi	Not available	Not available because project is ongoing.

Table 4.1: Project outcome

As can be seen in Table 4.1, in cases Delta, Theta, Lambda, Sigma, Alpha, Beta, Omicron, Rho, Xi, Epsilon, Mu and Pi, the ability of the project manager to meet cost, time and scope objectives were salient criteria for defining the project as a failure or success from their perspective. The project manager in case Delta stated: "It was a failure because the project was postponed." (Interview ref. Delta). However, as case Beta shows, although the project was suspended, the project manager perceived the project as being successful for the reason that their pioneering position in dealing with a new technology put them ahead of their competitors with resulting of follow up contracts "Although the project was suspended, it was successful for us. Because of our pioneering position in this technical environment we have already received follow up orders." (Interview ref. Beta)

As a result, the cases show that despite the emphasis of project managers on the widely used success criteria of scope, cost and time, this view represented by the majority of the literature is too narrow. The project manager in case Kappa explained:

"Are we within variances, within tolerances and being accepted by stakeholders, and also things like customer satisfaction is extremely important and also team motivation, team satisfaction is very important because if your team is not happy then your customer is not going to be happy. Time and budget are too narrow. I do believe it is very important but there are other things which come in and need to be looked at as well and they can have sometimes a more important factor. Obviously, projects that had been late and over budget and everybody loves them because they deliver something which is fundamentally valuable to the end users..." (Interview ref. Kappa)

Table 4.2 shows a comparison of the findings in existing literature and from the exploratory research in this study. It also gives an overview of the main criteria to be used in the questionnaire as part of the explanatory phase of the research.

Project outcome factors identified in the literature review	Project outcome factors through exploratory research	Main criteria[25]
Implementation of the project Project Efficiency	Time, cost and scope Other pre-stated objectives	Producing to specification, within budget and on time Meet its pre-stated objectives
Stakeholder satisfaction Impact on stakeholders	Satisfaction of project team Satisfaction of client Satisfaction of all parties involved	Satisfying the needs of the project team Satisfying the needs of the owners and users Satisfying the needs of stakeholders
Perceived value of the project Business and direct success	Maintaining the relationship Follow on contracts Learning experience	Provision of satisfactory benefit to the owner Project achieved its purpose

Table 4.2: Comparison between project outcome factors identified in the literature review and in the exploratory research

Project management literature (see Literature Review) tends to suggest that the project outcome is defined by scope, cost and time. However, as the findings show, the focus on only scope, cost and time objectives as suggested by some authors is too narrow. As a result of the findings in this study, the measurement of the project outcome from the IT project manager's

---

[25] These main features were used as measures in the questionnaire as part of the explanatory research.

point of view includes several main criteria (see Table 4.2): producing to specification, within budget and on time, meeting pre-stated objectives, satisfying the needs of the project team, owners, users and stakeholders, the provision of satisfactory benefit to the owner, and the project achieving its purpose.

4.2. Project risk management

Project risk management is one of nine key processes in project management (Project Management Institute, 2004) that project managers can apply to achieve the desired project outcome. In 14 out of the 18 cases, project risk management was applied in some format similar to best practice standards. Table 4.3 gives a broad overview of what kind of project risk management was applied in the investigated projects.

Case	Actions
Alpha	No project risk management applied
Beta	Trial runs were organised and based on these risk were identified, analysed and response actions defined and executed.
Gamma	Risks were identified and analysed. Response actions included the definition of contingencies.
Delta	Technical test were carried out. Each system was tested. Based on these tests, risks were analysed and risk response actions taken.
Epsilon	No project risk management applied.
Zeta	No project risk management applied.
Eta	Risk registers were produced. Each risk was quantified and risk response action recommended.
Theta	Risks were identified, analysed and risk response actions defined and executed.
Iota	Application of standard risk process (Prince II)
Kappa	Risks were identified, analysed (with subjective probabilities) and risk response actions defined and executed.
Lambda	Risks were identified, analysed and risk response actions defined and executed.
Mu	Application of project risk management including a risk scoring system.
Nu	Formal project risk management process followed.
Xi	Risks were identified, analysed and risk response actions defined and executed.
Omicron	Risk registers were produced. Each risk was quantified and risk response action recommended on a weekly basis.
Pi	Application of formal project risk management approach called "Orca".
Rho	Risks were identified, analysed and risk response actions defined and executed
Sigma	No project risk management applied.

Table 4.3: The application of project risk management

In 14 cases, a process of identification, analysis and response took place, in a way similar to that suggested by PMI, APM or the UK Government Centre for Information Systems. In 4 cases, no formal project risk management process was applied. In order to establish whether project risk management as described in Table 4.3 contributed to the project outcome in the cases investigated, project managers were asked whether they had applied project risk management, and then to describe to what extent project risk management had or would have contributed to the actual project outcome.

4.2.1. Contribution of project risk management to the project outcome

Referring to Table 4.4, I categorised the respondents' answers about the degree of contribution of project risk management to project success and failure into high, medium or low based on their comments and illustrated the categorisation by including a quotation. The assessment of the degree of contribution relates is based on my interpretation of their answers.

Case	Project risk management applied	Project outcome	Contribution of project risk management to the project outcome
Beta	Yes	Success	High "The risk management was successful and enabled the negative consequences for the project to be minimised." (Interview ref. Beta)
Gamma	Yes	Success	High "The efficiency of risk management contributed greatly to the overall success, because we increased pressure on the subcontractor and the hardware supplier in order to stick to deadlines." (Interview ref. Gamma)
Eta	Yes	Success	High "It did exactly what I was aiming for it to do and apart from this was the due diligence. It was such an important part." (Interview ref. Eta)
Omicron	Yes	Success	High "I would say enormously, greatly." (Interview ref. Omicron)
Rho	Yes	Success	High "... so in that sense it (project risk management) did contribute very significantly." (Interview ref. Rho)
Theta	Yes	Failure	High "I think pretty much as I said before. I think lack of proper planning and understanding and inappropriate risk assessment." (Interview ref. Theta)
Lambda	Yes	Failure	High "I would say number one, reason for the failure of the project was project governance and number two, risk management." (Interview ref. Lambda)
Delta	Yes	Failure	High "The project risk management was highly effective, because we worked together with the client. We could not really plan for a problem we didn't anticipate - that of internal process definition with (provider)." (Interview ref. Delta)
Mu	Yes	No clear categorisation	High "It was significant but it was not everything." (Interview ref. Mu)
Kappa	Yes	Success	Medium "I think it contributed in terms that we were much more proactive. We were much more in control, perceived to be in control by the stakeholders and by the partner. From that point of view it gave us much more, better credibility with stakeholders. A much higher level of perceived professionalism and much more of a trusted position in terms of, it enabled us to articulate what the key top ten issues would be, what impact they would have, how we would resolve them, what are the trigger events." (Interview ref. Kappa)
Nu	Yes	Failure	Medium "...I think that project risk management was necessarily there (to influence the project outcome)." (Interview ref. Nu)
Xi	Yes	No clear categorisation	Medium "Difficult to quantify. Project risk is one of a number of project control mechanism I believe were important to use in managing a project. If you used project risk only and ignore everything else, than the impact is minimal. You have very little difference. If you put in all of the other project controls and ignore project risk, you probably actually do eighty to eighty five percent of the job but you are leaving yourself exposed to the fact that there is something big out there that you may not know about that really come and screw you. I would be reluctant to quantify the extent which project risk makes contributions on its own but it is an essential part of the project control tool kit." (Interview ref. Xi)
Alpha	Yes	Success	Low "In truth, project risk management didn't play much of a role." (Interview ref. Alpha)
Pi	Yes	Not available	Not available because project is still ongoing
Iota	Yes	Success	Not available
Zeta	No	Failure	"It would have been worthwhile, for the simple reason that, at some point, we would have abandoned this project or would have had to." (Interview ref. Zeta)
Sigma	No	Success	Not available
Epsilon	No	No clear categorisation	"It would not have helped." (Interview ref. Epsilon)

Table 4.4: Overview of project outcome and the contribution of project risk management to project outcome

As can be seen in Table 4.4, in successful projects, the contribution of project risk management tended to be high: "I would say enormously, greatly." (Interview ref. Omicron).

In contrast, in failed projects, project managers seem to rate the failings in project risk management as a main contributor for project failure: "I would say number one, reason for the failure of the project was project governance and number two, risk management." (Interview ref. Lambda).

The findings suggest that project risk management manifests as an essential factor in influencing the project outcome. The importance of project risk management is consistent with earlier findings highlighted in chapter 2 suggesting that project risk management is a key discipline in project management (Project Management Institute, 2004) and highly contributes to project success but inadequate risk management also significantly contributes to project failure. Baccarini (2004, p. 287) argues: "Risk management is an essential part in achieving the successful delivery of IT projects". However, the findings also indicate that even in projects that project managers considered a success, they seem not to have achieved all project objectives, in particular they appear not to have met scope, cost and time targets. One project manager argued: "Although the project was suspended, it was successful for us. Because of our pioneering position in this technical environment we have already received follow up orders." (Interview ref. Beta). Therefore, taking the overall importance of project risk management as a main contributor to project success and failure into account, the findings underline the importance of investigating the research problem concerning the influence of risk mediators on project risk management and consequently on the project outcome.

4.2.2. Perceived effectiveness of project risk management

According to best practice standards, project risk management is thought to ensure project success. In most of the cases investigated, IT projects were considered to be a success although time, cost and scope targets appear to not have been met by project managers, indicating that project managers did not prevent risks from adversely influencing the project outcome. Project risk management includes four major stages: planning, identification, analysis and response. In more detail, project risk management can be deconstructed into nine process stages (Ward, 1999): risk management planning, identification of risks, analysis of the likelihood (probability) of a risk to occur and effects of the risk, evaluation of best response alternative, determination of response owner, monitoring risks and executing risk actions.

In order to determine in detail how effective the IT project managers have perceived the use of project risk management they were questioned about the effectiveness of each of the nine stages of the project risk management process. The premise behind this part of the analysis is that project managers may perceive each stage of the project risk management process different differently in managing risks. The results could show during which stage of the process the project manager's encountered problems in managing risks.

Table 4.5 presents the data on the perceived effectiveness of each of the nine process stages. Ordered by case I reduced the answers of the respondents regarding their perceived effectiveness to several indices (see below). For example, I interpreted the comment of the project manager in case Alpha regarding the effectiveness of identifying risks as "not effective": "Unfortunately the measures were not very effective, because the wrong risks had been identified. Only technical risks were taken into account and the main factor that was missing was the human aspect, the client." (Interview ref. Alpha). The findings about the perceived effectiveness of each of the project risk management stages is displayed according to the effect of risks on the project outcome.

Case	Planning	Identify Threat	Attach Probability	Determine Effects	Evaluate Response	Determine Response Owner	Monitor Risk	Execute Actions	Effect of risks on the project outcome
Delta	NA	✓	✓		✓	✓	✓	X	High
Alpha	NA	X		✓	✓	X	✓	X	High
Beta	NA	X	X	✓	NA	NA	✓	✓	High
Iota	✓	✓		✓	✓	X	✓	✓	High
Nu	NA	✓	✓	NA	X	X	X	X	High
Xi	NA	✓	X	NA	NA	✓	NA	X	High
Lambda	✓	X	X	X	X	NA	NA	X	High
Sigma	X - n	X - n	X - n	X - n	X - n	X - n	X - n	X - n	High
Epsilon	X - n	X - n	X - n	X - n	X - n	X - n	X - n	X - n	High
Theta	✓	X	X	X	X	X	X	X	High
Eta		✓	X			NA	✓		Medium
Kappa	✓	✓	X	✓	✓	X	✓		Medium
Mu	✓	X	X	X				X	Medium
Zeta	X - n	X - n	X - n	X - n	X - n	X - n	X - n	X - n	Medium
Rho	NA	X	NA	NA	NA	X	X	X	Low
Gamma	NA	✓	✓	NA	✓	✓			Low
Omicron		✓	NA					✓	Low
Pi	X	✓	X	✓	X	X	X	NA	Low

X = Not effective
✓ = Effective
X - n = no effectiveness - No project risk management applied
NA = Not available
Blank = No unambiguous effectiveness cited

Table 4.5: Summed indices - perceived effectiveness of project risk management stages

As shown in Table 4.5, the most ineffective process stages are the identification of risks, attaching a probability to risks, determining a response ownership and executing risk response actions. Regarding the stage of identifying of risks, one project manager stated:

"This was not easy. As we were introducing a new technology, it was unclear whether these products would satisfy the client's requirements. We were not aware of most of the risks." (Interview ref. Beta).

"Other problems occurred from the project manager's point of view when they attempted to attach probabilities to risks. This (probability) was merely an estimate. I have to say that, because we had little experience with this technology, it was barely possible to calculate probabilities. It was very difficult." (Interview ref. Beta).

Whereas project managers tended to perceive the definition of effects of risks and response alternatives as effective, they faced difficulties in allocating response ownership. One project manager argued: "There was no responsibility assigned for the risks and there was no deadline for mitigating that risk." (Interview ref. Nu). The problems in the initial stages of identifying, analysing risks, and determining a response owner appear to have created difficulties with the execution of response actions, the final and ultimate stage to prevent risks from influencing the project outcome. Project managers perceive this stage in the majority of cases as ineffective. Response actions to respond to the risks on the project outcome were not taken:

"What happened with the consequences with the risk management process that went wrong because the risk management process should have initiated measures, countermeasures to correct the problems, but that was not allowed to happen for other reasons." (Interview ref. Mu)

The findings suggest that regardless of whether project risk management significantly contributed to project success or failure, from the project manager's point of view, in all cases there appeared to be problems in identifying, analysing and ultimately in reducing the impact of risk on the project outcome.

In most of the cases, a low overall effectiveness seem to relate to the magnitude of disruption in a project. That is to say the lower the overall effectiveness of project risk management stages, the higher the degree of disruption. Nevertheless, in two cases (case Delta and Iota) the overall perceived effectiveness of project risk management was relatively high although severe disruptions were sustained. An explanation for this "paradox" may be related to the project manager's expectations about the breadth (different kind of uncertainties) and depth (to what extent) of uncertainty reduction through project risk management. The project manager in case Iota explained that they were not able anyway to identify "all" uncertainty which may have an adverse consequence on the fulfilment of the project objectives:

"Well, the only unidentified risk was that the customer had no interest and myself and the rest of the project team just could not and did not foresee." (Interview ref. Iota)

The project manager did not blame the risk management process for the failure to identify the customer as a risk because he excluded him as a possible threat to be managed:

"You automatically assume that the customer is engaging in the project because they want to succeed." (Interview ref. Iota)

This explains why his expectations about the identification of risks were met although severe disruptions occurred because of the customer. As a result, the degree of expectation of project managers is measured in the explanatory phase of the study (see section 5.1)

Project management, including the key process of project risk management, is described as self-evidently correct (Williams, 2004). Although project risk management enables project managers to effectively manage risk (e.g. Boehm, 1991), from the project manager's point of view, even in successful projects, this does not seem to be the case. Project manager do not seem to be able to effectively manage risks as project risk management standards claim they should. As the findings suggest, project risk management is either not performed at all or is perceived at some stages as ineffective, underlining Pender's (2001) argument that project risk management as it is presented by PMI or CCTA is inadequate. Referring back to the rational claims of risk management,

- rational actors assign (objective or subjective) probabilities to various outcomes;

The findings show that project managers encountered difficulties in assigning probabilities to risk as well as in defining the outcome (effect) of risks. In extreme cases, no probabilities were attached, because the threat remained unidentified due to lack of information. Otherwise, project managers encountered problems in attaching probabilities because of the lack of reliable historical information.

- rational actors can order possible actions according to their preferences (preference to meet cost, time and scope objectives). Preferences for actions involve some degree for risk aversion for specific choice situations;

In the cases investigated, project managers were often not able to effectively rank possible risk response actions because threats, their probabilities and their potential effect on the

94

project outcome remained uncertain and ambiguous. A ranking of risks was often problematic.

In addition, the preference of project managers to meet cost, scope and time objectives tended to collide with other preferences such as the preference to maintain a good relationship with the customer. In this respect, the degree of risk aversion was lower than the desire of project managers to pursue other objectives than to meet cost, scope and time objectives.

- rational actors can choose between different possible actions, each of which may lead to one or several possible outcomes. Actions as well as outcomes may differ in kind and scale;

The rational claim that rational actors or in this study project managers can choose between possible actions seemed, to a certain degree, not to occur in reality. Project managers often found it difficult to decide which action to choose because first, the outcome of those actions remained uncertain and controversial.

- rational actors try to choose an action, which is optimal according to their preferences.

The project managers' attempts to execute risk response actions appeared to be hindered by lack of risk ownership and the preference of stakeholders not to proactively manage risk. The preference of the project manager interfered with other stakeholders' preferences with the result that actions were chosen that were not optimal according to the project manager.

In consequence, the use of project risk management by IT project managers appeared to be less optimal than claimed or expected by project risk management standards. However, before I describe what causes the lack of effectiveness perceived by project managers, I will describe whether the project managers think that risks were effectively managed, that is to say, to what extent project risks were thought to have influenced the project outcome.

4.2.3. Under- and overestimation of risk

The findings so far suggest that project managers seem not to have been able to effectively reduce the adverse effects of risk on the project outcome in the cases investigated. In successful and failed IT projects, project managers encountered problems in effectively identifying, analysing and responding to risks. Under these circumstances, where project managers perceived the lack of effective project risk management in their ability to identify risks, attach probabilities to risk, establish response ownership and execute risk response actions, project managers were asked how effectively risk was actually managed in terms of whether threats and their effects on the project outcome materialised as predicted and whether the predicted response actually had the forecasted impact on preventing risks from influencing the project outcome and in how predicted risk deviated from those risks actually influencing the project outcome. Thus, I judge the effectiveness of project risk management in terms of its effects on the project outcome and not by its actions during the project risk management process. The findings could show whether risks were under- or overestimated and on what criteria of the project outcome these risks had an influence.

Table 4.6 displays the findings of underestimated and overestimated risks, highlighting in which cases risks were under- and overestimated. In chapter 2, I investigated three types of underestimation of risk: underestimation of state, effect and response uncertainty. Underestimated risks include threats which were not identified in advance, but which influenced the project outcome (underestimation of state uncertainty), actual effects having a greater influence on the project outcome than predicted (underestimation of effect uncertainty) or responses having a lesser influence on the response to risk than predicted (underestimation of response uncertainty). Overestimation of risk relates to threats which were identified in advance, but which did not influence the project outcome (overestimation of state uncertainty), effects that had a lesser impact on the project outcome (overestimation of effect uncertainty) and responses that had a bigger influence in the response to risk (overestimation of response uncertainty) than was predicted.

Case	Under-estimation state uncertainty	Under-estimation effect uncertainty	Under-estimation response uncertainty	Over-estimation state uncertainty	Over-estimation effect uncertainty	Over-estimation response uncertainty
Alpha	X	X	X	X[26]		
Beta	X					
Gamma		X				
Delta	X					
Epsilon	X					
Zeta	X					
Eta	X					
Theta	X					
Iota	X					
Kappa	X			X		
Lambda	X			X		
Mu	X			X		
Nu	X					
Xi			X			
Omicron	X					
Pi	X					
Rho	X					
Sigma	X					

Table 4.6: Overview of under- and overestimation of risk

In the majority of cases, project managers appear to have underestimated risks. The project manager in case Alpha stated:

> "Because we underestimated the risks at the outset, (we) classed as the project as easy to carry out and lots of unforeseen incidents occurred …" (Interview ref. Alpha)

In the majority of cases, risks were overlooked. This means, the project manager underestimated state uncertainty. The project manager in case Kappa, for example, argued:

> "Yes, definitely unidentified risks materialised and they came usually out of areas which were not within our scope." (Interview ref. Kappa)

Other risks were not overlooked, but the response did not have the desired influence on reducing the effect of risk on the project outcome:

> "We had a reasonable knowledge what were the big risks that caused serious damage to the project and we managed those as well as we could in that environment, under those circumstances. We still had risks, which were identified, but were not managed as effectively as they could have been." (Interview ref. Xi)

---

[26] Multiple answers are possible because risks may be simultaneously over- and underestimated within one project.

Project risks may not only be inadequately managed because they are underestimated, but also because they are overestimated. In contrast to overlooking risks (underestimation of state uncertainty), risks were also overestimated by project managers, that is to say that risks were identified, which actually did not occur. A project manager in case Alpha explained: "Nothing we identified occurred ..." (Interview ref. Alpha)

Despite project risk management, in the vast majority of cases risks materialised which were not identified in advance. It appears that project managers predominantly underestimated state uncertainty. However, the findings also suggest that in some of the cases, risks were also overestimated. Project managers committed resources to the identification of risks that did not materialise. Unsurprisingly, in the three cases, in which no project risk management was applied, threats materialised that were not identified in advance. However, over- and underestimation of risk by project managers may not be of interest in this study unless the risks had an actual effect on adversely influencing the project outcome. Therefore, I investigated to what extent over- and underestimated risks adversely influenced the project outcome. In the interviews I asked each project manager what influence over- and underestimated risks had on what aspect of the project outcome.

Table 4.7 gives an overview of the extent of influence over- and underestimated risk had on the project outcome. The degree of influence on the project outcome is the researcher's interpretation of respondent's answers. Again, I categorised the answers of the project managers into High, Medium and Low. Moreover, I highlighted the most salient criterion of the project outcome on which risks had an impact.

Case	Type of underestimation	Degree of influence	Influence on ...	Type of overestimation	Degree of influence	Influence on ...
Alpha	Underestimation of state uncertainty Underestimation of effect uncertainty Underestimation of response uncertainty	High	Costs	Overestimation of state uncertainty	Low	
Beta	Underestimation of state uncertainty	High	Time			
Delta	Underestimation of state uncertainty	High	Time			
Iota	Underestimation of state uncertainty	High	Time			
Kappa	Underestimation of state uncertainty	High	No unambiguous answer	Overestimation of state uncertainty	Low	
Lambda	Underestimation of state uncertainty	High	Time Cost	Overestimation of state uncertainty	Low	
Mu	Underestimation of state uncertainty	High	Scope Cost Time	Overestimation of state uncertainty	Low	
Nu	Underestimation of state uncertainty	High	Time Blame, Scapegoating			
Xi	Underestimation of response uncertainty	High	Scope Cost Time			
Gamma	Underestimation of effect uncertainty	Low	Time			
Omicron	Underestimation of state uncertainty	Low	No impact			
Sigma	Underestimation of state uncertainty	Low	No impact			
Epsilon	Underestimation of state uncertainty	Medium	Time			
Theta	Underestimation of state uncertainty	Medium	People's morale			
Eta	Underestimation of state uncertainty	No unambiguous answer	No unambiguous answer			
Zeta	Underestimation of state uncertainty	Not available	Not available			
Rho	Underestimation of state uncertainty	Not available	Not available			
Pi	Underestimation of state uncertainty	Project is still ongoing	Not available			

Table 4.7: Overview of underestimation of risk and its influence on the project outcome

As can be seen in Table 4.7, project managers perceived that underestimated risk predominantly influenced the project outcome in the sense that it constrained project managers in their ability to meet scope, cost and time objectives: "…our costs went through the roof" (Interview ref. Alpha). However, in cases Sigma and Omicron, risks were underestimated, but did not adversely influence the project outcome. Reasons for this may be that first, the effects of those risks were relatively low, and second that once the risk had materialised, the effect was immediately mitigated.

Not only the underestimation of risk, but also the overestimation of risk by project managers may influence the project outcome because scarce resources may have been committed, for example, for the identification of threats that do not materialise. In contrast to the effect of underestimated risks on the project outcome, there is little evidence that overestimation of uncertainty had any influence at all on the project outcome. In fact, none of the interviewees mentioned that resources were "wasted" (possible result of overestimation of risk) on risk management and therefore adversely influenced the project outcome: "The project was not really at threat from these (overestimated) risks." (Interview ref. Alpha). This pattern can be explained by reasoning that the impact of the overestimation of uncertainty on the project outcome by risk actors is far less severe than the underestimation of risk.

In the majority of cases, regardless whether project managers considered the project outcome a success or failure, underestimated risk was perceived to have adversely influenced the project outcome. It influenced the project manager's ability to meet cost, scope and time objectives. The findings suggest that project risk management was ineffective in the respect that underestimated risks adversely influenced the project outcome. According to Ritchie and Marshall (1993, p. 215) the key issue of managers is to "optimise the match between perceived risk and actual risk at the time of choosing between alternatives." However, the findings in this study indicate that project managers tended to be unable to first match perceived risk with actual risk and second, to prevent underestimated risks having an adverse influence on the project outcome.

Overall, taking also the findings of the perceived effectiveness of each of the project risk management process stages into account, project managers acted less rationally than project risk management standards (inexplicitly) claim they should, raising the questions of why or under which mediators do project managers lack effectiveness in preventing risks from adversely influencing the project outcome. In the next section, I will describe which mediators or risk mediator constrained project managers in effectively managing risks.

4.3. Risk mediators influencing project risk management

According to what has been previously discussed, project managers perceived specific project risk management stages to lack effectiveness in relation to the perceived effectiveness that can be assumed under perfect conditions of EUT. Risks were not optimally managed in the sense that underestimated risks in particular adversely influenced the project outcome. The next step in the analysis of the data was to ascertain why risks were perceived not to be effectively managed and under- and overestimated. For example, in case Zeta, my question concerned why risks were overlooked or why some of the project risk management stages were ineffective. The project manager's answer showed that he deliberately overlooked risks because he did not want to unnerve the customer or cast doubt on the competence of the provider to successfully complete the project: "Not just unnerve them, but also loose the project, because there was very strong competition from other providers." (Interview ref. Zeta). At the time of the analysis of the interviews, this phenomenon seemed to contradict other phenomena which emerged in the interviews such as the lack of knowledge of project manager's to accurately predict risks. However, the notion of project manager refusing to take actions to risks they are aware of re-emerged in following interviews and seemed to manifest as a pattern.

Overall, in the analysis of the interviews conducted by the researcher, a five-fold typology was defined, describing risk mediators that intervened in, or interrupted the rational and orderly management of risk during their projects. These are summarised in Table 4.8 below and subsequently discussed in detail, drawing on relevant quotations from the interviews in order to illustrate particular points.

Risk mediators	Definition	Description
Denial of uncertainty	The refusal of risk actors to reveal risks that may hold negative or discomforting connotations to other stakeholders.	**Risk as a "taboo** Denial of uncertainty in order not to expose stakeholders to something perceived as negative. Denial of uncertainty in order not to jeopardise long-term relationship with stakeholders. Denial of uncertainty in order not to be perceived as a "doomsayer". Denial of uncertainty in order to present the project as being "certain" and "certainly" successful to stakeholders.
Avoidance of uncertainty[27]	Lack of attention to risks	**Lack of trust in risks** Avoidance of uncertainty because of mistrust between risk actors. Avoidance of uncertainty because of contradictory confidence levels in risk estimates between risk actors. Avoidance of uncertainty because of contradictory perceptions of risk actors about the legitimacy of managing certain risks.
Delay of uncertainty	Failure to consider or resolve risk	**Opposing risk management preferences** Delay of uncertainty because of different expectations of risk actors about how to manage risk (proactive or reactive).
Being ignorant of uncertainty	Incomplete knowledge of risk.	**Lack of information** Ignorance of uncertainty because of the inability to scan and interpret the environment.
Ignoring uncertainty		Ignorance of uncertainty because of limited scanning of the environment.

Table 4.8: Overview of risk mediators

4.3.1. Denial of uncertainty

This was first type of mediator that emerged related to risk as an 'object' of 'fear' by those involved in projects. It seemed that project managers were unwilling to expose their customers to risks because those risks might have created anxiety and doubts among the stakeholders about the competence of the service provider:

> "We presented ourselves in such a way that we would seem as reasonable and competent as possible. And problems and risks don't go down so well. We wanted to come across as people who could get the project under way and complete it. The first aim was to win the tender, no matter what the cost ... I didn't want to be the

---

[27] Not to be mistaken with avoidance as a risk response strategy (see literature review)

doomsayer in the euphoric preliminary phase ... Problems were kept to a minimum, simply in order to come across as a competent provider." (Interview ref. Epsilon)

The refusal to admit that risks existed, or their concealment in order to avoid exposing stakeholders to an object perceived as a 'dread' and, consequently, a threat to the viability of the project, was categorised as *denial of uncertainty*. This can be defined as a refusal by project managers to expose other project stakeholders to negative or discomforting risk related information. The underlying mediator of denial was the refusal of project managers to acknowledge uncertainties with possible adverse consequences on the project outcome, rooted in the desire not to expose themselves or other stakeholders to something that was perceived as "worrisome".

This attitude to risk has been described as one of treating it as "taboo". "Taboo matters are literally what people must not know or even inquire about. Taboos function as guardians of purity and safety through socially enforced sanctioned rules of (ir)relevance." (Smithson, 1989, p. 8)

In another instance,

"His words to me (were) "You're the project manager, a professional project manager, you must have seen this problem happening before now". I had no choice but to say "Yes David, I did see it happening before now, but there were very good reasons why I chose not to escalate to you about that at a different time"." (Interview ref. Iota)

In this particular case, the risk was not actively managed because it was considered that in mentioning the very subject of risk, the customer would become aware of it and this awareness would jeopardise the relationship between the customer and the project management team. The relationship between the understanding and perception of risk appeared to lead to cautiousness among project managers in developing more understanding about specific risks and their implications for their particular projects. Another interviewee elaborated on this issue:

"The question is how specific you want to go. Pulling out a generic risk is fine and people can see the red flag go up, but unless an absolute showstopper sat right in my arena of operations then I would not necessarily think it was my case to raise it.

Informally I would say it to the project risk assessor: "you need to talk to so and so because I think they have an issue"." (Interview ref. Nu)

In summary, it was found that project managers responsible for the management of risk in some cases acted to reduce anxiety among customers and other stakeholders by not confronting them with uncertainties and risks, in other words, they concealed or denied the presence of risk and uncertainty. This mediator was either purposeful (they would make a decision not to mention specific, project-related risks) or unconscious (they did not dwell on the presence of risk, thereby not having to mention it as an issue).

As a result of discomforting risks, the relationship between knowledge and perceived risk (Simmons, 2003; Wildavsky & Dake, 2002) may result in a cautiousness by risk actors to 'create' more knowledge about possible negative perceived uncertainties as happened in case Epsilon. In this case, the project manager mentioned: "I didn't want to be the doomsayer in the euphoric preliminary phase." (Interview ref. Epsilon). One way to guard stakeholders from the influence of negative perceived uncertainties or a way to reduce anxiety among stakeholders that may arise through confronting them with uncertainties with possible negative consequences, is to deny risks (Slovic, 1987; Slovic, Fischhoff, & Lichtenstein, 1980). This choice of denial by stakeholders lies in the "freedom to choose whether or not to expose oneself (and others) to the dangers which lie in the activity (of risk management)" (Hale, 1987, p. 76). As a result of the apparent benefit of not knowing whether uncertainties are upsetting or scary, or in the words of Schneidermann (1980, p. 22) because of the "fear of the unknown" (Ghosh & Ray, 1997) individuals tend to be unwilling to manage risks (White, Pahl, Buehner, & Haye, 2003). Their unwillingness relates to the temptation to give people the answers they want to hear, and the answers are apparent certainty or a perception of a safe and predictable world (Beierle, 2004; Fischhoff et al., 1981; Slovic et al., 1980). Because stakeholders may perceive risk (management) to be a gloomy and negative affair (Raftery, 1994) or because stakeholders are more concerned with the exposure to potential adverse external opinion of failure than with the possible impact of uncertainties on the project (Parker & Mobey, 2003) they downgrade their actual perceived risk to a desired external accepted level of risk (Machlis & Rosa, 1990) that can be "safely" engaged through risk management without the side effects of "dread". In so far as risks that may have an influence on the project outcome are suppressed, they are not managed for the sake of avoiding discomfort among stakeholders.

4.3.2. Avoidance of uncertainty

The second mediator influencing project risk management seem to relate to conflicting risk estimates. In one case, where the customer was presented with a risk estimate, he strongly objected to risks. The project manager said:

> "The client did not accept the risks, or rather the risk analysis, wherever it concerned him. So when we had a risk that required the client to play an active role, which would have meant investing money or resources, he opposed the prevention of that risk. He said it wasn't necessary, the project could run without it." (Interview ref. Alpha)

What I found is similar to what has received attention in literature. The lack of consensus on perceptions of risk among those involved was found elsewhere to relate to the disbelief or lack of faith in the message (risk) or the source of the message (person who manages the risk) (Poortinga & Pidgeon, 2003). This can be described as *avoidance of uncertainty*. Differing perceptions of risks, influencing their treatment, arose elsewhere. In this case, the project team failed to come to an agreement about risks. Hence they chose not to manage them: "This was a problem, though it wasn't really possible to assess the risks. We couldn't come to any opinion." (Interview ref. Epsilon)

However, in cases where consensuses about risk estimates were found, some risks were managed and others were avoided.

> "We looked for risks that were easily identifiable, but didn't actually have serious consequences for the project. The project was not really at threat from these risks." (Interview ref. Alpha)

Risks were avoided in this project, because the project manager focused on "easily" assessable risks in order to achieve consensus within the project team. Another interviewee noted how risks were avoided in his project:

> "They were internal risks. But they should not have been deleted. They should have been managed internally, not just excluded or even ignored. They did not go even in the internal risk register." (Interview ref. Eta)

In this case, the sales department and senior management perceived the risk estimates produced by the project manager as something unrealistic. The project manager's risk estimates were regarded as being 'non-legitimate' with the result that they were not perceived as worth being managed.

Elsewhere, differences in perception of the legitimacy of risk estimates occurred along the supply chain, between subcontractors and prime contractors. In some instances, this led to those risks being left unmanaged. One interviewee explained why he thought this was the case:

> "(Our) partner has a much wider scope than we have. They are looking at other issues which are much more critical to them in the bigger picture and our issues although they are extremely important for us are not perceived as being important to (them)" (Interview ref. Kappa)

It was found that lack of trust in estimates of risk was indicative of a more general lack of trust between individuals within their own project team, between customers and subcontractors. One project manager even suggested that the risk management process was used to deliberately deceive other parties:

> "A lack of trust means that some of the risk, which might have been identified by various parties on the project, would not necessarily be given much weight, even if they were raised to project management. If there is a lack of trust then risks get tainted to people's belief that there are hidden agendas behind that." (Interview ref. Nu)

He went on to say:

> "There was a large element of mistrust in this project. We had multiple consultancies operating in the one consortium. Some of the consultancies were natural competitors outside of this consortium and therefore within the consortium there was a lot of mistrust. As a result, the client had a degree of mistrust with regard to the various hidden agendas that might have been operating within that consortium." (Interview ref. Nu)

Unlike denial of uncertainty, the salient characteristic of this risk mediator of project managers appears to be the lack of agreement on risks. In the literature, the lack of agreement on whether the message of risk is considered to be reliable, legitimate, fair or the deliverer of the message to be open and forthcoming, consistent honest, caring, concerned and competent

(Kasperson, Kasperson, Pidgeon, & Slovic, 2003; Metlay, 1999; Warg & Wester-Herber, 1999) as well as the lack of *ex-post* decision control at the *ex ante* stage of predicting risks and planning responses to risk is likely to lead to a "relative credibility" of risks, that is to say that risk actors may perceive the risk's "true" value differently. In all the above cases, no consensus was achieved among stakeholders about the credibility of risks. In the literature, the lack of consensus between risk actors' perceptions of risk relates to the disbelief or a lack of faith into the message (risk) or the source of the message (person who produces the risk) (Margolis, 2003; Marks et al., 2003; McLain & Hackman, 1999; Poortinga et al., 2003; Sheppard & Sherman, 1998); it is a question of trust (Kadefors, 2004).

Trust appears to be the root cause of risk conflicts (Slovic, 1993) and disagreements about risk's true nature (Bostrom, 1999). The problem of mistrust is addressed by Ritchie and Marshall (1993, p. 118) who argue: "There is a natural tendency to define a problem in such a way that the analytical results are valid and credible. ..., hazards which can be evaluated with confidence have been given comparatively more attention than other hazards". Lack of trust may therefore also be identified by the lack of attention towards risk estimates and their actual mitigation. Short (1989, p. 401) further suggests: "All too often such measures rest upon what can easily be counted, rather than on what is meaningful to those who are at risk, ...". Those risks that attract more attention than others may be "unusually visible, sensational, and easy to imagine" (Fischhoff et al., 1981, p. 29).

The management of risks by project managers may be influenced in the sense that risks that are not salient to the decision maker(s) may be avoided and the decision maker may not be motivated to manage those risks (e.g. Bobbitt et al., 1980; Elliot & McKee, 1995; Rowe, 1994). Rothstein (2002) mentions in another context, that risk actors tended to focus on the better known and readily-resolvable risks, obvious risks or these being perceived as legitimate. Hence, the disbelief in risk by risk actors or the disbelief in the source of risk is likely to relate to the risk actors' agreement on the management of risks that are clearer (Heath & Tversky, 1991), more obvious and controllable (Michalsen, 2003) or easier to measure (Rowe, 1994). This relative credibility of risk estimates (March et al., 1987) perceived by stakeholders tended to lead in the cases investigated in the first instance, to lack of cooperation and acceptance (Earle, 2004); Risks that were identified and analysed were not proactively responded to as happened in case Epsilon:

"... it was very easy to describe the effects, but they were just technical risks and the ones we assessed were not the most important later on in the project and that's what counts. Instead of identifying the important risks, the obvious ones were identified (and managed)." (Interview ref. Alpha).

On the other hand, attention was drawn to risks that in retrospect had a relative low influence on the project outcome:

"We looked for risks that were easily identifiable, but didn't actually have serious consequences for the project. The project was not really at threat from these risks." (Interview ref. Alpha).

4.3.3. Delay of uncertainty

In some instances, it was revealed that there was a tendency for the project managers to simply fail to actively manage certain risks, even where those risks were not regarded as a threat or 'taboo' and where there was consensus on what constituted a risk and how it should be measured. This manifested as apathy towards risk management, relying instead on trouble-shooting problems if and when they arose. For example, one interviewee noticed how a project culture encouraged this approach:

"In this particular environment, it was one that was used to 'flying by the seat of its pants' and managing issues and crises as they arrived rather than actually taking the time to stand back and look ahead and say 'What can we do to prevent that?'. If their focus and culture is one of fire fighting and crisis management, the step to take pre-emptive action to prevent a risk or to reduce a risk is never going to be at the top of their personal priority list." (Interview ref. Xi)

Elsewhere, the client did not regard the management of risk to be particularly important as it was felt that the project manager would simply deal with any problems that arose due to their brand exposure:

"My general feeling, it does come down to the brand. Fundamentally our name is on that piece of hardware which is deployed on the end customer's desk. They will see our brand name every day so the brand name is very important and something we want to protect so from that point of view there is that association that we have internally and is very strong for us. From the customer's point of view I suspect that there, they may be aware of this, they may be using that to a certain degree in that way that we will be very protective, that we will always jump in to save the situation, so there may a certain degree of abuse going on there." (Interview ref. Iota)

Thus, the customer delayed any active risk response that may have entailed costs and relied on the supplier, who was contractually obliged to react to any occurring problems.

The mediator noted in these cases can be described as *delay of uncertainty* by stakeholders in projects. Delay of uncertainty occurs when decision makers choose to wait until uncertainty resolves itself (Bobbitt et al., 1980). While this suggests a purposeful decision to 'wait and see', the interviews illustrated that, in some cases it was not a decision to be reactive to risk but, rather something that could be characterised as "inattention":

> "The manager was a "techie" person. He loved technology. If it had been technology driven, then I thought we would not have the issues that we had but because it was a commercial project, for him, the technology was standard and mundane. He had no interest at all in proactive risk management." (Interview ref. Iota)

Elsewhere, risk management was treated as a "box-ticking" exercise, suggesting that risk management was held in low regard as an activity. Risk management was treated as an administrative task rather than a management task:

> "I do not think there was a huge driver. I think this might have been a reason why the project risk assessment team might not have been really that well regarded. They were interested in finding the risk, the solutions were not really something that they were too bothered with. Their attitude was, find the risk, rate the risk but then feed that back into senior management and programme board and let them come up with a solution." (Interview ref. Nu)

and elsewhere:

> "It becomes an administrative process and as long people feel there is a risk register somewhere and lip service is being paid to it on a reasonably frequent basis, then they are managing risk." (Interview ref. Rho)

In summary, mitigating activities in response to identified risks were delayed or deferred because reactive (risk) management was the preferred mode of operation or there was a lack of interest, or inattention, in exercising active risk management. Delay of uncertainty tended to cause project managers to suspend any proactive actions because of their or other stakeholders' attitude towards proactive project risk management. In the extreme project managers did not apply project risk management at all because they could not justify the costs that would be incurred by managing risks: "At the beginning, we had so much to do that no one gave a thought to tackling risks at that point. It simply did not happen." (Interview ref. Epsilon). With the suspension of the proactive management of risk, risks adversely influenced the project.

The delay of project risk management actions appears to occur because project managers do not pay attention to active risk management and in other cases project managers may adopt reactive risk management as their preferred risk management method. Hansson (2004, p. 357) argues:

> "The search for new knowledge never ends and there is almost no end to the argument of information that one may wish to have in a risk-related decision. Since the premise of the delay argument ("If we wait we will know more about X") is true on all stages of a decision process, this argument can almost always be used to prevent risk-reducing actions."

Stakeholders may have strong and sometimes opposing preferences as to how to manage risk: proactive or reactive. Whereas on the one hand, some stakeholders' preference lies in identifying, analysing and responding in advance, other stakeholders appear to wait until uncertainty resolves itself (Bobbitt et al., 1980; Yang, Burns, & Backhouse, 2004) and to react to actual materialising risks. Smallman (1996, p. 260) summarises the apparent emphasis of risk actors on reactive risk management: "It is hardly surprising that reactive risk management is dominant at the present time; it is, apparently, more certain and easier to manage and cost than the holistic approach." Their preference may lie in saving costs and time by reducing the scope of risk management rather than trying to manage all possible risks with the purpose of reducing the possibility of adverse consequences on the project objectives of cost, scope and time (Redmill, 2002).

4.3.4. Ignorance of uncertainty

The fourth risk mediator that appears to constrain project risk management can be labelled ignorance of uncertainty. *Ignorance of uncertainty* can be seen as a lack of awareness of risk-related information on the part of project managers and other stakeholders, which could include incomplete knowledge. Ritchie and Marshall (1993, p. 117) note that "large uncertainties, and even ignorance, dominate areas of risk to the extent that the very lack of knowledge is unsuspected". In the interviews, this phenomenon appeared to be widespread, and was either being implied or overtly mentioned by several of the interviewees. For example:

"But when I think of the difficulties we had, we could only have anticipated some of them when we had problems with the server that could have been identified as a risk. You can make a note of something like that as being a risk, but you can't assess it. You can't provide a probability for this risk, because, at that time, information simply isn't available for you to be able to predict problems. If we had sat down at the beginning and tried to carry out a risk analysis, not 10% of it would have matched the problems we ended up having. Most of them simply could not have been foreseen. I think that the main problems we had could not have been predicted." (Interview ref. Epsilon)

"In a way nobody had a problem in the risks and everybody believed that it was so thoroughly researched that they would cover all the risks that they found. The problem was that when some of the risks, when it became clear that there were risks for the project which had not been anticipated because they had nothing to do with the project but which significantly impacted on the project. It's not that they had not been not thought of, they had been ignored, they had been so outside the project thinking that nobody considered them." (Interview ref. Mu)

"To a very great extent, with exception of the actual business-related risks, we were able to assess all the technical risks, but were not always able to assess other, non-technical risks." (Interview ref. Delta)

"Because we did not even know about it. We did not even think about it that it would be wrong and in fact that the only reason we knew that it was there was when they started producing their invoices." (Interview ref. Omicron)

Explanations for ignorance of risk are varied. A number of writers (Jaafari, 2001. Palmer et al., 1999) suggest that this ignorance may have its cause in organisational contexts of complexity and dynamism.

Freudenberg (1992) and Smallman (1996), for example, relate ignorance of uncertainty to the failure of risk actors to foresee interactions and interdependencies. In the context of project management, a project manager may face difficulties in forecasting how each component (e.g. a project task) may influence another (complexity) and remain stable over time (dynamism). This implies that a project manager may be unable to increase his knowledge about risk because of environmental constraints. In terms of complexity characterised by the interrelatedness of project components, the project manager in case Sigma argued:

> "... if one went wrong there is a geometric effect because another piece of software that was dependent on it was also delayed which then had a knock on effect. We did not get down to the level of understanding of all the interactions between all those components." (Interview ref. Sigma).

As the project progressed and components of the project such as the number of IT systems in the project changed, the lack of understanding about the complexity and dynamics of the project caused a sudden disruption:

> "Suddenly we were just caught out. We incrementally added boxes and it does not sound much if you add one PC, but when you add thirty, the power demand is huge and nobody even thought about it because none of us were electricians and in an office environment you plug your laptop in and it works, you do not even think about electricity having a capacity limit. That is why we got caught out on this one." (Interview ref. Sigma)

Ignorance of uncertainty is characterised by incomplete knowledge by project managers (Smithson, 1989). Ritchie and Marshall (1993, p. 117) argue: "Large uncertainties, and even ignorance, dominate areas of risk to the extent that the very lack of knowledge is unsuspected". The mediator in these specific cases was characterised by the passive and in deliberate unawareness of risks, the mediator of "being ignorant". Hence I define it as being ignorant of uncertainty. The risk mediator of being ignorant of uncertainty may be caused by environment related conditions of complexity and dynamism (Duncan, 1971, 1972; Farber, 2003; Jaafari, 2001; Palmer et al., 1999; Rowe, 1994).

In another case, a project manager stated, that he would not have been able to predict all the major problems which actually occurred in the IT project:

"But when I think of the difficulties we had, we could only have anticipated some of them (risks). When we had problems with the server that could have been identified as a risk. You can make a note of something like that as being a risk, but you can't assess it. You can't provide a probability for this risk, because, at that time, information simply isn't available for you to be able to predict problems. If we had sat down at the beginning and tried to carry out a risk analysis, not 10% of it would have matched the problems we ended up having. Most of them simply could not have been foreseen. I think that the main problems we had could not have been predicted." (Interview ref. Epsilon)

As a result, the mediator of being ignorant of uncertainty arises because individuals do not realise that a threat exists because they are unaware of it (Cooper, 2003) due to environmental related conditions such as complexity and dynamism.

However, project managers might not only ignore risks because of environmental dynamism and complexity but also because of their own set constraints or their own unwillingness to manage risk (White et al., 2003). Other cases illustrated that project managers sometimes also set their own set constraints and boundaries. Margolis (2003, p. 35) argues: "experts in general learn to concentrate on what is critical in their experience with the domain at hand and ignore anything else." Thus, it would appear that ignorance of risk arises for two reasons. Firstly, project teams are unable to predict risk because of contextual conditions such as complexity and dynamics. Secondly, they are unwilling to look for risks outside their defined scope of project management skills. In the cases investigated, project managers tended to exclude risks from being managed not because they believed that the risks were not "true" (avoidance of uncertainty), but because of their unwillingness to look for risks outside their defined scope of project risk management: "They looked purely at the implementation and not from a technical point of view. They had not looked at it from a business point of view." (Interview ref. Pi). Hence, I define this mediator as ignoring uncertainty; it describes the action of risk actors of "ignoring", the deliberate inattention of project managers towards risk. It is different from being ignorant of uncertainty in that project managers may be aware of risks, but they may exclude them from management because they consider them as out of the scope of their responsibility.

Being ignorant of uncertainty and ignoring uncertainty seemed to constrain project managers in identifying and analysing risks in the cases investigated. Due to incomplete knowledge, the influence of risks on the project outcome could not be minimised in advance because project managers overlooked risks as a whole or were unable to accurately estimate the effects or response to risks. Similarly, the project outcome tended to be influenced by risks that had been excluded from project risk management because they did not fit into the scope of project risk management.

Risk mediator as described above appears to constrain project managers in their ability to effectively manage risk. Lack of knowledge, for example, as a criterion of being ignorant of uncertainty seems to lead to risks being overlooked by project managers. Overall, this risk mediator imposes a constraint on the management of risk by project managers despite the benefits of managing risks for the purpose of reducing uncertainty (with the possibility of adverse consequences on the project performance). Project managers in IT projects are also confronted with "barriers to preventive action" (Adler et al., 1992, p. 234), barriers which have been described as mediators of denial, avoidance, delay and ignorance. These mediators may be not be created deliberately by risk actors but can also be described as "affective impulses" (Slovic, Finucane, Peters, & MacGregor, 2002, p. 10). Freudenberg (1992, p. 249) suggests:

> "Instead, the problem is that a variety of factors that are far more subtle - unseen, unfelt, and yet unfortunate in their consequences - exert an influence that could scarcely be more disturbing even if they were based on deliberate malice".

The risk mediators of denial, avoidance, delay and ignorance of uncertainty by risk actors in IT projects, whether created deliberately or not, tended to constrain project managers in preventing risks from adversely influencing the project outcome. All salient risk-related risk mediators, constraining project risk management in the research context of IT projects, show similarities with the problems identified in the literature review and underline the evidence that the actions of project managers often deviate from expected utility theory. Table 4.9 provides a comparison between the problems of project risk management that have been discussed in the literature review and the risk mediators that intervene in project risk management as identified in this study.

Problems with project risk management identified in the literature review	Explored risk mediator	Main criteria[28]
Problem of hindsight	Being ignorant of uncertainty	Risks not visible until they materialised.
Problem of ownership	Ignoring uncertainty	Risks outside the scope of risk management.
Problem of cost justification	Delay of uncertainty	Risks managed once they materialised rather than before.
Problem of arousal	Denial of uncertainty	Risks perceived as being uncomfortable for one or more project stakeholders.
Problem of ambiguity in risk estimates	Avoidance of uncertainty	Risks not agreed on by one or more project stakeholders.

Table 4.9: Comparison between problems identified in the literature review and risk mediator identified in the exploratory research

According to Table 4.9, most of the types of risk mediator reveal similarities with the problems of project risk management identified in the literature review: risks not visible until they materialise, risks outside the scope of risk management or managed once they materialise rather than before, risks perceived as being uncomfortable for one or more project stakeholders, and risks that are not agreed on by one or more project stakeholders.

Table 4.10 provides an overview of all findings. The table ranks the degree to which project managers thought project risk management contributed to a project and its success. The perceived ineffectiveness of the project risk management process stages is also displayed. Moreover, whether the project manager under- or overestimated risks, the type of risk mediator constrained the project manager's ability to manage risk and contributed to the influence of risk on the project outcome.

---

[28] Those main features were used as measures in the questionnaire as part of the explanatory research

Case	Contribution of project risk management to the project outcome	Project Outcome	Project risk management stages ineffective	Under- and overestimation of risk	Risk Mediator	Influence of (over- and) underestimated risks on the project outcome
Delta	High	Failure	EA	US	I	High
Theta	High	Failure	IT, AP, DE, DRA, DRO, MO, EA	US	A, I	High
Lambda	High	Failure	IT, AP, DE, DRA, EA	US, OS	D	Low
Beta	High	Success	IT, AP	US	I	High
Gamma	High	Success		UE	I	High
Eta	High	Success	AP	US	A, I	High
Omicron	High	Success		US	I	No unambiguous answer
Rho	High	Success	IT, DRO, MO, EA	US	I, Del	Not available
Mu	High	No clear categorisation	IT, AP, DE	US	I, Del	Low
Nu	Medium	Failure	DRA, DRO, MO, EA		D, A, Del	Medium
Xi	Medium	No clear categorisation	AP, EA	UR	Del	Medium
Kappa	Medium	Success	AP, DRO	US, OS	A, I	Low
Alpha	Low	Success	IT, DRO, EA	US, UE, UR, OS		High
Zeta	No project risk management applied	Failure	No effectiveness	US	I, D	High
Epsilon	No project risk management applied	No clear categorisation	No effectiveness	US	D, A, I	High
Sigma	No project risk management applied	Success	No effectiveness	US	I	Project is still ongoing
Pi	Not available	Not available	P, DE, DRO, MO	US	I	Not available
Iota	Not available	Success	DRO	US	I, D. Del	High

Effectiveness project risk management stages	Under- and overestimation of uncertainty	Risk mediators
P – Planning project risk management	US – Underestimation of state uncertainty	I - Ignorance of uncertainty
IT – Identify threat	UE - Underestimation of effect uncertainty	A – Avoidance of uncertainty
AP – Attach probabilities	UR - Underestimation of response uncertainty	Del – Delay of uncertainty
DE – Determine effects	OS - Overestimation of state uncertainty	D – Denial of uncertainty
DRA – Determine response alternative	OE - Overestimation of effect uncertainty	
DRO – Determine response ownership	OR - Overestimation of response uncertainty	
EA - Execute actions		
MO – Monitor risks		

Table 4.10: Overview of all findings from the exploratory study

Regardless of whether the project was a success or failure, risks appear to have adversely influenced the IT project outcome. Project managers encountered problems in identifying, analysing and responding to risks and risks were both over- and underestimated. Project managers believed that their inability to adequately identify, analyse and respond to risks was caused by specific risk mediators such as ignorance of uncertainty. As a consequence of their constrained ability to manage risks, underestimated risks in particular were thought to have influenced the project manager's ability to specifically meet cost and time objectives.

4.4. Summary and conclusions

The first phase of this study was designed to explore issues related to the research problem. The findings reveal that project managers tended not to be able to effectively manage risk because of a series of interventions. These interventions manifest as risk mediators which tended to lead to activity and decisions that deviated from, or intervened within, the risk management process described. These barriers are defined as denial, avoidance, delay and ignorance of uncertainty.

The exploratory study indicates that the norm of rationality claimed by best practice standards can be troubling when considering the influence of risk mediators. On the basis of the findings in this study, it appears that effective or rational project risk management with the purpose of preventing risks from adversely influencing the project outcome is constrained by risk mediator, underlining the criticism of researchers that EUT does not reflect how project managers actually behave. Table 4.11 displays a comparison between the theoretical claims of project risk management, its criticism by researchers and what has been found out in this exploratory study.

	Theory	Practice (Findings)
Project Risk Management	Rational actors assign (objective or subjective) probabilities to various outcomes.	Project managers tended to encounter difficulties in effectively assigning probabilities to various outcomes.
	Rational actors can order possible actions according to their preferences (preference to meet, cost, scope and time objectives). Preferences for actions involve some degree of risk aversion for specific choice situations.	Project managers tended to encounter difficulties in effectively ordering possible response actions according to the preference to meet cost, time and scope objectives because of interference with other preferences.
	Rational actors try to choose an action, which is optimal according to their preferences (preference to meet, cost, scope and time objectives).	Project managers tended to encounter difficulties in effectively choosing between different possible response actions because of the influence of other preferences.
	Rational actors can choose between different possible actions, each of which may lead to one or several possible outcomes. Actions as well as outcomes may differ in kind and scale.	Project managers tended to encounter difficulties in effectively choosing and executing a response action.
Project Risks	Match between perceived and actual risks. No influence of actual risks on the project outcome.	IT project managers thought to have under- and overestimated risks which tended to influence the project outcome.
Violations of theory/ reasons for ineffective project risk management	The uncertainty of taking any given action and whether or not negative outcomes will result. Cognitive and emotional overload that results from awareness of risk in many (if not most) mediators. The complex and varied dynamics associated with performing any given mediator.	Tendency for ... • Denial of uncertainty • Delay of uncertainty • Ignoring uncertainty • Being ignorant of uncertainty • Avoidance of uncertainty

Table 4.11: Comparison between theory of project risk management and reality

This study underlines the criticism of researchers that the normative model of expected utility theory is troubling when applied in practice. The risk mediators investigated in this study strengthen the argument that project managers are not able to fully prevent risk from adversely influencing the project outcome.

The exploratory study has provided insights into the process whereby a project manager's actions tend to deviate from EUT due to specific mediators. These insights were established on the basis of 18 interviews. In the extreme, the exploratory findings may not relate to any other case such as the investigated 18 cases. Thus, the degree of validity of the findings is limited. The exploratory study has not effectively revealed to what extent project managers in general perceive project risk management as ineffective, to what extent they under- and overestimate risk, to what extent risks adversely influence the project and to what extent risk mediators play a role in project managers ineffectiveness in reducing the mediators' influence on the project outcome. Hence, these patterns were tested in the explanatory phase of the study on a much wider population of project managers. The findings of this next phase are described and discussed in the following chapter.

5. EXPLANATORY RESEARCH

The findings of the exploratory research offer a detailed but restricted view of how risk mediators influence project risk management and subsequently the project outcome. In order to test whether the patterns identified in the exploratory research also apply to a greater number of IT project managers, a survey was conducted.

This chapter describes the findings of the explanatory study. In this second phase of the research an E-Mail with a link to a web-based questionnaire was sent to approximately 2.200 project managers. This survey was to increase the predictive power of IT project managers' perceptions about project risk management, risk mediators, the project outcome and the relationship between those concepts explored in the exploratory study. Only project managers who carried out IT projects were asked to answer the questionnaire. Out of roughly 2.200 possible project managers, 102 responded.

The questionnaire consisted of four sections (see Appendix B). The first section dealt with background questions: type of project, time frame, value of project and the position of the respondent in the project. The objective in this section was to gather after background information about the sample. The second section of the questionnaire dealt with project risk management. Project managers were asked whether project risk management was applied, what were the reasons were for not applying project risk management, what type of formal process was applied and how confident they were about the accuracy of the identification of risks. In addition, project managers were asked to locate on a scale from 0 (not at all) – 5 (to a great extent) to what extent in the exploratory phase risk mediators identified occurred. Section three of the questionnaire addressed the perceived effectiveness of project risk management. In section four, project managers were asked to what extent risks were under- and overestimated. In section five the project outcome was investigated. Project managers were questioned to what degree they achieved specific outcome criteria, whether they considered the project a success or failure, the main reasons for project success and failure and to what extent project risk management contributed to the project outcome.

In section 5.1 of this study, I describe to what extent IT project managers used a formal project risk management process and what reasons they gave not to do so. Furthermore, this section includes to what degree they expected to effectively manage risk. In section 5.2, I investigate the extent to which the five categories of risk mediator occurred. Section 5.3 offers a description of the perceived effectiveness of each stage of the project risk management process. In section 5.4, I elaborate on the findings of over- and underestimation of risk and section 5.5 offers an overview of the project outcome. Section 5.6 provides an analysis of the relationship between the key concepts of risk mediators, over- and underestimation of uncertainty, perceived effectiveness and the project outcome. In section 5.7, I analyse the contribution of project risk management to the project outcome to determine the overall importance of the findings in this study. In section 5.8, I summarise and comment on the key findings of the explanatory research.

5.1. The application of project risk management and expectations of IT project managers

In the exploratory study, in three cases the IT project manager's attitude towards project risk management had the result that all proactive actions to manage risks were suspended. In order to test this tendency on a wider population of IT project managers, they were first asked whether a formal project risk management process was applied. Figure 5.1 shows how many project managers applied a formal project risk management process:

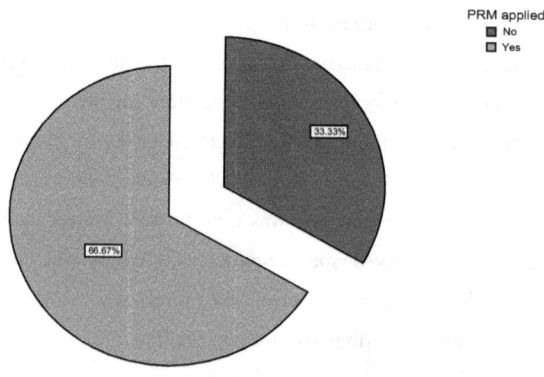

Figure 5.1: Application of project risk management (Survey Question 5)

In a third of the 102 cases, no formal project risk management approach was applied. This number seems rather surprising taking into account the amount of money that is at stake in those projects (see section 3.8). The findings can be explained by the reasons given by the respondents. In question 6, project managers were asked about their reasons for not applying a formal project risk management process. Table 5.1 displays the answers given by the respondents. It also includes my interpretation of those answers:

Reason for not applying project risk management	Risk mediator
"We haven't got time left."	Delay of uncertainty
"No executive call for risk measurements."	Delay of uncertainty
"Company doesn't see the value in adding the additional cycles to a project."	Delay of uncertainty
"Upper management did not think it required it."	Delay of uncertainty
"Ignorance that such a thing existed or was necessary."	Delay of uncertainty
"Decision made by pre-sales team."	Delay of uncertainty
"At the time, no one thought that was an important thing to do. It was the project manager's job to manage all risks, by himself, without help from others. It was what he was paid the '"big bucks" to do."	Delay of uncertainty
"An initial risk analysis was done but PM didn't bother to follow-up."	Delay of uncertainty
"Too many different companies had "ownership" of different elements, semi-formal risk management to work individual packages was applied but was not really effective, as it was not rolled up to the highest level."	Delay of uncertainty
"A single risk identification workshop was held early in the project before my arrival. Reason for not following the process was most probably the attitude of the members of the team."	Delay of uncertainty
"The principal reason why a formal project risk management process was not applied had more to do with the organizational culture than anything else. The organization is culturally focused on getting things done. Thus, there was no "formal project risk management process" required."	Delay of uncertainty
"Not enough time to prepare a plan. Accelerated implementation was the key, not cost."	Delay of uncertainty

Table 5.1: Reasons for the non-application of project risk management (Survey question 4)

As can be seen in Table 5.1, the most dominant reason for the non-application of project risk management appears to be the risk mediator of delay of uncertainty. Proactive project risk management was not carried out because project managers and other risk actors appeared not to consider project risk management as worthy of pursuit under time and cost constraints. Regarding the application of project risk management, the findings seem to confirm the tendency in the explorative cases that project risk management was not applied because of the mediator of delay of uncertainty in such a way that IT project managers and other risk actors emphasised a reactive project risk management approach and/or paid little attention to proactively managing project risks.

In the other two thirds of the investigated cases, project risk management was applied. IT project managers were asked which specific process they applied. Figure 5.2 shows which specific project risk management process was applied.

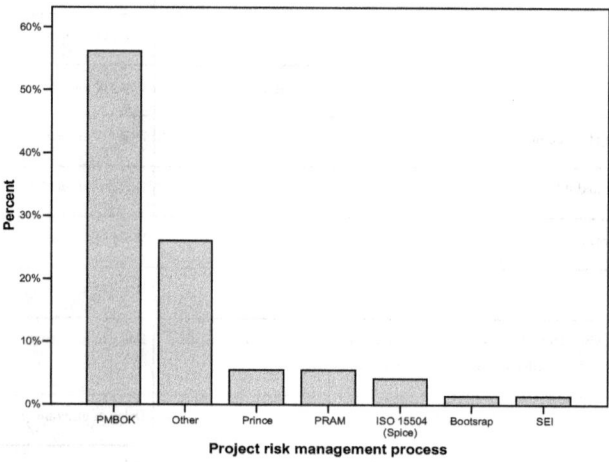

Figure 5.2: Applied project risk management process (Survey question 7)[29]

In over half of all cases, a PMI project risk management process was used, thus underlining the dominance of this best practice standard in IT project and project risk management in the chosen sample.

In those cases in which project managers applied project risk management, the explorative results give some indication that project manager's expectations were met because they reduced their aspiration levels by excluding some risks from project risk management, that is to say they do not expect all risks to be predicted. In the questionnaire project managers were asked how confident they were about the accuracy of predicted risks. Figure 5.3 displays how confident project managers were in predicting risk events (threats), effects and responses.

---

[29] Process PMBOK is published by Project Management Institute
Process PRINCE is published by The UK Government Centre for Information Systems
Process PRAM is published by the U.K. Association for Project Management
Process SPICE is published by the International Committee on Software Engineering Standards

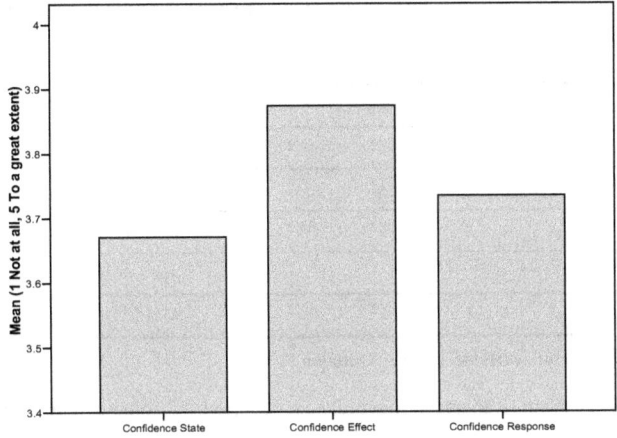

Figure 5.3: Overview of confidence levels - state, effect and response uncertainty (Survey Question 8)[30]

Project managers were moderately confident about their accuracy to identify and respond to risks. The findings seem to confirm the exploratory results that project managers do not expect to accurately identify, analyse and respond to risks that will influence the project outcome.

5.2. Risk mediators

In the exploratory study, five different types of risk mediator were identified: denial, delay, ignorance (unaware), ignorance (absent) and avoidance of uncertainty. In the survey, project managers were asked to what extent these mediators occurred in the project. In part II (question 9) of the questionnaire (see Appendix B), IT project managers were asked to what extent risks were perceived as being uncomfortable for one or more project stakeholders[31], outside the scope of risk management[32], not agreed on by one or more stakeholders[33], managed once they materialised rather than before[34], and as not visible until they materialised[35].

Process BOOTSTRAP is an adaptation of the standard process of the European Space Agency
Process SEI is published by the Software Engineering Institute
[30] The results of the variables confidence state, effect and response are not significantly different (Analysis of variance) – for further details see Appendix D.
[31] relates to denial of uncertainty
[32] relates to ignoring uncertainty
[33] relates to avoidance of uncertainty
[34] relates to delay of uncertainty
[35] relates to being ignorant of uncertainty

Table 5.2 gives an overview of the extent to which each mediator occurred in the investigated projects.

Variable	Mean[36] (SD)
Denial of uncertainty (Q9a)	3.59 (1.15)
Ignoring uncertainty (Q9b)	3.00 (1.20)
Avoidance of uncertainty (Q9c)	2.65 (1.89)
Delay of uncertainty (Q9d)	3.18 (1.23)
Being ignorant of uncertainty (Q9e)	3.12 (1.27)

Table 5.2: Mean values of risk mediators variables (Survey Question 9)[37]

On average, most of the risk mediators apart from avoidance, occurred "to some extent". The next step is to determine the relationship between risk mediators (see Table 5.3).

Variable		1	2	3	4
1	Denial of uncertainty	1			
2	Ignoring uncertainty	.047	1		
3	Avoidance of uncertainty	.124	.207	1	
4	Delay of uncertainty	.046	.434**	.278**	1
6	Being ignorant of uncertainty	-.093	.294**	.271*	.473**

**. Correlation is significant at the .01 level
*. Correlation is significant at the .05 level

Table 5.3: Correlations between risk mediator variables

Denial of uncertainty is not significantly correlated with other risk mediators. However, both types of ignorance of uncertainty are significantly correlated with delay of uncertainty while avoidance of uncertainty is less significantly related with being ignorant of uncertainty and delay of uncertainty. Although it is difficult to determine which variable causes which (George & Mallery, 2003), risk actors' attention towards reactive risk management or the mere inattention towards proactive project risk management is likely to lead to the ultimate ignorance of risks. Project managers may not even attempt to identify threats for the reason that they are not interested in pursuing a proactive risk management approach. Hence, delay of uncertainty may ultimately trigger ignorance of uncertainty by risk actors.

---

[36] Scale: 1 – not at all, 5 – to a great extent
[37] The results of the variables being ignorant of uncertainty, ignoring uncertainty, delay of uncertainty and denial of uncertainty are not significantly different (Analysis of variance) – for further details see Appendix D.

A factor analysis (see Table 5.4) resulted in the extraction of one factor including the variables of ignoring uncertainty, avoidance of uncertainty, delay of uncertainty and being ignorant of uncertainty.

Rotated Component Matrix[a]

	Component	
	1	2
Delay	.813	.014
Being ignorant	.753	-.244
Ignoring	.700	.132
Avoidance	.532	.339
Denial	-.010	.940

Extraction Method: Principal Component Analysis.
Rotation Method: Varimax with Kaiser Normalization.
a. Rotation converged in 3 iterations.

Table 5.4: Rotated component matrix of risk mediators variables[38]

Denial of uncertainty as a variable was dropped. However, no conceptual reason behind this decision can be stated with confidence (see section 6.4).

5.3. Perceived effectiveness of project risk management

The exploratory study revealed that certain risk mediators appeared to have an influence on project risk management. They seemed to influence the effectiveness of the project risk management stages perceived by IT project managers as well as how adequately they thought that risk was managed. Therefore, in the explanatory study the project managers were questioned as to what extent they perceived each project risk management process stage as effective.

Table 5.5 displays an overview of all project risk management stages and their perceived effectiveness.

---

[38] For a detailed factor analysis see Appendix C

Variable	Mean[39] (SD)
Effectiveness of planning project risk management (Q10b)	3.91 (1.06)
Effectiveness of identification risk (Q10c)	3.65 (1.16)
Effectiveness of attaching probabilities (Q10d)	2.98 (1.33)
Effectiveness of defining effects (Q10e)	3.83 (0.88)
Effectiveness of defining response alternatives (Q10f)	3.49 (1.04)
Effectiveness of determining response ownership (Q10g)	3.52 (1.21)
Effectiveness of determining best response (Q10h)	3.46 (0.88)
Effectiveness of monitoring (Q10i)	3.88 (1.05)
Effectiveness of executing actions (Q10j)	3.34 (1.15)

Table 5.5: Mean values of perceived effectiveness variables (Survey Question 10)[40]

The stage of Attaching Probabilities is the one with the lowest perceived effectiveness. The stages of Identification and Response Ownership reveal a higher, but relatively low perceived effectiveness with a mean of just 3.52 and 3.65. The ultimate stage to prevent risks from materialising and adversely influencing the project outcome is the stage of executing actions. However, as can be seen in Table 5.5, the perceived effectiveness of executing actions was only perceived as effective to "some extent". Project managers may question the utility of the whole project risk management process because response actions are perceived as moderately effective.

As a follow up step, correlations were run to investigate the relationship between the perceived effectiveness variables (see Table 5.6). However, the stages of planning project risk management and monitoring have been excluded because they are supportive project risk management stages and do not directly enable a project manager to estimate state, effect and response uncertainty.

---

[39] Scale: 1 – not at all, 5 – to a great extent

Variable	1	2	3	4	5	6
1 Effectiveness of identification risk	1					
2 Effectiveness of attaching probabilities	.680**	1				
3 Effectiveness of defining effects	.526**	.513**	1			
4 Effectiveness of defining response alternatives	.426**	.385**	.630**	1		
5 Effectiveness of determining response ownership	.556**	.469**	.543**	.537**	1	
6 Effectiveness of determining best response	.357**	.294**	.658**	.647**	.516**	1
7 Effectiveness of executing actions	.540**	.444**	.393**	.372**	.670**	.440**

**. Correlation is significant at the .01 level
*. Correlation is significant at the .05 level

Table 5.6: Correlation between perceived effectiveness variables

The correlations between perceived effectiveness variables indicate shared common factors. A subsequent factor analysis is shown in Table 5.7.

Component Matrix[a]

	Component
	1
Effectiveness identification risk	.773
Effectiveness attach probabilities	.714
Effectiveness define effects	.825
Effectiveness define response alternatives	.761
Effectiveness determine response ownership	.800
Effectiveness determine best response	.747
Effectivness execute actions	.742

Extraction Method: Principal Component Analysis.
a. 1 components extracted.

Table 5.7: Component matrix of perceived effectiveness variables[41]

It resulted in one single factor including all variables displayed in Table 5.6.

---

[40] Only the stage of attaching probabilities shows a significant difference to the results of all other perceived effectiveness variables (Analysis of variance) – for further details see Appendix D.
[41] For a detailed factor analysis see Appendix D

5.4. Under- and overestimation of risk

Risk mediators as discussed in chapter 4 also appeared to have an impact on how adequately risks were managed. As discussed earlier, IT project managers thought they had encountered problems in managing risks, risks appeared to be under- and overestimated. In the explanatory study, IT project managers were required to answer to what extent they over- and underestimated risks. Specifically, in terms of underestimation of uncertainty, they were asked to what extent unpredicted risk events actually materialised (underestimation of state uncertainty), to what extent the actual consequences of risk events were more severe than predicted (underestimation of effect uncertainty) and to what extent the actual risk mitigation actions were did worse than predicted (underestimation of response uncertainty). In contrast, concerning the overestimation of risk, to what extent predicted risk actually not materialised (overestimation of state uncertainty), to what extent the actual consequences of risk events were less severe than predicted and to what extent actual risk mitigation actions did better than predicted.

The degree of over- and underestimation is displayed in Table 5.8.

Variable[42]	Mean[43] (SD)
Underestimation of state uncertainty (Q12)	3.23 (1.13)
Underestimation of effect uncertainty (Q11b)	2.97 (1.28)
Underestimation of response uncertainty (Q11e)	3.06 (1.49)
Overestimation of state uncertainty (Q11a)	2.99 (1.18)
Overestimation of effect uncertainty (Q11c)	2.53 (1.31)
Overestimation of response uncertainty (Q11d)	3.34 (1.32)

Table 5.8: Mean values of over- and underestimation of uncertainty variables (Survey Question 11 and 12)[44]

Apart from overestimation of response uncertainty, project managers tended to under- and overestimate uncertainty to some extent. Their predictions of risk, their predictions about the existence of threats effect and responses tended to vary from the actual threats, effects and responses. This seems to underline the findings of the exploratory study that threats were overlooked which later materialised. The findings regarding the degree of over- and

---

[42] Multiple answers are possible because risks may be simultaneously over- and underestimated
[43] Scale: 1 – not at all, 5 – to a great extent
[44] The results of the variables overestimation of effect uncertainty is significantly different to all other over- and underestimation of uncertainty variables (Analysis of variance) – for further details see Appendix D.

underestimation may also reflect the lack of effectiveness and the level of difficulty project managers encountered during the process of managing risks.

Whereas the results of underestimation of state, effect uncertainty and overestimation of state and response uncertainty are similar, the amount of overestimation of effect uncertainty is significantly lower. This could be explained by the fact that due to the pressure to portray an IT project in a positive light, the effects of risks were kept to a minimum.

A subsequent step before the factor analysis was to determine the correlation between all over- and underestimation of uncertainty variables (see Table 5.9).

Variable		1	2	3	4	5
1	Underestimation of state uncertainty	1				
2	Underestimation of effect uncertainty	.371**	1			
3	Underestimation of response uncertainty	.291**	.234**	1		
4	Overestimation of state uncertainty	.181	.154	.203	1	
5	Overestimation of effect uncertainty	-.185	.150	-.027	.344**	1
6	Overestimation of response uncertainty	-.165	-.103	.099	.303**	.334**

**. Correlation is significant at the .01 level
*. Correlation is significant at the .05 level

Table 5.9: Correlations between over- and underestimation of uncertainty variables

The results show that all overestimation of uncertainty variables and all underestimation of uncertainty variables are significantly related. The factor analysis underlines this pattern of correlations. According to Table 5.10, two factors can be extracted.

Rotated Component Matrix[a]

	Component	
	1	2
Overestimation Effect	.840	-.059
Overestimation Response	.739	.126
Overestimation State	.576	.418
Underestimation State	-.295	.856
Underestimation Response	.293	.635
Underestimation Effect	.427	.561

Extraction Method: Principal Component Analysis.
Rotation Method: Varimax with Kaiser Normalization.
a. Rotation converged in 3 iterations.

Table 5.10: Rotated component matrix of under- and overestimation of uncertainty variables[45]

The first factor or composite consists of all three underestimations of uncertainty, the second of all overestimation of uncertainty variables.

5.5. The project outcome

Having looked at the extent to which risk mediators occurred in IT projects, how IT project managers perceived the effectiveness of project risk management and to what degree, and whether risks were under- and overestimated, this section looks at the findings regarding the perceived project outcome.

First, project managers were asked whether they considered the outcome of the project they were referring to in the survey to be a failure or a success (see Figure 5.4).

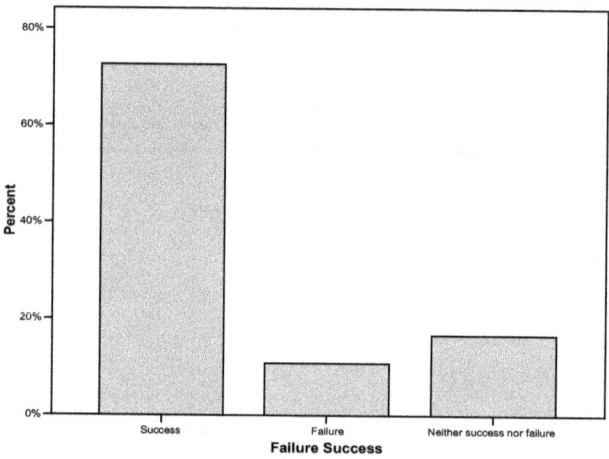

Figure 5.4: Resulting failure / success of projects (Survey Question 14)

Overall, only a relatively small number of projects were considered to have failed. As a further step to determine the project outcome in more detail, project managers were asked to what extent the project achieved its purpose, provided satisfactory benefit to the owner, satisfied the needs of the owner, users and stakeholders, met the pre-stated objectives, produces to specification, within budget and on time and to what extent the project satisfied

---

[45] For a detailed factor analysis see Appendix D

the needs of the project team. Those criteria used in the questionnaire were established in the exploratory study. Table 5.11 provides an overview of the project outcomes in the cases investigated.

Variable	Mean[46] (SD)
Achievement of Purpose (Q13a)	4.13 (1.00)
Benefit to Owner (Q13b)	4.10 (0.99)
Satisfaction of owners, users and stakeholders (Q13c)	3.92 (1.12)
Meeting pre-stated objectives (Q13d)	3.83 (1.20)
Scope, cost, time (Q13e)	3.21 (1.25)
Satisfaction of team (Q13f)	3.81 (1.00)

Table 5.11: Mean values project outcome variables (Survey Question 13)[47]

None of the project outcome criteria were achieved to a great extent. Furthermore, according to the respondents, scope, cost and time targets were only partially achieved. The findings may either show that the objectives of cost, scope and time are of secondary importance or that IT project managers have "learned" to fail. Regarding the first issue, one may expect on the one hand that the projects investigated tended to be considered as having failed by project managers because scope, cost and time objectives had predominantly not been met. However, as the findings show, this was not the case, underlining the tendency established in chapter 5, for project managers to include other outcome criteria than only scope, cost and time when categorising IT projects as failed or successful. In the light of these findings, the overall rate of failure of IT projects introduced in chapter 1 may also be questioned as they may not reflect the rate of failure from a project manager's point of view may not be reflected.

On the other hand, one could conclude that IT project managers have learned to fail to accomplish cost, scope and time objectives. Lyytinen and Robey (1999) argue that because sustained failure in previous projects occurred, failure in reaching objectives such as time, cost and scope objectives may be considered by project managers to become a normal situation. Hence, normality in failing objectives could be interpreted as being successful. Therefore, the findings may show that the achievement of scope, cost and time objectives is indeed secondary, but also that IT project managers have accepted the circumstance of failing

---

[46] Scale: 1 – not at all, 5 – to a great extent
[47] The results of the variables of scope cost, time is significantly different to all other project outcome variables (Analysis of variance) – for further details see Appendix D.

to accomplish these objectives as normal so that despite failure in these areas the outcome of the project may be considered a success.

Table 5.12 displays the correlations between all project outcome variables.

	Variable	1	2	3	4	5
1	Achievement of Purpose	1				
2	Benefit to Owner	.710**	1			
3	Satisfaction of owners, users and stakeholders	.644**	.721**	1		
4	Meeting pre-stated objectives	.736**	.501**	.620**	1	
5	Scope, cost, time	.545**	.413**	.397**	.642**	1
6	Satisfaction of team	.576**	.536**	.485**	.576**	.537**

**. Correlation is significant at the .01 level
*. Correlation is significant at the .05 level

Table 5.12: Correlations between project outcome variables

As can be seen, all project outcome variables significantly influence each other. The factor analysis is displayed in Table 5.13.

Component Matrix[a]

	Component
	1
Outcome Achievement Purpose	.897
Outcome Prestated Objectives	.859
Outcome Satisfaction owner, users, stake.	.841
Outcome satisf. benefit customer	.832
Outcome satisfy Needs of Team	.773
Outcome Scope, Cost Time	.720

Extraction Method: Principal Component Analysis.
a. 1 components extracted.

Table 5.13: Component matrix of project outcome variables[48]

It results in one single composite variable which is composed of all project outcome variables as shown in Table 5.12.

---

[48] For a detailed factor analysis see Appendix D

5.6. Modelling

In the previous sections, I provided descriptive statistics about the means and relationship of variables used in the survey and the extraction of composite variables. This section is concerned with providing an overview of the composite variables and the analysis of how the developed composite variables influence each other. Table 5.14 shows the means and the reliability Alpha factor of each composite variable.

Variable	Mean[49] (Cronbach's Alpha)[50]
Project Outcome composite	3.83 (0.899)
Overestimation of uncertainty composite	2.95 (0.647)
Underestimation of uncertainty composite	3.26 (0.524)
Perceived effectiveness composite	3.48 (0.875)
Risk mediators composite	2.98 (0.663)

Table 5.14: Mean values and reliability analysis of composite variables

The results of the reliability analysis show, that except for the underestimation of uncertainty composite, all coefficients are over 0.5 (see Appendix C), therefore showing a satisfying reliability.

Findings in the exploratory study already indicated that risk mediators appear to influence whether project managers perceive project risk management as effective. Hence, in order to shed more light on this relationship I ran correlations and step wise regressions on all composite variables. Table 5.15 displays the correlations between the composite variables of project outcome, overestimation of uncertainty, underestimation of uncertainty, and perceived effectiveness and risk mediators.

---

[49] Scale: 1 – not at all, 5 – to a great extent
[50] For detailed analysis see Appendix

Variable		1	2	3	4
1	Project Outcome composite	1			
2	Overestimation of uncertainty composite	.279*	1		
3	Underestimation of uncertainty composite	-.288*	.471**	1	
4	Perceived effectiveness composite	.607**	.089	-.520**	1
5	Risk Mediators composite	-.362**	.075	.487**	-.569**

**. Correlation is significant at the .01 level
*. Correlation is significant at the .05 level

Table 5.15: Correlations between composite variables

Risk mediators are significantly related to the degree of underestimation of uncertainty but rather inexplicably do not have an influence on overestimation of uncertainty. This appears to contradict the exploratory findings. Furthermore, the exploratory findings indicated that overestimated risk does not appear to have an influence on the project outcome. However, this is not the case due to the significant relationship between the project outcome composite and the overestimation of uncertainty composite.

Two different types of project risk management related outcomes are defined that appear to have been influenced by risk mediators: over- and underestimation of uncertainty and perceived effectiveness. As outlined in the literature review, the perceived effectiveness of project risk management relates to the action of project risk management itself whereas over- and underestimation of uncertainty relates to the outcome of actions. The exploratory findings of the research indicated that risk mediators firstly drive the degree of over- and underestimation of uncertainty and secondly appear to reduce the perceived effectiveness of project risk management by IT project managers. As a consequence, Figure 5.5 shows the first proposed step testing the impact of risk mediators on the over- and underestimation relationship and perceived effectiveness of project risk management.

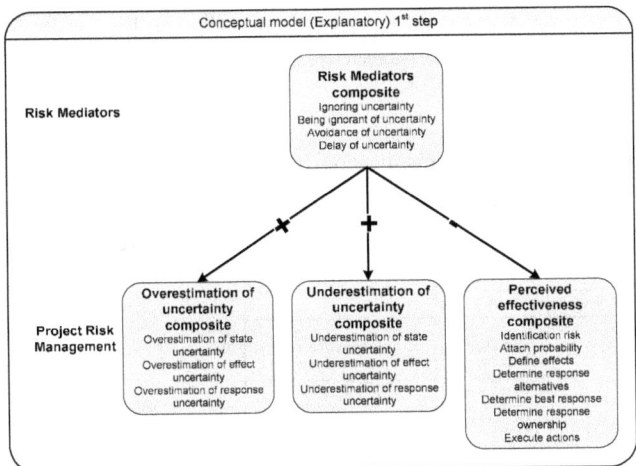

Figure 5.5: Conceptual model (explanatory) 1ˢᵗ step

As can be seen in Figure 5.5, the composite variables of over- and underestimation and perceived effectiveness have been defined as the dependent variables. The composite variable of project outcome has been excluded from this first step, but will be considered as a dependent variable in the second step of the modelling (see Figure 5.6).

	Dependent Variables		
Independent variables	Perceived Effectiveness composite	Overestimation of uncertainty composite	Underestimation of uncertainty composite
Risk Mediators composite	-.556***	.111	.417***
R^2	.309	.012	.174
Adjusted R^2	.300	-.001	.164
F for ΔR^2	34.393***	.959	16.252***

Regression coefficients are standardised. *p<.05 **p<.01 ***p<.001

Table 5.16: Regressions on perceived effectiveness, over- and under estimation of uncertainty and risk mediators composite variable

The findings on the influence of risk mediators of delay, ignorance and avoidance of uncertainty on the perceived effectiveness of project risk management by IT project managers and over- and underestimation of uncertainty state that risk mediators significantly and positively affect the degree of underestimation of uncertainty. This confirms the exploratory findings. The non-significant relationship between risk mediators and overestimation of uncertainty remains open to debate. However, one possible explanation is that due to the influence of risk mediators, risks are rather downplayed and (deliberately) overlooked rather than vice versa.

The second step of modelling includes an investigation into the influence of over- and underestimation of uncertainty and perceived effectiveness on the project outcome. Based on the exploratory findings the following conceptual model can be drawn (see Figure 5.6).

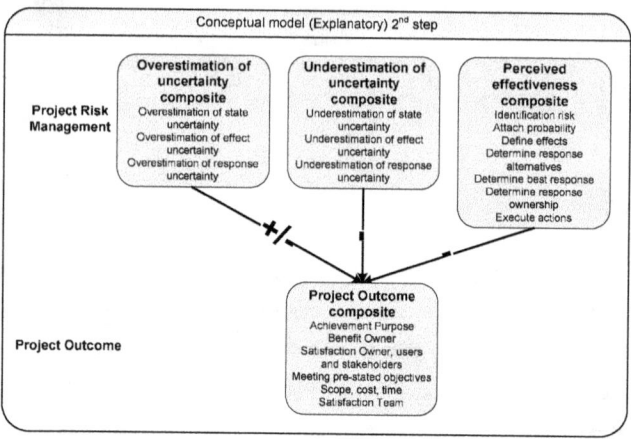

Figure 5.6: Conceptual model (explanatory) 2nd step

As can be seen in Figure 5.6, the project outcome composite is defined as the dependent variables. The exploratory findings suggested that overestimation of uncertainty appeared to have no influence on the project outcome. Furthermore, they suggested that underestimation of uncertainty and perceived effectiveness is negatively related to the project outcome. Regressions may shed further light on these relationships (see Table 5.17).

Dependent Variables

Independent variables	Project Outcome composite
Perceived Effectiveness composite	.377**
Overestimation of uncertainty composite	.530***
Underestimation of uncertainty composite	-.436**
R^2	.498
Adjusted R^2	.478
F for ΔR^2	24.780***

Regression coefficients are standardised. *p<.05 **p<.01 ***p<.001

Table 5.17: Regressions on project outcome composite and over- and underestimation of uncertainty composite and perceived effectiveness composite

According to the regressions, perceived effectiveness positively influenced the project outcome. Remarkably, overestimations of uncertainty not only lead to an insignificant influence on the project outcome as suggested but also had a significant positive impact on the project outcome. In contrast, underestimation of uncertainty significantly and negatively affected the project outcome confirming the tendency drawn from the interviews where underestimated risks negatively influenced the project outcome, especially the achievement of scope, cost and time objectives.

The explanatory findings show that driven by risk mediators, IT project managers underestimated risks and perceived the effectiveness as less optimal as is suggested by the assumptions of EUT. However, whereas underestimated risks and perceived effectiveness negatively influenced the project outcome, overestimated risks positively influenced the project outcome.

5.7. Contribution of project risk management to the project outcome

The importance of the findings about risk mediator influencing project managers in their ability to prevent projects from failing would be negligible if the contribution of project risk management to the project outcome is considered small by project managers when evaluated alongside the other eight project management disciplines.

Overall, with a mean of 3.03, project managers perceived the contribution of project risk management to the project outcome as moderately high. By separating the survey sample into a Failure and Success sample, with a mean of 3.38 project managers thought that the use of project risk management contributed more to the success than to the failure of their project (mean = 2.40). This may indicate that project managers of failed projects thought that other reasons contributed more to the outcome of the project than they did in successful projects. Figure 5.7 displays to what extent project managers thought that project risk management contributed to successful IT projects.

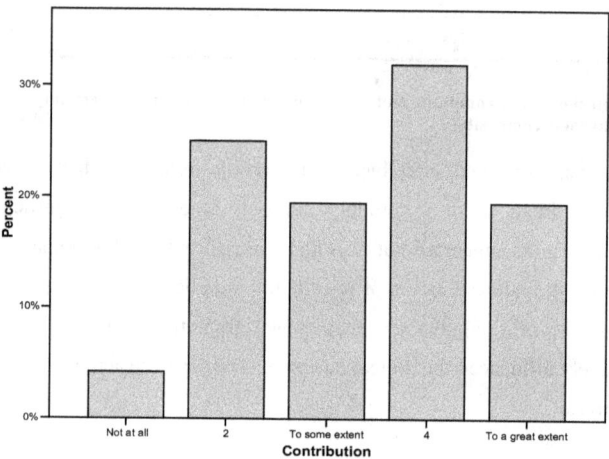

Figure 5.7: Overview of the contribution of project risk management to projects that are considered a success (Survey Question 16)

Under the consideration of the rate of success displayed in Figure 5.4, over three quarters of project managers thought that the use of project risk management contributed at least to some extent to the successful outcome of the project. Hence, they may not dismiss project risk management as a pointless activity despite the degree of under- and overestimation of risk.

5.8. Summary and conclusion

To sum up, most of the findings of the exploratory phase were confirmed through the statistical analysis of the survey data. The analysis of the data of 102 IT project managers confirmed that project managers faced difficulties in identifying, analysing and responding to risks; risks were over- and underestimated. As suggested, intervening risk mediators influenced the effective use of project risk management; due to risk mediators project risk managers seemed to underestimate risk. However, whereas underestimation of risk was negatively associated with the project outcome, overestimation positively influenced the achievement of the perceived project outcome. Hence, the risk mediators of ignorance, avoidance and delay of uncertainty manifested as deliberately or coincidentally imposing barriers for project managers to effectively estimate state, effect and response uncertainty and ultimately as barriers to achieving project objectives.

Furthermore, if project failure is only defined by the project manager's ability to meet cost, scope, and time objectives, one may conclude that because of the risk mediators of ignorance of uncertainty, avoidance and delay of uncertainty, project managers may have been able to prevent the IT project from failing. However, because of the inclusion of outcome criteria other than scope, cost and time a clear statement that project manager did not succeed in effectively preventing IT projects from failing needs to be seen in perspective. What can be said is that despite best practice project risk management standards, project managers failed to prevent risks from influencing the project outcome. Risks adversely influenced the project outcome because of specific risk mediators as outlined earlier. These risk mediators appeared to constrain project mangers in making rational and sensible decisions regarding risks.

6. CONCLUSIONS

"In the face of uncertainty, man may be an intellectual cripple, whose intuitive judgements and decisions violate many of the fundamental principles of optimal behaviour." (Hedge, 1987, p. 151)

Research has shown that many IT projects fail because scope, cost and time objectives are not met despite the existence of best practice project management standards. This study aimed to investigate the influence of risk mediators on the specific project management process of project risk management on the outcome of IT projects. Literature indicates that project managers in general appear to have problems optimally preventing risks from adversely influencing the project outcome. The exploratory and explanatory findings of this study suggest that IT project managers face specific risk mediators which tend to adversely influence the effective use of project risk management and which ultimately affect the project outcome of IT projects.

In section 6.1, I draw all the findings together, present the main conclusions, principles, relationships, correlations and generalisations and the interpretation of the results and their relationship to the research questions. In sections 6.2 and 6.3 respectively, I describe the theoretical and practical implications of the study's findings. Section 6.4 proposes limitations to this research and to the findings. Section 6.5 offers a proposal for future research. In section 6.6, I conclude this study with some final words.

6.1. Addressing the research problem and research questions

This study addresses the research problem of whether risk-related interventions influence the effective application of project risk management by project managers. The answer is that according to the findings in this study risk mediators of delay, ignorance and avoidance indeed influence the use of project risk management by project managers in IT projects. In more detail, this research problem can be answered by addressing each research question and proposition.

6.1.1. How do IT project managers define project outcome (success and failure)?

Some literature in project management suggests that the project outcome is defined and measured in terms of time, cost and scope. However, the criticism has also been raised that this view is too narrow and does not include project outcome criteria such as team

141

satisfaction. In order to investigate the influence of risk mediators in project risk management and the project outcome, comprehensive project outcome criteria have to be defined. However, because literature does not provide a single interpretation of project outcome, this concept was explored in this study by asking IT project managers how they define project success and failure.

The findings of the exploratory research show that objectives beyond time, cost and scope play an important role from the project manager's point of view in assessing the project outcome. Scope, cost and time were mentioned by the respondents to the questionnaire as important in defining project success and failure. However, IT project managers went beyond these criteria and also emphasised the maintenance of a good relationship with stakeholders, the learning experience, the opportunity to obtain follow on contracts and the satisfaction of all parties involved in the project outcome.

The view that project outcome should not only include the criteria of scope, cost and time is strengthened by the findings of the explanatory research. Although the explanatory research revealed that IT project managers achieved time, cost and scope objectives only to some extent, the outcome of most of the IT projects were described by the IT project managers involved as a success. This seems to imply that project outcome criteria other than scope, cost and time are heavily emphasised in assessing the project outcome.

However, the findings about the project outcome may also highlight the issue of learning. As discussed, because of the possible historical failure of IT project managers to accomplish the project objectives of scope, cost and time, they may have learned to accept these circumstances as unavoidable. Failure to meet scope, cost and time objectives, although strictly speaking a sign of failure, may have been accepted as normal practice and therefore part of a project being considered to be a success, that is to say, the outcome turned out as expected.

Taking the findings of the exploratory and explanatory research into account, the rate of failure of IT projects as introduced in chapter 1 may be interpreted with caution. Indeed, by excluding other project outcome criteria such as the satisfaction of the team from any statistics, a restricted view of the overall failure rate of IT projects might result in inaccurately overestimating the degree of failure and because of that possibly casting a shadow of doubt over the success of an industry that may not be justified.

6.1.2. Do IT project managers perceive that the use of project risk management processes contribute to the project outcome?

Organisations such as PMI suggest nine key processes to ensure project success. Some literature, although inconclusive, suggests that inadequate project risk management is one of the main contributors to project failure. In order to justify the focus on project risk management in this study, the degree of the overall contribution of project risk management to the project outcome was investigated. Arguably, if an IT project manager felt that project risk management did not play a major role in achieving the project outcome, the justification for considering the concept of project risk management in this study may have been doubtful.

The findings show that IT project managers perceived project risk management contribute considerably to the project outcome. Project risk management does seem to make a difference (Voetsch & Cioffi, 2002). The findings show that project risk management manifests as one of the key disciplines in project management to achieve the desired project outcome and this underlines Whittaker's (1999) claim mentioned in the introduction that project risk management is indeed a major contributor to the project outcome. Proposition 1 can be accepted insofar as it claims that IT project managers will perceive that the use of project risk management contributes to the project outcome. Beyond this, because of the overall contribution of project risk management among other project management disciplines to the project outcome as described in chapter 1, the findings about the effectiveness of project risk management, over- and underestimation of uncertainty and the influence of risk mediators on project risk management and ultimately on the project outcome are of importance.

6.1.3. Do IT project managers perceive the use of project risk management as effective for managing risks?

Organisations such as the Project Management Institute or the Association of Project Management claim in their best practice standards that through planning, identification, analysis of and response to risk, project managers can effectively achieve the planned project outcome. The general project risk management process includes four major process stages: planning of the project risk management, identification of threats, analysis of effects and probabilities and the response to risks.

The project risk management process has its foundation in EUT. Following the risk management process, project managers should perceive each stage of the project risk management process as effective. However, some project management literature indicates that project managers face difficulty in effectively managing project risks.

The findings on the perceived effectiveness of project risk management are mixed. Project managers have difficulties in optimally predicting project threats, their effects on the project outcome and executing an optimal response to reduce either the probability of the risk materialising or the impact of the effects on the project outcome. However, proposition 2 (IT Project managers will perceive the use of project risk management as effective) needs to be seen in the context of multiple process stages. In particular, the stage of attaching probabilities to risk was only perceived to be effective by project managers to some extent. Whether this degree of effectiveness can be described as either effective or ineffective may be open to debate. Nevertheless, taking EUT into consideration, the perceived level of effectiveness appears to be less than optimal. As a result, based on their experience of how effective IT project managers perceive project risk management, they may dismiss the process as a whole unless they take into consideration the fact that this process may only work under optimal conditions; conditions that are unlikely to prevail in a project environment characterised by a high degree of complexity and dynamism.

6.1.4. Are project risks effectively managed?

The risk literature shows that individuals may misestimate risk. Regarding this study, in contrast to determining how IT project managers perceive the effectiveness of their actions in relation to the management of project risk, the outcome of their actions in terms of over- and underestimation may also reveal to what extent IT project managers optimally apply project risk management. Overestimation of uncertainty implies that project managers attach a greater probability, consequence and/or response to a threat than is actually necessary and vice versa, underestimation of uncertainty means that project managers assess a risk's probability, consequence and/or response lower than it's actual value.

According to EUT, project managers should in principal not under- or overestimate risk. However, taking the findings of this study into consideration, in particular the level of risk that IT project managers under- and overestimated and second, to what degree underestimated risk adversely influenced the project outcome, proposition 3 (IT project managers will perceive that project risks were not over- or underestimated) can be rejected. Overall, the results show that project managers thought they had over- and underestimated risk. Although in most cases the choice to apply risk management to respond to some identified and assessed uncertainties was made by IT project managers, other uncertainties often materialised with severe effects on the performance of the project. These uncertainties were not "optimally" managed. That is to say that ultimately no reasonable risk response or optimal action was taken to minimise their impact on the project outcome. In terms of overestimation of risk, the effect on the project performance can be considered to be low; indeed the explanatory results show that it has a positive effect on project performance. With hindsight, this could mean that the costs of underestimation of risk were far higher than the costs of committing project resources to risks which did not exist, had a lower actual probability or effect than predicted or whose response had a greater effect than planned.

6.1.5. Do IT project managers think that risk-related factors constrain the effective use of project risk management by project managers?

Some evidence in the literature already indicates that project managers face problems that may constrain them in effectively managing risk. These are the problem of hindsight, problem of ownership, problem of cost justification, lack of expertise, problem of arousal and the problem of ambiguity in risk estimates. The findings regarding the perceived effectiveness of project risk management also seem to indicate that some risk mediators interfered with the IT project manager's management of project risk. In extreme cases, risk mediators influenced the IT project manager to the extent that no formal project risk management was applied at all.

The fifth research question asks what type of risk mediators influence project managers' actions to manage risk (project risk management). Whereas denial of uncertainty by risk actors relates to risk related information that risk actors found troubling because of its discomforting character, avoidance of uncertainty applies to risk estimates that are conflicting. Delay of uncertainty emphasises the preference of risk actors regarding reactive risk management and their preference to wait until uncertainty resolves itself. Ignorance of uncertainty includes the exclusion and lack of awareness of risks by risk actors.

Risk mediators tend to lead to a decreased level of perceived effectiveness and to underestimation of uncertainty, subsequently adversely influencing the project outcome. Furthermore, the findings also show that risk mediators do not appear to facilitate the application of project risk management in the sense that risk mediators lead to risk being overestimated by IT project managers and consequently to a positive influence on the project outcome. Hence, proposition 4 which states that IT project managers will perceive that risk mediators constrain the effective minimisation of risk by IT project managers can be accepted.

6.2. Theoretical implications

The influence of risk mediators appears to confirm findings in disciplines such as organisation theory. Organisations tend to create their own environment through interpretation and cognition of their members. They take decisions according to their beliefs and attitudes in order to create a "desirable" environment that may not reflect a true or objective environment (Bobbitt et al., 1980; Goffman, 1971; Meyer & Rowan, 1977; Weick, 1977, 1979). The construction of the environment through social factors also leads to "elements of foolishness" (March, 1981, p. 572), underlining bounded rationality as described in this study. Ansoff and McDonnell (1990, p. 403) determined sources of resistance to acting under uncertainty and contradicted the claim that "reasonable people will do reasonable things". This resistance to act or to change may be caused because uncertainty is intolerable for managers, so it is assumed away or denied (Nutt, 1993): because uncertainty is considered as outside a manager's control, it is ignored (Ford et al., 1984). Avoidance of uncertainty as investigated in this study was addressed in an organisational context by Bobbit and Ford (1980) who argue that decision makers perceive their environment differently and may attempt to force other decision makers to conform to their perception and vice versa. If a decision maker is not willing to conform to another decision maker's created environment, he may refuse to deal with it. Decision makers in organisations may not even actively confront uncertainty, but wait until uncertainty materialises (Bobbitt et al., 1980).

Overall, the key discipline of project risk management lacks the optimality that is assumed in best practice standards. Renn (1998, p. 64) argues in this context that the set of assumptions of a mainly objective analysis of risk "is a virtue as much as it is a shortcoming". The findings underline the criticism of some researchers such as Ritchie (1993), that the normative model of EUT is inadequate to describe how decision makers manage risks. In addition, it appears that the findings of this study about the influence of risk mediators on project risk management also apply in a wider context and are not confined to the specific context of IT project management. In other areas such as organisation theory, the resistance to managing uncertainties because of denial, avoidance, delay and ignorance seems to be confirmed through research being conducted in various settings. This firstly may underline the robustness of the findings of this research and secondly indicates that the optimal conditions of EUT as underlying assumptions of best practice standards in project risk management tend to be violated.

The findings about risk mediators influencing the degree of over- and underestimation confirm the problems of project risk management and underline deviations from optimal project risk management as discussed in the literature review. Under the optimal conditions described in the literature review, one can assume that risk actors always choose to respond to risks and minimise the influence of risk on the project outcome because A (the utility of no disruption) is assumed to be greater than G (the utility of no project risk management) and P (probability of avoiding risks through the execution of risk response actions) to be greater than Q (probability of avoiding risks without the execution of risk response actions). However, Pitz (1992) argues that the expected utility of G or the choice of a risk actor not to manage risk although being faced with uncertainties with possible adverse consequences in a project may be greater than A if either A is reduced or G increased. As shown in Figure 6.1, by reducing A the relative expected utility for avoiding disruptions in the project will be reduced and vice versa. By increasing G the relative expected utility for not applying risk management in the project will be greater. Hence, considering that G is relatively large enough, a risk actor in a project may decide not to manage risks although they will probably have an effect on the project outcome.

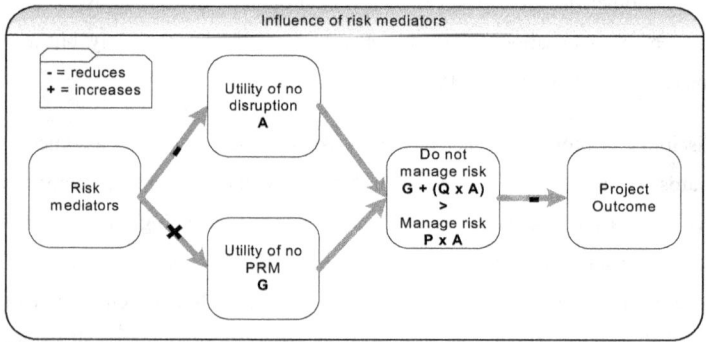

Figure 6.1: Influence of risk mediators on the expected utility

Risk mediators appear to lead to the relative reduction in A or the increase in G and therefore lead to a severe underestimation of state uncertainty with considerable adverse influences on the project objectives of time, cost and scope. Delay of uncertainty by risk actors, for example, may increase G and/or reduce A. A risk actor's benefit in not exposing one or more stakeholders to information perceived as negative may be so great that he trades off the benefit of avoiding disruptions with the benefit of not managing risks.

On the one hand, an action by an IT project manager to delay risk response actions may be described as irrational, at least under the premise that those mediators may not lead to the optimal choice of reducing the impact of uncertainties on the project objectives of scope, cost and time. On the other hand, Otway (1992) argues that a person who only focuses on the statistical probability of threats and their impacts and ignores any other information would be truly irrational. Hence a project manager would act sensibly by, for example, rating the importance of a long term relationship between provider and customer higher than the actual short-term avoidance of disruptions through the management of project risk. Therefore, if people persistently act in violation of EUT, the account of rationality according to EUT may be questioned (Anand, 1993). Furthermore, the practical implications of the mediators established in this study have to be taken into account in order to understand the limitations of project risk management and, if possible, to manage them.

6.3. Practical implications

Project risk management as a process among other 8 processes could be neglected unless project managers perceive it as a contributing discipline for achieving set project objectives such as time and cost. However, as the results reveal, project risk management is considered by IT project managers to be an important factor which influences the project outcome. Hence, the importance of project risk management and the findings of the research cannot be underestimated.

According to Figure 6.2, two extreme approaches to project risk management can be pursued in principle by project managers in IT projects and in general taking the influence of risk mediators into consideration: "better safe than sorry" (precautionary approach) and "waste not, want not, can not" (fatalistic approach).

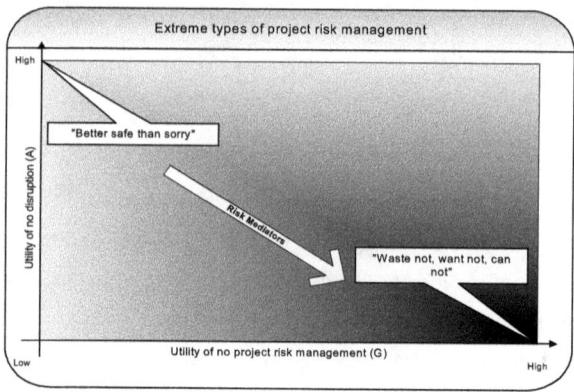

Figure 6.2: Extreme types of project risk management and the influence of risk mediators
(adapted from Margolis, 2003)

The first extreme signals extreme caution, the latter not to "waste" any resources such as time or money on project risk management. This can be described as fatalism. On the one hand, fatalism, that is to say in the context of project risk management extreme proactive in-activity towards uncertainty by project managers is probably not useful to pursue because uncertainties would have unlimited adverse influence on the project manager's achievement of the project objectives. On the other hand, the approach of extreme precaution "better safe than sorry" implies that even if the cause-effect relationships of risks are not fully established scientifically, precautionary risk reduction actions should be taken (Goldstein & Carruth, 2004). However, this approach can also be criticised:

> "There is some important truth in the precautionary principle. Sometimes it is much better to be safe than sorry. Certainly we should acknowledge that a small probability (say, 1 in 100,000) of a serious harm (say 100,000 deaths) deserves extremely serious attention. It is worthwhile to spend a lot of money to eliminate that risk. The fact that a danger is unlikely to materialise is hardly a good objection to regulatory controls. But everything depends on the size of the investment and the speculativeness of the harm. Unless the harm would be truly catastrophic, a huge investment makes no sense for a harm that has one in one billion chance of occurring. Taken literally, the precautionary principle would lead to indefensibly huge expenditures, exhausting our budget well before the menu of options could be thoroughly consulted. If we take costly steps to address all risks, however improbable they are, we will quickly impoverish ourselves" (Sunstein, 2002, p. 103)

Risk mediators impose a barrier or constraint on the effective use of project risk management by project managers, leading to a supposedly higher degree of fatalism in project risk management. The findings show that because of mistrust or because of unawareness of risk by project managers, risks remain unmanaged. Indeed, it appears that because of the apparent tendency towards underestimation of risk in IT projects by project managers, risks are under regulated. Because of risk mediators such as ignorance of uncertainty in IT projects, the degree of underestimation suggests that the measures to manage risk are not stringent enough. One could argue that project managers should increase their degree of "precaution", that is to say the degree of risk response actions. In particular, under the circumstances that the cost of overestimating and over regulating risks by risk actors tends to be negligible and the cost of underestimating considerable, risk actors may need to invest more money in the response to risk because with hindsight, it appears that from a purely monetary point of view, the relative resulting costs of A are far greater than those of G. Taking into account the fact that risk mediators as described tend to increase the "utility of no project risk management" or fatalism as displayed in Figure 6.2, two practical recommendations can be suggested in order to prevent from having unlimited adverse influence on the project performance: prevention of risk mediators and compensation for risk mediators.

6.3.1. Prevention of risk mediators

Under the assumption that risk mediators can be prevented, the influential risk mediator of avoidance, ignorance and denial of uncertainty may be averted by risk actors through the prevention of decision-maker related factors of uncertainty (see chapter 2): tolerance of ambiguity, experience and locus of control.

Tolerance of ambiguity refers to the extent to which an individual seeks clarity and specifies vague and unclear information. Research has shown that persons with a higher degree of tolerance towards ambiguity spend more time scanning the environment for the purpose of uncertainty reduction (Ashill et al., 1999, 2001; Dollinger, 1984; Govindrajan, 1989; Ramgopal, 2003; Wang & Chan, 1995). In a project environment, risk actors with a higher tolerance of ambiguity may perceive uncertainty as an opportunity instead of a threat and may seek to overcome uncertain situations and try to seek consensus on conflicting risk related information with the result that the mediators of avoidance, ignorance and denial of risks are decreased.

A further way of preventing risk mediators from influencing project risk management is *experience*. Ignorance and avoidance of uncertainty may impose fewer barriers to optimal project risk management depending on the amount of variety and duration of experience risk actors have gained. The problem of complete unawareness of threats as well as conflicts about what risks are "true" may be avoided through the involvement of risk actors with greater experience or the greater accumulation of relevant historic data in the decision-making process in project risk management.

In addition, delay, avoidance and denial of uncertainty by risk actors may be decreased with increased *locus of control*. Locus of control is the amount of control, which an individual has over his life (Miller et al., 1986). In a project, this may be the extent to which a project manager has control over internal and external factors. If managers perceive their environment as more controllable (internal locus of control), they tend to be more proactive (e.g. Govindrajan, 1989; Miller et al., 1986). Lack of perceived control might arise through disagreements or lack of consensus, a characteristic of the mediator of avoidance of uncertainty (Morgan et al., 1990). Furthermore, risk actors who find their environment to be less controllable may perceive it as more threatening with the result that they may deny risks (Ashill et al., 1999, 2001). Hence, in a project environment, risk actors with a high degree of internal locus of control may contribute to reducing the mediator of delay, avoidance and denial of uncertainty.

6.3.2. Compensation for the influence of risk mediators

Risks may, however, always remain inadequately managed and cause disruptions to projects. Two suggestions to compensate for the impact of materialised uncertainty is the arrangement of multi-layer reserves to absorb the impact of unforeseen events (Pender, 2001) or adding contingencies to establish a fit between the environment and the project's structural and process characteristics (Barki, Rivard, & Talbot, 2001). The adaptation to unforeseen situations may include project managers being flexible and dealing with situations only as they arise and with information only when it becomes available (Pavlak, 2004). With the prospect of unsuspected changes in the project, the project manager may want to prepare himself to be able to react to any unpredicted disruptions in the project. In this respect, flexibility is considered an important way of dealing with uncertainty (e.g. Carlsson, 1989; Dreyer & Gronhaug, 2004; Eppink, 1978; Gustavsson, 1984; Holt, 2002; Leuuw & Volbreda, 1996; Sharfman & Dean, 1997; Slack & Correa, 1992). In project management, although considered to be a critical success factor, flexibility is unacknowledged (Hornby, 2001). Although the concept of flexibility addresses residual uncertainty caused by risk mediators on the management of risk, it has been given little attention in project risk management literature so far.

In the cases researched, the data points towards flexible actions of risk actors in the IT projects. This was the case in project Sigma where unforeseen risk events "forced" project managers to adapt to reactive risk management techniques:

> "It would have been nice to do it differently (proactive risk management instead of reactive risk management), but because we were quite vulnerable in terms of software development and because most of that was driven by the States, we were never in the position to be pro active. The Americans would say, 'We have got an update to that system and we just released it to you', rather than telling us a week in advance that something was happening. We were never ahead enough to be able to really plan. We could plan our testing. We could plan certain aspects that very quickly became obvious to virtually everybody that if you plan for a week in advance you will probably be wasting your time. We were just so vulnerable to external shocks." (Interview ref. Sigma)

The time between the forecasting of problems and the actual occurrence of problems merged so that the problem had first to occur before it could be solved:

> "I think the risk management that we put in place which was this sort of a daily check up and the daily accountability and responsibility and the portioning of the workloads to ensure we solved problems worked remarkably well. Yes, it was slightly reactive, but until we found the problems we could not fix them. That was one of the problems we had." (Interview ref. Sigma)

This case shows that the project manager adapted to unforeseen events. Despite the underestimation of risk due to ignorance of uncertainty, unfortunate results on the achievement of project objectives may have been partially compensated for through the project managers' reactive ability to adapt to materialising uncertainty. This may be an indication why, in this particular case, despite a high level of disruption the project manager considered the project a success.

6.3.3. Balance between prevention and compensation

"It is desirable to be as open, explicit and cautious as possible in decision-making on risk in an attempt to allow for the un-anticipated." (Beard, 2004, p. 30)

The extremes of fatalism and precaution have problematic side effects. Project managers should find a reasonable balance between the fatalistic approach of not taking any action to proactively manage risks and taking an infinite number of actions to achieve maximum precaution (Wiener, 2002); which means making risky decisions with the maximum of precision and reliability (O'Hagan, 2004). An overall approach for risk actors could be to apply risk management as carefully as possible, but also to be prepared for the unexpected (Bourgeois et al., 1988), that is to say to apply project risk management as "best" as possible, but also be flexible enough to react to unfolding events and unforeseen uncertainties. This also means that the project risk manager may have to acknowledge the limitations risk mediators impose on risk management (Douglas, 1986) and consequently reduce their expectations of the degree of desired precaution. The project risk management process may have to change to give credit to the lack of historical information available to make any statistical forecasts as the main purpose of the project risk management processes discussed. Otherwise, there is a danger that traditional project risk management processes are bound to fail and be dismissed as ineffective by those who apply project risk management.

6.4. Limitations of research

A research strategy-related limitation concerns retrospective qualitative data in the first stage of the research for the purpose of gaining a rich and detailed view of the influence of risk mediators on project risk management in IT projects. In achieving the ideal aim of a post-positivistic philosophy of being as objective as possible, it would have been worthwhile for more than one researcher to be involved in the study for the purpose of minimising biases. In addition, the aspect of "positive bias" of the respondents needs to be addressed. The project managers interviewed might have given information about mediators and risk actions in IT projects, which they see retrospectively in a more positive light than at the time when those mediators occurred and actions were taken. The IT project managers may have chosen to present the project risk management they applied "in a better light" in order not to be considered by the interviewer as a "bad" project manager.

A further limitation regarding the robustness of the exploratory findings may result from the limited amount of data that was available. Overall, 25 interviews were conducted to achieve the ambiguous stage of concept saturation. However, the depth and level of detail of the information gained through the interviews, although satisfactory from the point of view of the researcher (conceptual saturation) may be questioned by other researchers. It is open to debate, whether additional interviews would have resulted in a more complete view of risk mediators and their influence on project risk management and project outcome. In relation to this, one may even question the completeness of the survey. Driven by the findings of the exploratory research, the survey only tested those risk mediators that emerged in the exploratory phase of the research. As a result, the findings of the study may display overall only a restricted view of the IT project manager's reality of managing risks.

As discussed in the literature review, success and failure may be defined differently depending on the stakeholder's view. However, this study focuses on the perceptions of the main actor in a project, the IT project manager. Taking different stakeholders such as the sponsor of the project into account, the IT project manager's view about what constitutes success and failure may not be shared by other stakeholders. Hence, although this study may provide a single interpretation of success and failure from the specific viewpoint of the IT project manager, it may not incorporate the perceptions about the project outcome of other stakeholders.

Regarding the explanatory research, the accuracy of the scales used in this research remains open to debate. The scale development was predominantly based on the exploratory results and relied far less on existing empirical evidence due to the scarcity and insufficient credibility of existing measurements. Inadequate scale development of the risk mediator of denial of uncertainty may have resulted in its exclusion from the risk mediator composite. Even with the inclusion of the denial of uncertainty as a separate variable, regressions revealed that denial of uncertainty does not have a significant influence on any of the used variables. Possible inadequateness in accurately developing a scale for the risk mediator of denial of uncertainty may have resulted in the insignificance of this type of mediator.

A limitation related to the findings about the degree to which project managers adhered to the fundamental process of project risk management as suggested by organisations such as PMI or APM. Although the project risk management process is a self-evidently correct process, little evidence exists on the extent to which project managers followed the logic or rational process stages or to what degree their actions deviated from the optimal project risk management process. Project managers may have rolled dice to rank risk response responses. Hence, it may be premature to argue that the project risk management process itself is flawed. The findings about the effectiveness of project risk management are based on the assumption in this study that project managers followed the project risk management processes as outlined in best practice standards.

A limitation regarding the level of generality relates first, to the sample of the second phase of explanation which included a narrow segment of project managers; those IT project managers, who were members of the professional organisation of PMI and those of two major CSP in the UK. Second, limited generalisabilty arises through the use of subjective data. The IT project manager's reality which has been investigated in this study may not be transferable to other individuals. As a consequence, tendencies which have emerged and been tested about concepts such as risk mediators cannot be generalised beyond the chosen sample cluster (Bryman, 2001; Robson, 2002). In these circumstances, the degree of generalisation is limited to the respondents chosen in the first exploratory phase and respondents of the survey. That is to say, these findings may only apply to the IT project managers who were part of the cluster sample and not to any other IT project manager or project manager involved in projects such as construction or pharmaceutical projects.

6.5. Future research

The findings and conclusions presented in this study suggest several directions for further research. Regarding the scale development, the majority of composite variables used in the explanatory research show a satisfying Cronbach Alpha greater than 0.5. However, it is recommended that further research focus upon more reliable measurements of the key concepts in this study.

A further implication for future research is the limited degree of generalisation. One direction is to conduct additional research into risk mediators in other industries such as in the construction or the pharmaceutical industry. As it seems that the degree of uncertainty is different in these industries (Meyer et al., 2002), it may be worthwhile to determine whether the same mediators prevail and to what extent they contribute to risks adversely influencing the project outcome.

In addition, researchers may investigate how specific environment and decision-maker related conditions lead to denial, avoidance, ignorance and delay of uncertainty. Figure 6.3 shows a provisional and unconfirmed matrix, which gives a broad direction of whether a risk mediator is influenced by the environmental or decision-maker related sub conditions.

The findings about the project outcome revealed that IT project manager may consider the project a success despite the failure to fully achieve scope, cost and time objectives because they consider this to be normal practice. Further research may also investigate whether and to what extent an IT project manager or project manager in general learns to fail.

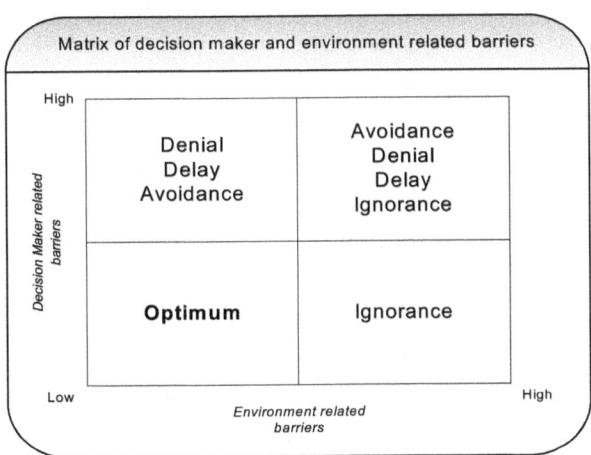

Figure 6.3: Matrix of decision maker and environment related barriers to optimal project risk management

As illustrated in Figure 6.3, ignorance of uncertainty seems to be predominantly influenced by environment-related factors such as complexity and dynamism, whereas denial, delay and avoidance might include a high degree of individual, decision maker related barriers. In addition, although these categories already show a broad but unconfirmed tendency about the underlying cause of each condition, sub conditions in terms of psychological biases such as overconfidence, optimism, pattern seeking, complacency and inertia (e.g. Borge, 2001; Rizzi, 2003) were also not explored because a psychological exploration was out of the scope of this study. The scope of this study was to explore and explain the influence of risk mediators on project risk management and the project outcome, but not the underlying mental patterns of those risk mediators. Nevertheless, these patterns related to human nature may reveal further useful information about what sub conditions are likely to lead to a divergence from "optimality" according to EUT.

Furthermore, on the assumption that uncertainty remains (residual uncertainty) and can not be eliminated and estimated to 100% (Yang et al., 2004) because of risk mediators, it is interesting how project managers manage materialising uncertainties. Often, no prediction and no proactive project risk management is possible, so project managers may adapt to developing situations. In the light of earlier discussion, namely that project managers should be flexible enough to react to unforeseen events, they may adopt different types of flexibility with different outcomes. In the extreme, in case of temporal and action convergence (reaction to materialised uncertainty) project managers may improvise (Crossan, 1998; Crossan, White, Lane, & Klus, 1996; Eisenhardt, 1997; Miner, 2001; Weick, 1998). Given its potential usefulness, the concept of flexibility improvisation as an extreme form of flexibility may compensate for the project manager's limited ability to proactively manage risk. For a project to be successful in an inherently uncertain environment, flexibility is assumed to be of major importance. The word flexibility is "ubiquitous" (Evans, 1991, p. 73). For example, Gustavsson (1984, p. 802) states that "flexibility comes from the Latin word for bendable. Other expressions are adjustable and mobile. In industry the word means adaptable and capable of change". Whereas Evans (1991, p. 73) suggests that "in everyday parlance, the term is generally used to refer to the ability to do something other than which was originally intended", Harvey (1997, p. 34) claims that flexibility refers to the "ability to change or react with little penalty in time, effort, cost or performance."

Studies investigating the concept of flexibility are various. Nutt (1993) and Sharfman & Dean (1997), for example, studied flexible decision styles of executives and flexibility in strategic decision-making. Both give evidence, which shows there is a distinctive correlation between uncertainty and flexibility. They point out, that the factor of uncertainty encourages flexible strategic decision-making although it should be mentioned, that other factors beside uncertainty also either encourage or discourage flexibility. Das (1995, p. 68) gives evidence, that flexibility is worth pursuing in environments with many changes. Eppink (1978, p. 9) proposes that flexibility is a response to the unforeseen, this means to uncertainty.

The recognition of flexibility by scholars and practitioners has led to new approaches in project management which can be seen in contrast to traditional approaches to management of risk suggested by organisations such as PMI or APM. A new type of project management approach has emerged. It can be defined as "lean" or "agile" project management (Williams, 1999). For example, in software development, prominent agile project management approaches are Scrum, Dynamic Systems Development Method (DSDM), Crystal methods, Feature-driven development (FDD), Lean development (LD), Extreme programming (XP) and Adaptive software development (ASD) (Highsmith, 2002). These agile approaches to managing a project have in common the fact that tasks are not planned in advance as suggested by traditional project management literature. Only prerequisites such as the allocation of resources for tasks are planned that will be revised on a daily or weekly basis. Changes are allowed late in the development cycle (Highsmith, 2002; Schwaber, 2004).

Although agile project management approaches appear to be a useful alternative to traditional project management which emphasises planning, evidence about its drawbacks is scarce. Problems such as the lack of planning may have to be taken into account. In the extreme, no prediction about the outcome of the project can be made in advance if changes are constantly allowed. This lack of certainty might not be appreciated by stakeholders.

6.6. Final words

Unless we stop being human and become godlike creatures, our environment is characterised by mediators such as lack of knowledge, distrust or discomfort. Those mediators faced by IT project managers may impose a barrier to effective and optimal project risk management. This research leads to a better understanding of which mediators exist in IT projects and how they influence the effective use of project risk management. Consequently, this understanding may result in an improvement in the application of project risk management by project managers. This means, that the fundamental principles of an expected utility-based project risk management process may have to be taken into account and questioned. As a result, IT project managers may have to reduce the impact of risk mediators on the use of project risk management or be prepared for materialising risk in order to minimise the effect of uncertainty which materialises during a project with adverse consequences on the achievement of project objectives, and ultimately to avoid project failure.

REFERENCES

Adams, J. 1995. Risk. London: UCL Press.

Adler, N. E., Kegeles, S. M., & Genevro, j. L. 1992. Risk taking and health. In F. J. Yates (Ed.), Risk-taking behaviour: 231 - 255. West Sussex: John Wiley & Sons Ltd.

Akintoye, A. S. & MacLead, M. J. 1997. Risk analysis and management in construction. International Journal of Project Management, 15(1): 31 - 38.

Aldrich, H. E. 1979. Organizations and environments. New Jersey: Prentice-Hall.

Ambery, D. 2003. Negotiating the research environment. Qualitative Research Journal, 3(1): 29 - 40.

Ami, L. 2000. Goals-oriented project management. IIE Solutions, 32(9): 39 - 41.

Anand, P. 1993. Foundations of rational choice under risk. Oxford: Clarendon Press.

Anderson, C. R. & Schneier, C. E. 1978. Locus of control, leader behaviour and leader performance among management students. Academy of Management Journal, 21(4): 690 - 698.

Andres, H. P. & Zmud, R. W. 2002. A contingency approach to software project coordination. Journal of Management Information Systems, 18(3): 41 - 70.

Ansoff, I. & McDonnell, E. J. 1990. Implanting strategic management (2nd ed.). Hemel Hempstead: Prentice Hall International.

Arrow, K. J. 1983. Behaviour under uncertainty and its implications for policy. In B. P. Stigum & F. Wenstop (Eds.), Foundations of utility and risk theory with applications: 19 - 32. Dordrecht: D. Reidel Publishing Company.

Ashill, N. J. & Jobber, D. 1999. The impact of environmental uncertainty perceptions, decision-maker characteristics and work environment characteristics and work environment characteristics on the usefulness of marketing information Systems (MkIS): A conceptual framework. Journal of Marketing Management, 15: 519 - 540.

Ashill, N. J. & Jobber, D. 2001. Defining the domain of perceived environmental uncertainty: An exploratory study of senior marketing executives. Journal of Marketing Management, 17: 543 - 558.

Atkinson, R. 1999. Project management: Cost, time and quality, two best guesses and a phenomenon, its time to accept other success criteria. International Journal of Project Management, 17(6): 337 - 342.

Baccarini, D. 1996. The concept of project complexity - a review. International Journal of Project Management, 14(4): 201 - 204.

Baccarini, D. 1999. The logical framework method for defining project success. Project Management Journal, 30(4): 25 - 32.

Baccarini, D., Salm, G., & Lover, P. E. D. 2004. Management of risks in information technology projects. Industrial Management & Data Systems, 104(4): 286 - 295.

Backman, K. & Kyngaes, H. 1999. Challenges of the grounded theory approach to a novice researcher. Nursing and Health Sciences, 1: 147 - 153.

Baker, B. N. & Fisher, D. 1988. Factors affecting project success. In D. I. Cleland & W. K. King (Eds.), Project Management Handbook. New York: Van Nostrand.

Barki, H., Rivard, S., & Talbot, J. 2001. An integrative contingency model of software project risk management. Journal of Management Information Systems, 17(4): 37 - 69.

BBC News; The tragic sequence; http://news.bbc.co.uk/1/hi/uk/1194340.stm; 28.02., 2001.

Beard, A. N. 2004. Risk assessment assumptions. Civil Engineering and Environmental Systems, 21(1): 19 - 31.

Beierle, T. C. 2004. The benefits and costs of disclosing information about risks: What do we know about right-to-know? Risk Analysis, 24(2): 335 - 346.

Ben-David, I. & Raz, T. 2001. An integrated approach for risk response development in project planning. Journal of the Operational Research Society, 52: 14 - 25.

Bhaskar, R. 1975. A realist theory of science. Leeds: Leeds Books.

Bobbitt, H. R. & Ford, J. D. 1980. Decision-maker choice as a determinant of organizational structure. Academy of Management Review, 5(1): 13 - 23.

Boehm, B. W. 1991. Software risk management: Principles and practices. IEEE Software, 8: 32 - 41.

Borge, D. 2001. The book of risk. New York: John Wiley & Sons.

Bostrom, A. 1999. Who calls the shots? Credible vaccine risk communication. In G. Cvetkovich & R. E. Löfstedt (Eds.), Social Trust and Management of Risk. London: Earthscan.

Bourgeois, L. J. & Eisenhardt, K. M. 1988. Strategic decision processes in high velocity environments: Four cases in the microcomputer industry. Management Science, 34(7): 816 - 834.

Bradbury, J. A. 1989. The policy implications of differing concepts of risks. Science, Technology, & Human Values, 14(4): 381 - 399.

Brehmer, B. 1987. The psychology of risk. In W. T. Singleton & J. Hovden (Eds.), Risk and Decisions: 25 - 39. Chichester: John Wiley & Sons.

British Standards Institute. 2000. Project management - Part 1: Guide to project management. London: British Standards Institute.

British Standards Institution. 2000. Project management - Part 3: Guide to the management of business related project risk. London: British Standards Institution.

Bryman, A. 2001. Social Research Methods. Oxford: Oxford University Press.

Bryman, A. & Cramer, D. 2001. Quantitative data analysis with SPSS release 10 for windows. East Sussex: Routledge.

Bryne, P. & Cadman, D. 1984. Risk, uncertainty and decision-making in property development. London: E, & F. N. Spon.

References

Buchko, A. A. 1994. Conzeptualization and measurement of environmental uncertainty: An assessment of the miles and snow perceived environmental uncertainty scale. Academy of Management Journal, 37(2): 410 - 425.

Buchok, J. 2000. Failed initiatives. Computing Canada, 28: 10.

Burchett, J. F., Tummala Rao, V. M., & Leung, H. M. 1999. A world-wide survey of current practices in the management of risk within electrical supply projects. Construction Management and Economics, 17: 77 - 90.

Burgess, R. G. 1984. In the field: An introduction to field research. London: George Allen & Unwin Ltd.

Burghardt, M. 1995. Einführung in Projektmanagement. Erlangen: Publicis MCD Verlag.

Buttrick, R. 1997. Project workout (2nd ed.). London: Pearson Education Ltd.

Carlsson, B. 1989. Flexibility and the theory of the firm. International Journal of Industrial Organisation, 7: 179 - 203.

CCTA - The UK Government Centre for Information Systems. 1995. An introduction to managing project risk. Norwich: CCTA - The Government Centre for Information Systems.

Chambers English Dictionary. 1990. Chambers English dictionary. New York: W & R Chambers Ltd.

Chapman, C. 1997. Project risk analysis and management - PRAM the generic process. International Journal of Project Management, 15(5): 273 - 281.

Chapman, C. & Ward, S. 2000. Managing risk. In J. R. Turner & S. J. Simister (Eds.), Gower Handbook of Project Management, 3rd. ed.: 375 - 394. Aldershot: Gower Publishing Limited.

Cicmil. 1997. Critical factors of effective project management. The TQM magazine, 9(6): 390 - 396.

Clawson, J. G. 1996. Chicago park district (c): The information systems project, Vol. UVA-OB-0620. Charlottesville: University of Virginia Darden School Foundation.

References

CNN; Chronology of death;
http://www.cnn.com/2001/US/09/11/chronology.attack/index.html; 12.09., 2001.

Cooke, S. & Slack, N. 1984. Making management decisions (2nd ed.). Hemel Hempstead: Prentice Hall International.

Cooper, D. 2003. Psychology, risk & safety. Professional safety, November: 39 - 46.

Corbin, J. & Strauss, A. 1990. Grounded theory research: Procedures, canons and evaluative criteria. Qualitative Sociology, 13(1): 3 - 21.

Cowan, D. A. 1986. Developing a process model of problem recognition. Academy of Management Review, 11(4): 763 - 776.

Crockford, N. 1986. An introduction to risk management. Cambridge: Woodhead-Faulkner Ltd.

Crossan, M. M., White, R. E., Lane, H. W., & Klus, L. 1996. The improvising organisation: Where planning meets opportunity. Organizational Dynamics, Spring.

Crossan, M. M. 1998. Improvisation in action. Organisation Science, 9(5): 593 - 599.

Crotty, M. 1998. The foundations of social research: Meaning and perspective in the research process. London: Sage Publications.

Czaja, R. & Blai, J. 1996. Designing surveys: A guide to decisions and procedures. Pine Forge: Thousand Oaks.

Daft, R. L. & Weick, K. E. 1984. Toward a model of organisations as interpretation systems. Academy of Management Review, 9(2): 284 - 295.

Dake, K. 1992. Myths of nature: Culture and the social construction of risk. Journal of Social Issues, 48(4): 21 - 37.

Dalal, S. R., Fowlkes, E. B., & Hoadley, B. 1989. Risk analysis of the Space Shuttle: Pre-Challenger prediction of failure. American Statistical Association, 84(408): 945 - 957.

Das, T. K. & Elango, B. 1995. Managing strategic flexibility: Key to effective performance. Journal of General Management, 20(3): 60 - 75.

Davidson, P. 1996. Reality and economic theory. Journal of Post Keynesian Economics, 18(4): 479 - 508.

DeCotiis, T. A. & Dyer, L. 1979. Defining and measuring project performance. Research Management, 16: 17 - 22.

Dedolph, M. F. 2003. The neglected management activity: Software risk management. Bell Labs Technical Journal, 8(3): 91 - 95.

Dequech, D. 2004. Uncertainty: Individuals, institutions and technology. Cambridge Journal of Economics, 28: 365 - 378.

Dermer, J. 1973. Cognitive characteristics and the perceived importance of information. The Accounting Review, July: 511 - 519.

Dollinger, M. J. 1984. Environmental boundary spanning and information processing effects on organisational performance. Academy of Management Journal, 27(2): 351 - 368.

Douglas, M. & Wildavsky, A. 1982. Risk and Culture. Berkeley: University of California Press.

Douglas, M. 1986. Risk acceptability according to social sciences. Padstow: T J Press.

Downey, K. H., Hellriegel, D., & Slocum, W. 1975. Environmental uncertainty: the construct and its application. Administrative Science Quarterly, 20: 613 - 629.

Downey, K. H. & Slocum, W. 1975. Uncertainty: Measures, research and sources of variation. Academy of Management Journal, 18(3): 562 - 578.

Dreyer, B. & Gronhaug, K. 2004. Uncertainty, flexibility, and sustained competitive advantage. Journal of Business Research, 57: 484 - 494.

Duncan, R. B. 1971. The implementation of different decision making structures in adapting to environmental uncertainty. Academy of Management Proceedings: 39 - 47.

Duncan, R. B. 1972. Characteristics of organizational environments and perceived environmental uncertainty. Administrative Science Quarterly, 17: 313 - 327.

Earle, T. C. 2004. Thinking aloud about trust: A protocol analysis of trust in risk management. Risk Analysis, 24(1): 169 - 183.

Easterby-Smith, M., Thorpe, R., & Lowe, A. 1991. Management research: An introduction. London: SAGE Publications.

Einhorn, H. J. & Hogarth, R. M. 1986. Decision making under ambiguity. Journal of Business, 59(4): 225 - 250.

Eisenhardt, K. M. 1989. Building theories from case study research. Academy of Management Review, 14(4): 532 - 550.

Eisenhardt, K. M. 1997. Strategic decisions and all that jazz. Business Strategy Review, 8(3): 1 - 3.

Ekenberg, L., Boman, M., & Linnerooth-Bayer, J. 2001. General risk constraints. Journal of Risk Research, 4(1): 31 - 47.

Elkington, P. & Smallman, C. 2002. Managing project risks: a case study from the utilities sector. International Journal of Project Management, 20: 49 - 57.

Elliot, S. R. & McKee, M. 1995. Collective risk decisions in the presence of many risks. Kyklos, 48: 541 - 554.

Eppink, J. D. 1978. Planning for strategic flexibility. Long Range Planning, 11: 9 - 15.

Estrada, J. 2000. The temporal dimension of risk. The Quarterly Review of Economics and Finance, 4: 189 - 204.

Evans, J. 1991. Strategic flexibility for high technology manoeuvres: A conceptual framework. Journal of Management Studies, 28(1): 69 - 89.

Fairley, R. 1994. Risk management for software projects. IEEE Software, 11(3): 57 - 67.

Farber, D. A. 2003. Probabilities behaving badly: Complexity theory and environmental uncertainty. University of California Davis Law Review, 37(1): 145 - 173.

Feldman, M. S. & March, J. G. 1981. Information in organizations as signal and symbol. Administrative Science Quarterly, 26: 171 - 186.

Field, M. & Keller, L. 1998. Project management. London: International Thomson Business Press.

Fischhoff, B., Lichtenstein, S., Slovic, P., Derby, S. L., & Keeney, R. L. 1981. Acceptable risk. Cambridge: Cambridge University Press.

Fishburn, P. 1994. A variational model of preference under uncertainty. Journal of Risk and Uncertainty, 8: 127 - 152.

Fleming, W. & Koppelman, J. 1996. Earned value project management. Newton Square: Project Management Institute.

Floricel, S. & Miller, R. 2001. Strategizing for anticipated risks and turbulence in large-scale engineering projects. International Journal of Project Management, 19: 445 - 455.

Ford, J. D. & Hegarty, H. W. 1984. Decision makers' beliefs about the causes and effects of structure: An exploratory study. Academy of Management Journal, 2: 271 - 291.

Fredrickson, J. & Mitchell, T. R. 1984. Strategic decision process: Comprehensiveness and performance in an industry with an unstable environment. Academy of Management Journal, 27(2): 399 - 423.

Freeman, M. & Beale, P. 1992. Measuring project success. Project Management Journal, 23(1): 8 - 18.

Freudenberg, W. R. 1992. Heuristics, biases, and the not-so-general public: Expertise and error in the assessment of risk. In S. Krimsky & D. Golding (Eds.), Social theories of risk: 229 - 249. Westport: Praeger Publishers.

Frosdick, S. 1997. The techniques of risk analysis are insufficient in themselves. Disaster Prevention and Management, 6(3): 165 - 177.

Furnham, A. & Ribchester, T. 1995. Tolerance of ambiguity: A review of the concept, its measurement and applications. Current psychology, 14(3): 179 - 200.

Gardiner, P. D. & Stewart, K. 2000. Revisiting the golden triangle of cost, time and quality: The role of NPV in project control, success and failure. International Journal of Project Management, 18: 251 - 256.

Garson, D. 2005. Factor Analysis: http://www2.chass.ncsu.edu/garson/pa765/index.htm, 15.08.2005.

Gaulke, M. 2002. Risikomanagement in IT-Projekten. Wien: Oldenbourg Verlag.

George, D. & Mallery, P. 2003. SPSS for windows step by step: A simple guide and reference. London: Pearson Education.

George, D. & Mallery, P. 2003. SPSS for Windows. London: Pearson Education.

Ghalayini, A. M. & Noble, J. S. 1996. The changing basis of performance measurement. International Journal of Operations & Production Management, 16(8): 63 - 80.

Ghosh, D. & Ray, M. R. 1997. Risk, ambiguity, and decision choice: Some additional evidence. Decision Sciences, 28(1): 81 - 104.

Glaser, B. G. & Strauss, A. L. 1967. The discovery of grounded theory: strategies for qualitative research. New York: Aldine Publishing Company.

Glendon, A. I. 1987. Risk cognition. In W. T. Singleton & J. Hovden (Eds.), Risk and Decisions: 87 - 108. Chichester: John Wiley & Sons.

Goffman, E. 1971. The presentation of self in everyday life. Harmondsworth: Penguin.

Goldstein, B. & Carruth, R. S. 2004. The precautionary principle and/or risk assessment in world trade organization decisions: A possible role for risk perception. Risk Analysis, 24(2): 491 - 499.

Goulding, C. 1998. Grounded theory: The missing methodology on the interpretivist agenda. Qualitative Market Research: An International Journal, 1(1): 50 - 57.

Govindrajan, V. 1989. Implementing competitive strategies at the business unit level: Implications of matching managers to strategy. Strategic Management Journal, 10: 251 - 269.

Graham, R. 1999. Managing the project management process in aerospace and construction: A comparative approach. International Journal of Project Management, 17(1): 39 - 45.

Grey, S. 1995. Practical Risk Assessment for Project Management. West Sussex: John Wiley & Sons Ltd.

Guba, E. G. & Lincoln, Y. S. 1994. Competing paradigms in qualitative research. In N. K. Denzin & Y. S. Lincoln (Eds.), Handbook of Qualitative Research: 105 - 117. Thousand Oaks: SAGE Publications.

Gustavsson, S.-O. 1984. Flexibility and productivity in complex production processes. International Journal of Production Research, 22(5): 801 - 808.

Habermas, J. 1970. Knowledge and Interest. In M. Easterby-Smith & R. Thorpe & A. Lowe (Eds.), Management Research: An Introduction: 25 - 26. London: SAGE Publications.

Hair, J., Anderson, R., Tatham, R., & Black, W. 1998. Multivariate data analysis. New Jersey: Prentice-Hall International.

Hale, A. R. 1987. Subjective risk. In W. T. Singleton & J. Hovden (Eds.), Risk and decisions: 67 - 85. Chichester: John Wiley & Sons.

Hall, W. K. 1975. Why risk analysis isn't working. Long Range Planning, 8(6): 25 - 29.

Hammersley, M. 1989. Herbert Blumer and the Chicago tradition. New York: Routledge.

Hannsson, S. O. 2004. Fallacies of risk. Journal of Risk Research, 7(3): 353 - 360.

Hartman, F. & Ashrafi, R. 2002. Project management in the information systems and information technologies industries. Project Management Journal, 33(3): 5 - 15.

Harvey, J. 1997. Flexibility and technology in services: a conceptual model. International Journal of Operations & Production Management, 17(1): 29 - 45.

Hauptmann, O. & Iwaki, G. 1990. The final voyage of the challenger: Harvard Business School.

Head, G. L. 1967. An alternative to defining risk as uncertainty. The Journal of Risk and Insurance, 34(2): 205 - 214.

Heath, C. & Tversky, A. 1991. Preference and belief: Ambiguity and competence in choice under uncertainty. Journal of Risk and Uncertainty, 4: 5 - 28.

Hedge, A. 1987. Major hazards and behaviour. In W. T. Singleton & J. Hovden (Eds.), Risk and decisions: 139 - 157. Chichester: John Wiley & Sons.

Heritage, J. 1984. Garfinkel and ethnomethodology. Cambridge: Polity.

Highsmith, J. 2002. Agile software development ecosystems. Boston: Addison-Wesley.

Hillson, D. A. 2002. Extending the risk process to manage opportunities. International Journal of Project Management, 20: 235 - 240.

Hillson, D. A. 2003. Effective opportunity management for projects: Exploiting positive risk. New York: Marcel Dekker.

Hoehn, J. P. 1988. Risk, utility concepts, and policy choices: Discussion. American Journal of Agricultural Economics, 70(5): 1118 - 1121.

Holt, R. 2002. Risk management: The talking cure. Organization, 11(2): 251 - 270.

Holzheu, F. & Wiedermann, P. 1993. Perspektiven der Risikowahrnehmung. In B. Rueckversichering (Ed.), Risiko ist ein Konstrukt: 9 - 19. Muenchen: Knesebek.

Hormozi, A. M., McMinn, R. D., & Nzeogwu, O. 2000. The project life cycle: The termination phase. SAM Advanced Management Journal, Winter 2000: 45-51.

Hornby, R. C. 2001. Oaks and Palms - Flexibility in project management. Paper presented at the Project Management Institute Annual Seminars & Symposium, Nashville, Tenn., USA.

Howard, J. 2001. Computer Services: 2001 Market Report: Key Note Ltd.

Hurley, A. E., Scandura, T. A., Schriesheim, C. A., Brannick, M. T., Seers, A., Vandenberg, R. J., & Williams, L. J. 1997. Exploratory and confirmatory factor analysis: Guidelines issues, and alternatives. Journal of Organizational Behaviour, 18: 667 - 683.

Jaafari, A. 2001. Management of risks, uncertainties and opportunities on projects: time for a fundamental shift. International Journal of Project Management, 19: 89 - 101.

Jaeger, C. C., Renn, O., Rosa, E. A., & Wehler, T. 2001. Risk, certainty, and rational action. London: Earthscan.

Jankowicz, A. D. 1991. Business research for students. London: Chapman & Hall.

Jasanoff, S. 1993. Bridging the two cultures of risk analysis. Risk Analysis, 13(2): 123 - 129.

Jelassi, T. & Dutta, S. 1993. Integrating global commercial operations with information technology at BP Chemicals, Vol. 695-009-1. Fontainebleau, France: INSEAD.

Jemison, D. B. 1987. Risk and the relationship among strategy, organizational processes, and performance. Management Science, 33(9): 1087 - 1101.

Jennings, D. & Wattam, S. 1994. Decision making: An integrated approach. London: Pitman Publishing.

Jiang, J. J., Klein, G., & Chen, H.-G. 2001. The relative influence of IS project implementation policies and project leadership on eventual outcomes. Project Management Journal, 32(3): 49 - 55.

Jick, T. D. 1979. Mixing qualitative and quantitative methods: Triangulation in action. Administrative Science Quarterly, 24: 602 - 611.

Johnston, A. K. 1995. A hacker's guide to project management. Oxford: Butterworth-Heinemann Ltd.

Kadefors, A. 2004. Trust in project relationships - inside the black box. International Journal of Project Management, 22: 175 - 182.

Kahneman, D. & Tversky, A. 1979. Prospect theory: An analysis of decision under risk. Econometrica, 47(2): 263 - 291.

Karlsen, J. T. & Gottschalk, P. 2003. An empirical evaluation of knowledge transfer mechanisms for IT projects. Journal of Computer Information Systems, Fall 2003: 112 - 119.

Karlsen, J. T. & Gottschalk, P. 2004. Factors affecting knowledge transfer in IT projects. Engineering Management Journal, 16(1): 3 - 10.

Kartam, N. A. & Kartam, S. A. 2001. Risk and its management in the Kuwaiti construction industry: A contractors' perspective. International Journal of Project Management, 19: 325-335.

Kasper, R. G. 1980. Perceptions of risk and their effects on decision making. In R. C. Schwing & W. A. Albers (Eds.), Societal risk assessment: 71 - 80. New York: Plenum Press.

Kasperson, J. X., Kasperson, R. E., Pidgeon, N., & Slovic, P. 2003. The social amplification of risk: Assessing fifteen years of research and theory. In N. Pidgeon & R. E. Kasperson & P. Slovic (Eds.), The social amplification of risk: 13 - 45. Cambridge: Cambridge University Press.

Kasperson, R. E., Renn, O., Slovic, P., Brown, H. S., Emel, J., Goble, R., Kasperson, J. X., & Ratick, S. 1988. The social amplification of risk: A conceptual framework. Risk Analysis, 8(2): 177 - 187.

Keil, M. 1995. Pulling the plug: Software project management and the problem of project escalation. MIS Quarterly, December: 421 - 447.

Keil, M., Mixon, R., Saarinen, T., & Tuunainen, V. 1995. Understanding runaway information technology projects: Results from an international research program based on escalation theory. Journal of Management Information Systems, 11(3): 65 - 85.

Keil, M., Cule, P. E., Lyytinen, K., & Schmidt, R. C. 1998. A framework for identifying software projects. Communications of ACM, 41(1): 76 - 83.

Keller, M. & Keller, L. 1998. Project management. London: International Thomson Business Press.

Kendra, K. & Taplin, L. J. 2004. Project success: A cultural framework. Project Management Journal, 35(1): 30 - 45.

Kerzner, H. 2003. Project management case studies. New Jersey: John Wiley & Sons.

Kiesler, S. & Sproull, L. 1982. Managerial response to changing environments: Perspectives on problem sensing from social cognition. Administrative Science Quarterly, 27: 548 - 570.

Kirkwood, A. S. 1994. Why do we worry when scientists say there is no risk? Disaster Prevention and Management, 3(2): 15 - 22.

KPMG Great Britain. 2001. Why do so many projects still fail when we invest so much training. KMWORLD, January: 5 - 7.

KPMG Management Consulting. 1994. Report on IT Runaway Systems: KPMG Management Consulting.

Lanza, R. B. 2000. Does your project risk management system do the job? Information Strategy: The executive' s journal, 17(1): 6 - 12.

Lawrence, P. R. & Lorsch, J. W. 1967. Organisation and environment. Boston: Harvard University, Graduate School of Business Administration, Division of Research.

Leblebici, H. & Salancik, G. R. 1981. Effects of environmental uncertainty on information and decision processes in banks. Administrative Science Quarterly, 26: 578 - 596.

Lee-Kelley, L. & Loong, K. L. 2003. Turner's five-functions of project-based management and situational leadership in IT services projects. International Journal of Project Management, 21: 583 - 591.

Leuuw, A. D. & Volbreda, H. 1996. On the concept of flexibility: A dual control perspective. Omega, 24(2): 121 - 139.

Lichtenstein, S., Slovic, P., Fischhoff, B., Layman, M., & Combs, B. 1978. Judged frequency of lethal events. Journal of Experimental Psychology: Human perception and memory, 4: 551 - 578.

Lidow, D. 1999. Duck alignment. Project Management Journal, 30(4): 8 - 14.

Liu, A. & Walker, A. 1998. Evaluation of project outcomes. Construction Management and Economics, 16: 209 - 219.

Lock, D. 2000. Project management (7th ed.). Aldershot: Gower Publishing Limited.

Lowrance, W. W. 1980. The nature of risk. In R. C. Schwing & W. A. Albers (Eds.), Societal risk assessment: 5 - 17. New York: Plenum Press.

Lyles, M. A. & Mitroff, I. I. 1980. Organizational problem formulation: An empirical study. Administrative Science Quarterly, 25: 102 - 119.

Lynn, G. & Reilly, R. 2000. Measuring team performance. Research Technology Management, 43(2): 48 - 56.

Lyons, T. & Skitmore, M. 2004. Project risk management in the queensland engineering construction industry: A survey. International Journal of Project Management, 22: 51 - 61.

Lyytinen, K. & Robey, D. 1999. Learning failure in information systems development. Info Systems, 9: 85 - 101.

MacCrimmon, K. R. & Wehrung, D. A. 1986. Taking risks. New York: The Free Press.

Macgill, S. M. & Siu, Y. L. 2004. The nature of risk. Journal of Risk Research, 7(3): 315 - 352.

Machlis, G. E. & Rosa, E. A. 1990. Desired risk: Broadening the social amplification of risk framework. Risk Analysis, 10(1): 161 - 168.

Manunta, G. 2000. Research: Concepts, issues and paradigms. Wiltshire: Cranfield Security Centre.

March, J. G. 1981. Footnotes to organizational change. Administrative Science Quarterly, 26: 563 - 577.

March, J. G. & Shapira, Z. 1987. Managerial perspectives on risk and risk taking. Management Science, 33(11): 1404 - 1419.

Margolis, H. 2003. Dealing with risk. London: The University of Chicago Press.

Marks, H., Coleman, M., & Michael, M. 2003. Further deliberations on uncertainty in risk assessment. Human and Ecological Risk Assessment, 9: 1399 - 1410.

Marshall, H. 2002. What do we do when we code data? Qualitative Research Journal, 2(1): 56 - 57-.

Maylor, H. 1999. Project management (2nd ed.). Essex: Pearson Education Ltd.

McGarity, T. O. 2002. Professor sunstein's fuzzy math, GEO.

McGrew, J. F. & Bilotta, J. G. 2000. The effectiveness of risk management: measuring what didn't happen. Management Decision, 38(4): 293 - 300.

McLain, D. L. & Hackman, K. 1999. Trust, risk, and decision-making in organisational change. PAQ, Summer: 152 - 176.

Metlay, D. 1999. Institutional trust and confidence: A journey into a conceptual quagmire. In G. Cvetkovich & R. E. Löfstedt (Eds.), Social Trust and the Management of Risk: 100 - 117. London: Earthscan.

Meyer, A. D., Loch, C. H., & Pich, M. T. 2002. Managing project uncertainty: From variation to chaos. IEEE Engineering Management Review, Third quarter: 91 - 98.

Meyer, J. W. & Rowan, B. 1977. Institutionalised organizations: Formal structure as myth and ceremony. American Journal of Sociology, 83: 340 - 360.

Michalsen, A. 2003. Risk assessment and perception. Injury control and safety promotion, 10(4): 201 - 204.

Milburn, M. A. 1978. Sources of bias in the prediction of future events. Organisational Behaviour and Human Performance, 21: 17 - 26.

Miles, M. B. & Huberman, M. A. 1994. Qualitative Data Analysis (2nd ed.). London: SAGE Publications Ltd.

Miller, D. & Jean-Marie, T. 1986. Chief executive personality and corporate strategy and structure in small firms. Management Science, 32(11): 1389 - 1409.

Miller, S. I. & Fredericks, M. 1999. How does grounded theory explain? Qualitative Health Research, 9(4): 538 - 551.

Milliken, F. J. 1987. Three types of perceived uncertainty about the environment: State, effect, and response uncertainty. Academy of Management Review, 12(1): 133 - 143.

Milliken, F. J. 1990. Perceiving and interpreting environmental change: An examination of college administrators' interpretation of changing demographics. Academy of Management Journal, 33(1): 42 - 63.

Miner, A. S. 2001. Orginizational improvisation and learning: A field study. Administrative Science Quarterly, 46(2001): 304 - 337.

Moore, P. G. 1983. The business of risk. Cambridge: Cambridge University Press.

Morgan, G. M. & Henrion, M. 1990. Uncertainty: A guide to dealing with uncertainty in quantitative risk and policy analysis. Cambridge: Cambridge University Press.

Morris, P. W. & Hough, G. H. 1987. A study of the reality of project management. London: John Wiley.

Naden, J. 2000. Have a successful APS implementation. IIE Solutions, 32(10): 46 - 57.

Navare, J. 2003. Process or behaviour: Which is the risk and which is to be managed? Managerial Finance, 29(5/6): 6 - 19.

Neumann, P. J. & Politser, P. E. 1992. Risk and optimality. In F. J. Yates (Ed.), Risk-taking behaviour: 27 - 47. West Sussex: John Wiley & Sons Ltd.

Nutt, P. 1993. Flexible decision styles and the choices of top executives. Journal of Management Studies, 30(5): 695 - 721.

Nylen, K.-O. 1999. Civil works - Unique projects or a repeatable process? Stockholm: Kungl Tekniska Hoegskolan.

O'Hagan, A. 2004. Probability is perfect, but can't elicit it perfectly. Reliability Engineering and System Safety, 85: 239 - 248.

Otway, H. & Thomas, K. 1982. Reflections on risk perceptions and policy. Risk Analysis, 2(2): 69 - 82.

Otway, H. 1992. Public wisdom, expert fallibility: Toward a contextual theory of risk. In S. Krimsky & D. Golding (Eds.), Social theories of risk. London: Praeger Publishers.

Pablo, A. L. 1997. Reconciling predictions of decision making under risk. Journal of Managerial Psychology, 12(1): 4 - 20.

Pablo, A. L. 1999. Managerial risk interpretation: Does industry make a difference? Journal of Managerial Psychology, 14(2): 92 - 108.

Palmer, T. B. & Wiseman, R. M. 1999. Decoupling risk taking from income stream uncertainty: A holistic model of risk. Strategic Management Journal, 20: 1037 - 1062.

Pandit, N. R.; The creation of theory: A recent application of the grounded theory method; http://www.nova.edu/ssss/QR/QR2-4/pandit.html.

Parker, D. & Mobey, A. 2003. Perceptions in risk evaluation for project management. Paper presented at the EurOMA - POMS Conference, Italy.

Partington, D. 2000. Building Grounded Theories of Management Action. British Journal of Management, 11: 91 - 102.

Patton, M. Q. 1980. Qualitative evaluation methods. London: SAGE Publications Ltd.

Patton, M. Q. 1990. Qualitative evaluation and research methods. London: SAGE Publications Ltd.

Pavlak, A. 2004. Project troubleshooting: Tiger teams for reactive risk management. Project Management Journal, 35(4): 5 - 14.

Pender, S. 2001. Managing incomplete knowledge: Why risk management is not sufficient. International Journal of Project Management, 19: 79 - 87.

Pidgeon, N. & Beattie, J. 1998. The psychology of risk and uncertainty. In P. Calow (Ed.), Handbook of environmental risk assessment and management: 289 - 318. London: Blackwell Science Inc.

Pinto, J. K. & Mantel, S. J. 1990. The causes of project failure. IEEE Transactions of Engineering Management, 37(4): 269 - 276.

Pitz, G. F. 1992. Risk taking, design, and training. In F. J. Yates (Ed.), Risk-taking behaviour: 283 - 320. West Sussex: John Wiley & Sons Ltd.

PMnetwork. 2003. Successful trends. February.

Poortinga, W. & Pidgeon, N. F. 2003. Exploring the dimensionality of trust in risk regulation. Risk Analysis, 23(5): 961 - 972.

Powell, P. & Klein, J. H. 1996. Risk management for information systems. Journal of Information Technology, 11: 309 - 319.

Project Management Institute. 2004. A guide to the project management body of knowledge (Third ed.). Pennsylvania: Project Management Institute.

Project Management Institute. 2005. Fact Sheet June 2005: http://www.pmi.org/prod/groups/public/documents/info/GMC_MemberFACTSheetJune05.pd f, 18.05.2005.

Raftery, J. 1994. Risk analysis in project management. London: Chapman & Hall.

Ramgopal, M. 2003. Project uncertainty management. Cost Engineering, 45(12): 21 - 24.

Raz, T. & Michael, E. 2001. Use and benefit of tools for project management. International Journal of Project Management, 19: 9 - 17.

Redmill, F. 2002. Risk analysis - A subjective process. Engineering Management Journal, April: 91 - 96.

Remenyi, D. & Heafield, A. 1996. Business process re-engineering: Some aspects of how to evaluate and manage risk exposure. International Journal of Project Management, 14(6): 349 - 357.

Renn, O. 1992. Concepts of risk: A classification. In S. Krimsky & D. Golding (Eds.), Social theories of risk. Westport: Praeger Publishers.

Renn, O., Burns, W. J., Kasperson, J. X., Kasperson, R. E., & Slovic, P. 1992. The social amplification of risk: Theoretical foundations and empirical applications. Journal of Social Issues, 48(4): 137 - 160.

Renn, O. 1998. Three decades of risk research: Accomplishments and new challenges. Journal of Risk Research, 1(1): 49 - 71.

Ritchie, B. & Marshall, D. 1993. Business risk management. London: Chapman & Hall.

Rizzi, J. V. 2003. Behavioural bias: The hidden risk in risk management. Commercial Lending Review, November: 2 - 8.

Robson, C. 2002. Real world research: A resource for social scientists and practitioner - researchers (2nd ed.). London: Blackwell Publishers.

Rosa, E. A. 2003. The logical structure of the social amplification of risk framework (SARF): Metatheoretical foundations and policy implications. In N. Pidgeon & R. E. Kasperson & P. Slovic (Eds.), The social amplification of risk: 47 - 79. Cambridge: Cambridge University Press.

Rothstein, H. 2002. Neglected risk regulation: the institutional attenuation phenomenon. London: Centre for analysis of risk and regulation.

Rouse, A. & Dick, M. 1994. The use of nudist, a computerised analytical toll, to support qualitative information systems research. Information Technology & People, 7(3): 50 - 62.

Rowe, W. D. 1994. Understanding uncertainty. Risk Analysis, 14(5): 743 - 750.

Royer, P. S. 2000. Risk management: The undiscovered dimension of project management. Project Management Journal, 31(1): 6 - 13.

Runde, J. 1998. Clarifying frank knight's discussion of the meaning of risk and uncertainty. Cambridge Journal of Economics, 22: 539 - 546.

Sapsford, R. 1999. Survey research. London: SAGE Publications.

Saunders, M., Lewis, P., & Thornhill, A. 1997. Research methods for business students. London: Pitman Publishing.

Scapens, R. W. 1990. Researching management accounting practice: The role of case study methods. In J. Hussey & R. Hussey (Eds.), Business Research: 66. Hampshire: MacMillan Press Ltd.

Schere, J. L. 1982. Tolerance of ambiguity as a discriminating variable between entrepreneurs and managers. Academy of Management Proceedings: 404 - 408.

Schmidt, R., Lyytinen, K., Keil, M., & Cule, P. 2001. Identifying software project risks: An international delphi study. Journal of Management Information Systems, 17(4): 5-36.

Schneiderman, M. A. 1980. The uncertain risks we run: Hazardous materials. In R. C. Schwing & W. A. Albers (Eds.), Societal risk assessment: 19 - 37. New York: Plenum Press.

Schwaber, K. 2004. Agile project management with scrum. Washington: Microsoft Press.

Seddon, P. 1997. A respecification and extension of the DeLone and McLean model of IS success. Information System Research, 8(3): 240 - 253.

Shakle, G. 1952. Expectation in economics (2nd ed.). Cambridge: Cambridge University Press.

Shapira, Z. 1986. Risk in Managerial decision making. Unpublished ms., Hebrew University.

Sharfman, M. P. & Dean, J. W. 1997. Flexibility in strategic decision making: informational and ideological perspectives. Journal of Management Studies, 34(2): 191 - 217.

Shenhar, A. J., Levy, O., & Dvir, D. 1997. Mapping the dimensions of project success. Project Management Journal, 28(2): 5 - 13.

Shenhar, A. J., Dvir, D., Levy, O., & Maltz, A. C. 2001. Project success: A multidimesnional strategic concept. Long Range Planning, 34: 699 - 725.

Shenhar, A. J., Tishler, A., Dvir, D., Lipovetsky, S., & Lechler, T. 2002. Refining the search for project success factors: A multivariate, typological approach. R & D Management, 2: 111 - 126.

Sheppard, B. H. & Sherman, D. M. 1998. The grammars of trust: A model and general implications. Academy of Management Review, 23(3): 422 - 437.

Short, J. F. 1989. On defining, describing and explaining elephants (and reactions to them): Hazards, disasters, and risk analysis. International Journal of Mass Emergencies and Disasters, 7(3): 397 - 418.

Simmons, E. 2003. The human side of risk. Paper presented at the 21st Annual Pacific Northwest Software Quality Conference, Portland.

Simon, H. 1978. Rationality as process and as product of thought. American Economic Association, 68(2): 1 - 16.

Simon, H. A. 1996. The sciences of the artificial (3rd ed.). Massachusetts: MIT Press.

Sitkin, S. B. & Weingart, L. R. 1995. Determinants of risky decision-making behaviour: A test of the mediating role of risk perceptions and propensity. Academy of Management Journal, 38(6): 1573 - 1592.

Slack, N. & Correa, H. 1992. The flexibilities of push and pull. International Journal of Operations & Production Management, 12(4): 82 - 92.

Slack, N., Chambers, S., & Johnson, R. 2001. Operations Management (Third edition ed.). Essex: Pearson Education Limited.

Slovic, P., Fischhoff, B., & Lichtenstein, S. 1980. Facts and fears: Understanding perceived risk. In R. C. Schwing & W. A. Albers (Eds.), Societal risk assessment: 181 - 214. New York: Plenum Press.

Slovic, P. 1987. Perception of risk. Science, 23: 280 - 285.

Slovic, P. 1993. Perceived risk, trust, and democracy. Risk Analysis, 13(6): 675 - 682.

Slovic, P., Finucane, M. L., Peters, E., & MacGregor, D. G. 2002. Risk as analysis and risk as feelings. Eugene: Decision Research.

Slovic, P. 2003. Going beyond the red book: The Sociopolitics of risk. Human and Ecological Risk Assessment, 9: 1181 - 1190.

Smallman, C. 1996. Risk and organizational behaviour: A research model. Disaster Prevention and Management, 5(2): 12-26.

Smallman, C. 1996. Challenging the orthodoxy in risk management. Safety Science, 22: 245 - 262.

Smith, K. & Biley, F. 1997. Understanding grounded theory: Principles and evaluation. Nurse Researcher, 4(3): 17 - 31.

Smithson, M. 1989. Ignorance and uncertainty. New York: Springer-Verlag.

Stake, R. E. 1995. The art of case study research. London: SAGE Publications Ltd.

Steeger, O. 2003. Risikomanagement - Das "Stiefkind" in der Projektarbeit. Projektmanagement aktuell, 2: 5 - 10.

Stewart, W. E. 2001. Balanced scorecard for projects. Project Management Journal, 32(1): 38 - 53.

Strauss, A. L. & Corbin, J. 1990. Basics of qualitative research: Grounded theory procedures and techniques. London: SAGE Publications.

Sunstein, C. R. 2002. Risk and reason. Cambridge: Cambridge University Press.

Teo, D. H. P., Quah, L. K., Torrance, V. B., & Okoro, M. I. 1991. Risk evaluation and decision support systems for tendering and building refurbishment contracts. In A. Bezelga & P. Brandon (Eds.), Management, quality and economics in building: 301 - 319. London: E. & F. N. Spon.

The Royal Society. 1983. Risk Assessment. London: The Royal Society.

The Standish Group International Inc. 1995. Chaos (Application project and failure): The Standish Group International Inc.

Tosi, H., Aldag, R., & Storey, R. 1973. On the measurement of the environment: An assessment of the Lawrence and Lorsch environmental uncertainty subscale. Administrative Science Quarterly, 18(1): 27 - 36.

Tukel, O. I. & Rom, W. O. 2001. An empirical investigation of project evaluation criteria. International Journal of Operations & Production Management, 21(3): 400 - 416.

Tummala Rao, V. M., Leung, H. M., Burchett, J. F., & Leung, Y. H. 1997. Practices, barriers and benefits of using risk management approaches in selected Hong Kong industries. International Journal of Project Management, 15(5): 297- 312.

Tung, R. L. 1979. Dimensions of organizational environments: An exploratory study of their impact on organization structure. Academy of Management Journal, 22(4): 672 - 693.

Turner, B. 1981. Some practical aspects of qualitative data analysis: One way of organising the cognitive processes associated with the generation of grounded theory. Quality and Quantity, 15: 225 - 247.

Turner, J. R. 1993. The handbook of project-based management. London: McGraw-Hill.

Turner, J. R. & Cochrane, R. A. 1993. Goals-and-methods matrix: coping with projects with ill defined goals and/or methods of achieving them. International Journal of Project Management, 11(2): 93 -102.

Tversky, A. & Kahneman, D. 1974. Judgement under uncertainty: Heuristics and biases. Science, 185: 1124 - 1131.

Tversky, A. & Kahneman, D. 1992. Advances in prospect theory: Cumulative representation of uncertainty. Journal of Risk and Uncertainty, 5: 297 - 323.

Valentine, N. 1991. BP chemicals commercial system: IT risk and project management, Vol. 391-033-1. Fontainebleau, France: INSEAD.

Voetsch, R. J. & Cioffi, D. 2002. Managing project integration: 1, 4 - 5: Project Management Institute.

Vogwell, D. 2003. Avoiding the risk of risk. Project, August/September: 36 - 37.

Wald, M. L. & Broad, W. J. 2003. Shuttle engineers debated chances of grave damage, New York Times, Feb. 27 ed.

Walsh, A. 1990. Statistics for the social sciences. New York: Harper & Row.

Wang, P. & Chan, P. S. 1995. Top management perception of strategic information processing in a turbulent environment. Leadership & Organization Development Journal, 16(7): 33 - 43.

Ward, S. & Chapman, C. 1991. Extending the use of risk analysis in project management. Project Management Journal, 9(2): 117 - 123.

Ward, S. 1999. Requirements for an effective project risk management process. Project Management Journal, 30(3): 37 - 44.

Ward, S. & Chapman, C. 2002. Project uncertainty management as a desirable future. Southampton: University of Southampton.

References

Warg, L.-E. & Wester-Herber, M. 1999. Restoring trust by participation: A comment based on social judgement theory. Paper presented at the Risk Analysis: Facing the new millennium, Rotterdam.

Waring, A. & Glendon, A. I. 1998. Managing Risk. London: Thomson Learning.

Wateridge, J. 1995. IT projects: A basis for success. International Journal of Project Management, 13(3): 169 - 172.

Wateridge, J. 1998. How can IS/IT projects be measured for success? International Journal of Project Management Association, 16(1): 59 - 63.

Watson, S. R. 1981. On risks and acceptability. Journal of the society for radiological protection, 1(4): 21 - 25.

Weick, K. E. 1977. Enactment processes in organisations. In B. M. Staw & G. S. Slancik (Eds.), New directions in organisational behaviour. Chicago: St. Clair.

Weick, K. E. 1979. The social psychology of organising (2nd. ed.). Reading: Addison-Wesley.

Weick, K. E. 1998. Improvisation as a mindset for organisational analysis. Organisation Science, 9(5): 543 - 555.

Weick, K. E. 2001. Making sense of the organisation. Oxford: Blackwell Publishers LtD.

White, B. & Leifer, R. 1986. Information systems development success: Perspective from project team participants. MIS Quarterly, September: 215 - 223.

White, D. & Fortune, J. 2002. Current practice in project management - an empirical study. International Journal of Project Management, 20: 1 - 11.

White, M. P., Pahl, S., Buehner, M., & Haye, A. 2003. Trust in risky messages: The role of prior attitudes. Risk Analysis, 23(4): 717 - 726.

Whittaker, B. 1999. What went wrong? Unsuccessful information technology projects. Information Management & Computer Security, 7(1): 23 - 29.

Wiener, J. B. 2002. Precaution in a multirisk world. In D. J. Paustenbach (Ed.), Human and ecological risk assessment: 1509 - 1531. New York: John Wiley and Sons.

Wildavsky, A. & Dake, A. 2002. Theories of risk perception: Who fears what and why? Daedalus, 129(4): 41 - 60.

Williams, L. J. 1995. Covariance structure modelling in organisational research: Problems with the method versus applications of the method. Journal of Organizational Behaviour, 16: 225 - 234.

Williams, R. C. & Walker, J. A. 1997. Putting risk management into practice. IEEE Software, 14(3): 75 - 81.

Williams, T. 1995. A classified bibliography of recent research relating to project risk management. European Journal of Operational Research, 85: 18 - 38.

Williams, T. 1999. The need for new paradigms for complex projects. International Journal of Project Management, 17(5): 269 - 273.

Williams, T. 2004. Assessing and building on the underlying theory of project management in the light of badly over-run projects. Proceedings PMI Research Conference.

Wirth, I. 1996. How generic and how industry-specific is the project management profession? International Journal of Project Management, 14(1): 7 - 11.

Wood, G. D. & Ellis, C. T. 2003. Risk management practices of lading cost consultants. Engineering, Construction and Architectural Management, 10(4): 254 - 262.

Wright, G. & Ayton, P. 1989. Immediate and short-term judgemental forecasting: Personologism, situationism, or interactionism. Personality and Individual Differences, 9: 109 - 120.

Yang, B., Burns, N. D., & Backhouse, C. J. 2004. Management of uncertainty through postponement. International Journal of Production Research, 42(6): 1049 - 1064.

Yates, F. J. & Stone, E. R. 1992. The risk construct. In F. J. Yates (Ed.), Risk-taking behaviour: 2 - 25. West Sussex: John Wiley & Sons Ltd.

Yin, R. K. 1994. Case study research: Design and methods. California: SAGE Publications.

Young, T. L. 1998. The handbook of project management. London: Kogan Page Ltd.

Zmud, R. W. 1980. Management of large software development projects. MIS Quarterly, June: 45 - 55.

APPENDIX A – INTERVIEW QUESTIONS, CHECKLIST

EXPLORATORY RESEARCH

Area of conceptual framework	Concepts	Questions[51]
Project manager, project	Asks about the *background of the project manager and project (context).*	Please describe the time frame, volume and content of the project Which position did you occupy in this project? What experience of project management did you have at the time this project commenced? How much experience was available in this project? (Project manager related experience) In what sense were other projects you have conducted similar to this one? (Experience in one particular project)
Risk / Uncertainty	Asks about the *phenomenon* Which factors might influence his perception, e.g. attitudes, experience, beliefs, peer group influence etc. (Components of risk)	How risky was the project at the beginning? What do you mean when you describe the project as risky in this way? What factors influenced your belief about the level of risk in the project? Which individuals or groups were you influenced by in your degree of perceived risk? (group experience)
Project risk management applied	Asks about the *actions / interactions PRM* taken in Phase 1 – Phase 6 of the risk management process. Asks about their *expectations regarding PRM*	In detail, what did you do to manage risk in this project? What were your expectations after doing this? Did you expect to be able to predict ALL project-related uncertainties? Did you expect to predict 100% of uncertainties?
Project risk management not applied	Asks why no *actions / interactions PRM* were taken. Asks about no *actions / interactions* on *project outcome.*	Why did you not take any actions? Did something unforeseen with negative effects occur? How did it influence the project outcome? Would project risk management have been useful in this project? Why not? With hindsight, is there anything that you should have done? As you did not apply PRM, how else did you manage uncertainty with possible negative consequences on the project outcome?

---

[51] Those questions were used as a broad guideline. Experience gained through the pilot interviews has shown, that an unstructured approach is more suitable to gain a detailed insight into the respondent's reality.

Area of conceptual framework	Concepts	Questions[51]
Perceived PRM effectiveness	Asks about the *perceived PRM outcome* (for each stage of PRM).	What factors make PRM effective?
		Do you think PRM was effective or ineffective?
		Did the project risk management fulfil your expectations?
		Do you think you effectively planned the risk management process? To what extent?
		Do you think you accurately identified and characterised risks? To what extent?
		Do you think you accurately attached probabilities to risks? To what extent?
		Do you think you accurately defined effects? To what extent?
		Do you think you accurately defined response alternatives to risks? To what extent?
		Do you think you determined response ownership to risks? To what extent?
		Do you think you effectively determined the most suitable response to the risk? To what extent?
		Do you think you effectively monitored and executed risk actions? To what extent?
Over- and underestimation of risk (influence on project performance)	Asks about *PRM performance* Ex post analysis of over- and underestimation of risk? (Can be used to cross check data about perceived effectiveness regarding the reduction of state, effect and response uncertainty). Asks about the relation between *PRM performance and actions/ interactions PRM.* With the "why not" question, PRM actions (ignorance, avoidance etc.) can be identified. Asks about the relation between *PRM performance* and *project outcome.*	What was the performance of PRM? Did identified risk materialise as predicted? Why not? (Over- and underestimation) How did it influence the project outcome? How much confidence did you have in your estimation of threats, effects and consequences? Did unidentified risk materialise? Why not? (Over- and underestimation) How did it influence the project outcome? Were you aware at all of that risk? How much confidence did you have in your estimation of threats, effects and consequences?

Area of conceptual framework	Concepts	Questions[51]
Success/Failure	Asks about the *project outcome* of the project Asks about *Intervening conditions* in relation to *project outcome*. Asks about the relation between *project outcome* and *performance PRM.*	What was the outcome of the project (internally and externally)? What does success / failure mean for you? From your point of view, was the project a success or failure? Are the stakeholders' views different? Overall, what were the main reasons for the project success / failure? Do you think PRM fulfilled your expectations? Why were your expectations fulfilled although you had problems? Were the reasons for failure not included in your PRM scope? In what sense would you have been able to avoid the failings of PRM? Did the project risk management contribute to the project success? To what extent?

Perceived risk ☐ High ☐ Medium ☐ Low
Further Comments:

Influence: _____

PRM applied ☐ Yes ☐ No _____

Confidence ☐ High ☐ Low

Effectiveness

Planning ☐ Effective ☐ Ineffective

Identification ☐ Effective ☐ Ineffective

Assessment ☐ Effective ☐ Ineffective

Response ☐ Effective ☐ Ineffective

Monitoring/Control ☐ Effective ☐ Ineffective

Underestimation

_____ Contr. ☐ High ☐ Low

_____ Contr. ☐ High ☐ Low

_____ Contr. ☐ High ☐ Low

Overestimation

_____ Contr. ☐ High ☐ Low

Project Outcome ☐ Failure ☐ Neither success nor failure ☐ Success

APPENDIX B – WEB BASED QUESTIONNAIRE

EXPLANATORY RESEARCH

Project Risk Management Survey

CONFIDENTIALITY: NOTHING YOU SAY WILL EVER BE IDENTIFIED
WITH YOU PERSONALLY OR YOUR ORGANISATION.

**PLEASE CHOOSE ONE PROJECT WHICH HAS BEEN COMPLETED AND IS
MOST VIVID IN YOUR MIND!!!**
**PLEASE TAKE A FEW MOMENTS TO ANSWER SOME QUESTIONS ABOUT
YOUR EXPERIENCES WITH RISK IN A SPECIFIC PROJECT OF YOUR
CHOICE.**

PART I: BACKGROUND QUESTIONS

Q1   **What was the type of project?**
Roll Out .... A
Software-Development.. A
Implementation of user help desk structures .... A
Outsourcing .... A
Other - please state

Q2   **What was the time frame of the project?**
less than 6 months .... A
between 6 month and 12 months.. A
between 2 months and 24 months .... A
over 24 months .... A

Q3   **What was the value of the project?**
less than £ 10,000 .... A
between £10,000 and £100,000 .... A
between £100,000 and £1,000,000.. A
more than £ 1,000,000 .... A

Q4   **What position did you occupy in the project?**

PART II: PROJECT RISK MANAGEMENT

Q5   **Was a formal project risk management process (including risk identification, analysis, response evaluation and monitoring and control) applied?**
Yes.. A   Go to Q7
No .... A

Q6   **If a formal project risk management process was not applied, what were the reasons for not using it? (e.g. too expensive, low project risk)**
_____ Go to Q12
_____
_____
_____
_____
_____
_____
_____
_____

Q7   **If a formal project risk management process was applied, which formal process was used?**
PMBOK... A
Prince... A
PRAM.. A
Bootstrap... A
ISO 15504 (Spice) .... A
SEI .... A
Other - please state   _____
_____
_____

Q8   **How confident were you about the accuracy of predicted ...**

	1 (Not at all)	2	3 (To some extent)	4	5 (To a great extent)
... risks as a whole?	A	A	A	A	A
... risk events?	A	A	A	A	A
... consequences of those risk events?	A	A	A	A	A
... risk mitigation actions and their effects?	A	A	A	A	A

Q9   **To what extent did the following apply to the project? The main risk factors that had a real or potential impact on the project were:**

	1 (Not at all)	2	3 (To some extent)	4	5 (To a great extent)
Risks perceived as being uncomfortable for one or more project stakeholders.	A	A	A	A	A

Risks outside the scope of risk management.	A	A	A	A	A
Risks not agreed on by one or more project stakeholders.	A	A	A	A	A
Risks managed once they materialised rather than before.	A	A	A	A	A
Risks not visible until they materialised.	A	A	A	A	A

Please state anything else about
the main risk factors that you
think is relevant.

_____

_____

_____

_____

_____

_____

_____

PART III: EFFECTIVENESS OF PROJECT RISK MANAGEMENT

Q10   **To what extent was it possible...**

	1 (Not at all)	2	3 (To some extent)	4	5 (To a great extent)
... to effectively manage risk in general in this project?	A	A	A	A	A
...to plan the risk management process?	A	A	A	A	A
...to identify risks?	A	A	A	A	A
...to attach probabilities to risks?	A	A	A	A	A
...to define effects of risks?	A	A	A	A	A
...to define response alternatives to risks?	A	A	A	A	A
...to determine response ownership to risks?	A	A	A	A	A
...to determine the most suitable response to risks?	A	A	A	A	A
...to monitor risks?	A	A	A	A	A
...to execute response actions?	A	A	A	A	A

PART IV: CONSEQUENCES

Q11 **To what extent ...**

	1 (Not at all)	2	3 (To some extent)	4	5 (To a great extent)	Do not know
... did predicted risk events actually NOT materialise?	A	A	A	A	A	A
... were the actual consequences of risk events MORE severe than predicted?	A	A	A	A	A	A
... were the actual consequences of risk events LESS severe than predicted?	A	A	A	A	A	A
... did actual risk mitigation actions BETTER than predicted?	A	A	A	A	A	A
... did actual risk mitigation actions WORSE than predicted?	A	A	A	A	A	A

Q12 **To what extent did ...**

	1 (Not at all)	2	3 (To some extent)	4	5 (To a great extent)	Do not know
... unpredicted risk events actually materialise?	A	A	A	A	A	A

PART V: OUTCOME OF PROJECT

Q13   **Did the project ...**

	1 (Not at all)	2	3 (To some extent)	4	5 (To a high extent)
...achieve its purpose?	A	A	A	A	A
...provide satisfactory benefit to the owner?	A	A	A	A	A
...satisfy the needs of the owners, users, and stakeholders?	A	A	A	A	A
...meet its prestated objectives?	A	A	A	A	A
... produce to specification, within budget and on time?	A	A	A	A	A
...satisfy the needs of the project team?	A	A	A	A	A

Other measures of success - please state

_____

_____

_____

_____

_____

_____

Q14   **Was the project considered a failure or success?**

Failure .... A

Success .... A

Neither nor (partially either) .... A

Q15   **What were the main reasons for the success / failure of the project?**

_____

_____

_____

Q16   **To what extent did project risk management contribute to the project outcome?**

	1 (Not at all)	2	3 (To some extent)	4	5 (To a high extent)
Contribution of PRM	A	A	A	A	A

Q17 **Do you have any other comments?**

_____

_____

_____

_____

_____

_____

_____

_____

_____

_____

THANK YOU FOR PARTICIPATING

APPENDIX C – ANALYSIS

List of variables

Question (Variable) Label

q1 (1) Type of Project
  Measurement Level: Nominal
    Value   Label

      1   Outsourcing
      2   Implementation of user help desk structures
      3   Software Development
      4   Roll Out

q2 (2) Time Frame
  Measurement Level: Ordinal
      Value   Label

      1   > 24
      2   12 - 24
      3   6 - 12
      4   < 6

q3 (3) Project Volume
  Measurement Level: Ordinal
      Value   Label

      1   > £1,000,000
      2   £100,000 - £1,000,000
      3   £ 10,000 - £ 100,000
      4   < £10,000

q5 (4) PRM applied
  Measurement Level: Nominal
      Value   Label

      0   No
      1   Yes

q7 (5) PRM Process
   Measurement Level: Nominal
      Value   Label

      1   Other
      2   SEI
      3   ISO 15504 (Spice)
      4   Bootsrap
      5   PRAM
      6   Prince
      7   PMBOK

q8a (6) Confidence Overall
   Measurement Level: Ordinal
      Value   Label

      1   Not at all
      3   To some extent
      5   To a great extent

q8b (7) Confidence State
   Measurement Level: Ordinal
      Value   Label

      1   Not at all
      3   To some extent
      5   To a great extent

q8c (8) Confidence Effect
   Measurement Level: Ordinal
      Value   Label

      1   Not at all
      3   To some extent
      5   To a great extent

q8d (9) Confidence Response
   Measurement Level: Ordinal
      Value   Label

      1   Not at all
      3   To some extent
      5   To a great extent

q9a (10) Denial of uncertainty
    Measurement Level: Ordinal
        Value   Label

        1   Not at all
        3   To some extent
        5   To a great extent

q9b (11) Ignoring uncertainty
    Measurement Level: Ordinal
        Value   Label

        1   Not at all
        3   To some extent
        5   To a great extent

q9c (12) Avoidance of uncertainty
    Measurement Level: Ordinal
        Value   Label

        1   Not at all
        3   To some extent
        5   To a great extent

q9d (13) Delay of uncertainty
    Measurement Level: Ordinal
        Value   Label

        1   Not at all
        3   To some extent
        5   To a great extent

q9e (14) Being ignorant of uncertainty
    Measurement Level: Ordinal
        Value   Label

        1   Not at all
        3   To some extent
        5   To a great extent

q10a (15) Effectiveness Overall
    Measurement Level: Ordinal
        Value   Label

        1   Not at all
        3   To some extent
        5   To a great extent

q10b (16) Effectiveness in planning project risk management
Measurement Level: Ordinal
Value   Label

1   Not at all
3   To some extent
5   To a great extent

q10c (17) Effectiveness in identification of risk
Measurement Level: Ordinal
Value   Label

1   Not at all
3   To some extent
5   To a great extent

q10d (18) Effectiveness in attaching probabilities
Measurement Level: Ordinal
Value   Label

1   Not at all
3   To some extent
5   To a great extent

q10e (19) Effectiveness in defining effects
Measurement Level: Ordinal
Value   Label

1   Not at all
3   To some extent
5   To a great extent

q10f (20) Effectiveness in defining response alternatives
Measurement Level: Ordinal
Value   Label

1   Not at all
3   To some extent
5   To a great extent

q10g (21) Effectiveness in determining response ownership
Measurement Level: Ordinal
Value   Label

1   Not at all
3   To some extent
5   To a great extent

q10h (22) Effectiveness in determining best response
    Measurement Level: Ordinal
        Value   Label

        1   Not at all
        3   To some extent
        5   To a great extent

q10i (23) Effectiveness in monitoring risks
    Measurement Level: Ordinal
        Value   Label

        1   Not at all
        3   To some extent
        5   To a great extent

q10j (24) Effectiveness in executing actions
    Measurement Level: Ordinal
        Value   Label

        1   Not at all
        3   To some extent
        5   To a great extent

q11a (25) Overestimation of state uncertainty
    Measurement Level: Ordinal
        Value   Label

        1   Not at all
        3   To some extent
        5   To a great extent
        6   Do not know

q11b (26) Underestimation of effect uncertainty
    Measurement Level: Ordinal
        Value   Label

        1   Not at all
        3   To some extent
        5   To a great extent
        6   Do not know

q11c (27) Overestimation of effect uncertainty
    Measurement Level: Ordinal
        Value   Label

        1   Not at all
        3   To some extent
        5   To a great extent
        6   Do not know

q11d (28) Overestimation of response uncertainty
Measurement Level: Ordinal
Value   Label

1   Not at all
3   To some extent
5   To a great extent
6   Do not know

q11e (29) Underestimation of response uncertainty
Measurement Level: Ordinal
Value   Label

1   Not at all
3   To some extent
5   To a great extent
6   Do not know

q12 (30) Underestimation of state uncertainty
Measurement Level: Ordinal
Value   Label

1   Not at all
3   To some extent
5   To a great extent
6   Do not know

q13a (31) Achievement of purpose
Measurement Level: Ordinal
Value   Label

1   Not at all
3   To some extent
5   To a great extent

q13b (32) Benefit to owner
Measurement Level: Ordinal
Value   Label

1   Not at all
3   To some extent
5   To a great extent

q13c (33) Satisfaction of owner, users, stakeholders
Measurement Level: Ordinal
Value   Label

1   Not at all
3   To some extent
5   To a great extent

q13d (34) Meeting prestated objectives
    Measurement Level: Ordinal
       Value   Label

         1   Not at all
         3   To some extent
         5   To a great extent

q13e (35) Scope, cost, time
    Measurement Level: Ordinal
       Value   Label

         1   Not at all
         3   To some extent
         5   To a great extent

q13f (36) Satisfaction of team
    Measurement Level: Ordinal
       Value   Label

         1   Not at all
         3   To some extent
         5   To a great extent

q14 (37) Failure / Success
    Measurement Level: Nominal
       Value   Label

         1   Neither success nor failure
         2   Success
         3   Failure

q16 (38) Contribution of project risk management
    Measurement Level: Ordinal
       Value   Label

         1   Not at all
         3   To some extent
         5   To a great extent

Paired samples t-test

T-Test - Mean comparisons between confidence variables

Paired Samples Statistics

		Mean	N	Std. Deviation	Std. Error Mean
Pair 1	Confidence State	3.67	79	1.022	.115
	Confidence Effect	3.87	79	.939	.106
Pair 2	Confidence State	3.67	79	1.022	.115
	Confidence Response	3.73	79	1.059	.119
Pair 3	Confidence Effect	3.87	79	.939	.106
	Confidence Response	3.73	79	1.059	.119

Paired Samples Correlations

		N	Correlation	Sig.
Pair 1	Confidence State & Confidence Effect	79	.664	.000
Pair 2	Confidence State & Confidence Response	79	.511	.000
Pair 3	Confidence Effect & Confidence Response	79	.662	.000

T-Test - Mean comparisons of outcome variables

Paired Samples Statistics

		Mean	N	Std. Deviation	Std. Error Mean
Pair 1	Achievement Purpose	4.13	101	1.007	.100
	Benefit owner	4.10	101	.995	.099
Pair 2	Achievement Purpose	4.13	101	1.007	.100
	Satisfaction owner, users, stakeholders	3.93	101	1.125	.112
Pair 3	Achievement Purpose	4.13	101	1.007	.100
	Meeting prestated objectives	3.83	101	1.201	.119
Pair 4	Achievement Purpose	4.13	101	1.007	.100
	Scope, cost, time	3.21	101	1.252	.125
Pair 5	Achievement Purpose	4.13	101	1.007	.100
	Scope, cost, time	3.21	101	1.252	.125
Pair 6	Achievement Purpose	4.13	101	1.007	.100
	Satisfaction team	3.81	101	.997	.099
Pair 7	Benefit owner	4.10	101	.995	.099
	Satisfaction owner, users, stakeholders	3.93	101	1.125	.112
Pair 8	Benefit owner	4.10	101	.995	.099
	Meeting prestated objectives	3.83	101	1.201	.119
Pair 9	Benefit owner	4.10	101	.995	.099
	Scope, cost, time	3.21	101	1.252	.125
Pair 10	Benefit owner	4.10	101	.995	.099
	Satisfaction team	3.81	101	.997	.099
Pair 11	Satisfaction owner, users, stakeholders	3.93	101	1.125	.112
	Meeting prestated objectives	3.83	101	1.201	.119
Pair 12	Satisfaction owner, users, stakeholders	3.93	101	1.125	.112
	Scope, cost, time	3.21	101	1.252	.125
Pair 13	Satisfaction owner, users, stakeholders	3.93	101	1.125	.112
	Satisfaction team	3.81	101	.997	.099
Pair 14	Meeting prestated objectives	3.83	101	1.201	.119
	Scope, cost, time	3.21	101	1.252	.125
Pair 15	Meeting prestated objectives	3.83	101	1.201	.119
	Satisfaction team	3.81	101	.997	.099

Paired Samples Correlations

		N	Correlation	Sig.
Pair 1	Achievement Purpose & Benefit owner	101	.766	.000
Pair 2	Achievement Purpose & Satisfaction owner, users, stakeholders	101	.732	.000
Pair 3	Achievement Purpose & Meeting prestated objectives	101	.746	.000
Pair 4	Achievement Purpose & Scope, cost, time	101	.542	.000
Pair 5	Achievement Purpose & Scope, cost, time	101	.542	.000
Pair 6	Achievement Purpose & Satisfaction team	101	.592	.000
Pair 7	Benefit owner & Satisfaction owner, users, stakeholders	101	.792	.000
Pair 8	Benefit owner & Meeting prestated objectives	101	.541	.000
Pair 9	Benefit owner & Scope, cost, time	101	.417	.000
Pair 10	Benefit owner & Satisfaction team	101	.553	.000
Pair 11	Satisfaction owner, users, stakeholders & Meeting prestated objectives	101	.643	.000
Pair 12	Satisfaction owner, users, stakeholders & Scope, cost, time	101	.415	.000
Pair 13	Satisfaction owner, users, stakeholders & Satisfaction team	101	.523	.000
Pair 14	Meeting prestated objectives & Scope, cost, time	101	.682	.000
Pair 15	Meeting prestated objectives & Satisfaction team	101	.616	.000

Paired Samples Test

		Paired Differences							
				Std. Error	95% Confidence Interval of the Difference				
		Mean	Std. Deviation	Mean	Lower	Upper	t	df	Sig. (2-tailed)
Pair 1	Achievement Pur Benefit owner	.030	.685	.068	-.106	.165	.436	100	.664
Pair 2	Achievement Pur Satisfaction owne stakeholders	.198	.788	.078	.043	.354	2.527	100	.013
Pair 3	Achievement Pur Meeting prestate objectives	.297	.807	.080	.138	.456	3.700	100	.000
Pair 4	Achievement Pur Scope, cost, time	.921	1.102	.110	.703	1.138	8.400	100	.000
Pair 5	Achievement Pur Scope, cost, time	.921	1.102	.110	.703	1.138	8.400	100	.000
Pair 6	Achievement Pur Satisfaction team	.317	.905	.090	.138	.495	3.519	100	.001
Pair 7	Benefit owner - Satisfaction owne stakeholders	.168	.694	.069	.031	.305	2.438	100	.017
Pair 8	Benefit owner - M prestated objecti	.267	1.067	.106	.057	.478	2.519	100	.013
Pair 9	Benefit owner - S cost, time	.891	1.232	.123	.648	1.134	7.268	100	.000
Pair 10	Benefit owner - Satisfaction team	.287	.942	.094	.101	.473	3.064	100	.003
Pair 11	Satisfaction owne stakeholders - Me prestated objecti	.099	.985	.098	-.095	.293	1.010	100	.315
Pair 12	Satisfaction owne stakeholders - Sc cost, time	.723	1.289	.128	.468	.977	5.634	100	.000
Pair 13	Satisfaction owne stakeholders - Satisfaction team	.119	1.042	.104	-.087	.325	1.146	100	.255
Pair 14	Meeting prestate objectives - Scop time	.624	.978	.097	.431	.817	6.408	100	.000
Pair 15	Meeting prestate objectives - Satis team	.020	.980	.097	-.174	.213	.203	100	.839

T-Test - Mean comparison of overestimation of uncertainty variables

Paired Samples Statistics

		Mean	N	Std. Deviation	Std. Error Mean
Pair 1	Overestimation state uncertainty	2.99	79	1.182	.133
	Overestimation effect uncertainty	2.53	79	1.309	.147
Pair 2	Overestimation state uncertainty	2.99	79	1.182	.133
	Overestimation response uncertainty	3.34	79	1.319	.148
Pair 3	Overestimation effect uncertainty	2.53	79	1.309	.147
	Overestimation response uncertainty	3.34	79	1.319	.148

Paired Samples Correlations

		N	Correlation	Sig.
Pair 1	Overestimation state uncertainty & Overestimation effect uncertainty	79	.427	.000
Pair 2	Overestimation state uncertainty & Overestimation response uncertainty	79	.323	.004
Pair 3	Overestimation effect uncertainty & Overestimation response uncertainty	79	.391	.000

T-Test - Mean comparison of underestimation of uncertainty variables

Paired Samples Statistics

		Mean	N	Std. Deviation	Std. Error Mean
Pair 1	Underestimation effect uncertainty	2.97	78	1.289	.146
	Underestimation state uncertainty	3.09	78	1.083	.123
Pair 2	Underestimation response uncertainty	3.08	78	1.493	.169
	Underestimation state uncertainty	3.09	78	1.083	.123
Pair 3	Underestimation effect uncertainty	2.97	78	1.289	.146
	Underestimation response uncertainty	3.08	78	1.493	.169

Paired Samples Correlations

		N	Correlation	Sig.
Pair 1	Underestimation effect uncertainty & Underestimation state uncertainty	78	.309	.006
Pair 2	Underestimation response uncertainty & Underestimation state uncertainty	78	.253	.026
Pair 3	Underestimation effect uncertainty & Underestimation response uncertainty	78	.271	.016

T-Test - Mean comparisons of risk mediators variables

Paired Samples Statistics

		Mean	N	Std. Deviation	Std. Error Mean
Pair 1	Denial of uncertainty	3.63	76	1.130	.130
	Ignoring uncertainty	2.96	76	1.205	.138
Pair 2	Denial of uncertainty	3.63	76	1.130	.130
	Avoidance of uncertainty	2.66	76	1.195	.137
Pair 3	Denial of uncertainty	3.63	76	1.130	.130
	Delay of uncertainty	3.17	76	1.237	.142
Pair 4	Denial of uncertainty	3.63	76	1.130	.130
	Being ignorant of uncertainty	3.12	76	1.265	.145
Pair 5	Ignoring uncertainty	2.96	76	1.205	.138
	Avoidance of uncertainty	2.66	76	1.195	.137
Pair 6	Ignoring uncertainty	2.96	76	1.205	.138
	Delay of uncertainty	3.17	76	1.237	.142
Pair 7	Ignoring uncertainty	2.96	76	1.205	.138
	Being ignorant of uncertainty	3.12	76	1.265	.145
Pair 8	Avoidance of uncertainty	2.66	76	1.195	.137
	Delay of uncertainty	3.17	76	1.237	.142
Pair 9	Avoidance of uncertainty	2.66	76	1.195	.137
	Being ignorant of uncertainty	3.12	76	1.265	.145
Pair 10	Delay of uncertainty	3.17	76	1.237	.142
	Ignorance of uncertainty (unaware)	3.12	76	1.265	.145

Paired Samples Correlations

		N	Correlation	Sig.
Pair 1	Denial of uncertainty & Ignoring uncertainty	76	.068	.562
Pair 2	Denial of uncertainty & Avoidance of uncertainty	76	.113	.332
Pair 3	Denial of uncertainty & Delay of uncertainty	76	.046	.695
Pair 4	Denial of uncertainty & Being ignorant of uncertainty	76	-.090	.437
Pair 5	Ignoring uncertainty & Avoidance of uncertainty	76	.222	.054
Pair 6	Ignoring uncertainty & Delay of uncertainty	76	.461	.000
Pair 7	Ignoring uncertainty & Being ignorant of uncertainty	76	.292	.011
Pair 8	Avoidance of uncertainty & Delay of uncertainty	76	.257	.025
Pair 9	Avoidance of uncertainty & Being ignorant of uncertainty	76	.265	.021
Pair 10	Delay of uncertainty & Being ignorant of uncertainty	76	.473	.000

Paired Samples Test

		Paired Differences							
					95% Confidence Interval of the Difference				
		Mean	Std. Deviatio	Std. Error Mean	Lower	Upper	t	df	Sig. (2-tailed
Pair 1	Denial of uncertai Ignoring uncertain	.671	1.595	.183	.307	1.036	3.668	75	.000
Pair 2	Denial of uncertai Avoidance of unce	.974	1.549	.178	.620	1.328	5.480	75	.000
Pair 3	Denial of uncertai Delay of uncertain	.461	1.637	.188	.087	.835	2.453	75	.016
Pair 4	Denial of uncertai Being ignorant of uncertainty	.513	1.770	.203	.109	.918	2.527	75	.014
Pair 5	Ignoring uncertain Avoidance of unce	.303	1.497	.172	-.039	.645	1.763	75	.082
Pair 6	Ignoring uncertain Delay of uncertain	-.211	1.268	.145	-.500	.079	-1.447	75	.152
Pair 7	Ignoring uncertain Being ignorant of uncertainty	-.158	1.470	.169	-.494	.178	-.936	75	.352
Pair 8	Avoidance of unce - Delay of uncerta	-.513	1.483	.170	-.852	-.174	-3.016	75	.003
Pair 9	Avoidance of unce - Being ignorant of uncertainty	-.461	1.492	.171	-.801	-.120	-2.691	75	.009
Pair 10	Delay of uncertain Being ignorant of uncertainty	.053	1.285	.147	-.241	.346	.357	75	.722

Factor analysis

Factor Analysis project outcome variables

Total Variance Explained

Component	Initial Eigenvalues			Extraction Sums of Squared Loadings		
	Total	% of Variance	Cumulative %	Total	% of Variance	Cumulative %
1	4.059	67.646	67.646	4.059	67.646	67.646
2	.798	13.307	80.954			
3	.449	7.484	88.438			
4	.313	5.219	93.657			
5	.246	4.096	97.754			
6	.135	2.246	100.000			

Extraction Method: Principal Component Analysis.

Component Matrix[a]

	Component
	1
Outcome Achievement Purpose	.897
Outcome Prestated Objectives	.859
Outcome Satisfaction owner, users, stake.	.841
Outcome satisf. benefit customer	.832
Outcome satisfy Needs of Team	.773
Outcome Scope, Cost Time	.720

Extraction Method: Principal Component Analysis.

a. 1 components extracted.

Communalities

	Initial	Extraction
Outcome Achievement Purpose	1.000	.804
Outcome satisf. benefit customer	1.000	.693
Outcome Satisfaction owner, users, stake.	1.000	.707
Outcome Prestated Objectives	1.000	.738
Outcome Scope, Cost Time	1.000	.518
Outcome satisfy Needs of Team	1.000	.598

Extraction Method: Principal Component Analysis.

Rotated Component Matrix

a. Only one component was extracted.
The solution cannot be rotated.

Factor Analysis over- and underestimation variables

Communalities

	Initial	Extraction
Overestimation State	1.000	.506
Underestimation Effect	1.000	.496
Overestimation Effect	1.000	.709
Overestimation Response	1.000	.562
Underestimation Response	1.000	.489
Underestimation State	1.000	.819

Extraction Method: Principal Component Analysis.

Total Variance Explained

Compon	Initial Eigenvalues			ction Sums of Squared Loa			tion Sums of Squared Load		
	Total	of Varian	umulative	Total	of Varian	umulative	Total	of Varian	umulative
1	2.270	37.836	37.836	2.270	37.836	37.836	1.937	32.289	32.289
2	1.311	21.845	59.680	1.311	21.845	59.680	1.644	27.392	59.680
3	.945	15.746	75.427						
4	.706	11.774	87.201						
5	.442	7.361	94.562						
6	.326	5.438	100.000						

Extraction Method: Principal Component Analysis.

Component Matrix[a]

	Component	
	1	2
Overestimation State	.712	-.001
Underestimation Effect	.675	.202
Overestimation Response	.671	-.333
Overestimation Effect	.644	-.542
Underestimation Response	.611	.340
Underestimation State	.265	.865

Extraction Method: Principal Component Analysis.

a. 2 components extracted.

Rotated Component Matrix[a]

	Component	
	1	2
Overestimation Effect	.840	-.059
Overestimation Response	.739	.126
Overestimation State	.576	.418
Underestimation State	-.295	.856
Underestimation Response	.293	.635
Underestimation Effect	.427	.561

Extraction Method: Principal Component Analysis.
Rotation Method: Varimax with Kaiser Normalization.

a. Rotation converged in 3 iterations.

Component Transformation Matrix

Component	1	2
1	.808	.589
2	-.589	.808

Extraction Method: Principal Component Analysis.
Rotation Method: Varimax with Kaiser Normalization.

Factor Analysis perceived effectiveness variables

Communalities

	Initial	Extraction
Effectiveness identification risk	1.000	.598
Effectiveness attach probabilities	1.000	.510
Effectiveness define effects	1.000	.680
Effectiveness define response alternatives	1.000	.579
Effectiveness determine response ownership	1.000	.640
Effectiveness determine best response	1.000	.557
Effectivness execute actions	1.000	.551

Extraction Method: Principal Component Analysis.

Total Variance Explained

Component	Initial Eigenvalues			Extraction Sums of Squared Loadings		
	Total	% of Variance	Cumulative %	Total	% of Variance	Cumulative %
1	4.115	58.785	58.785	4.115	58.785	58.785
2	.967	13.817	72.601			
3	.731	10.443	83.045			
4	.370	5.287	88.331			
5	.329	4.698	93.030			
6	.266	3.795	96.824			
7	.222	3.176	100.000			

Extraction Method: Principal Component Analysis.

Component Matrix[a]

	Component 1
Effectiveness identification risk	.773
Effectiveness attach probabilities	.714
Effectiveness define effects	.825
Effectiveness define response alternatives	.761
Effectiveness determine response ownership	.800
Effectiveness determine best response	.747
Effectivness execute actions	.742

Extraction Method: Principal Component Analysis.

a. 1 components extracted.

Rotated Component Matrix[a]

a. Only one component was extracted.
The solution cannot be rotated.

Factor Analysis risk mediators variables

Communalities

	Initial	Extraction
Denial	1.000	.883
Ignoring	1.000	.507
Avoidance	1.000	.398
Delay	1.000	.661
Being ignorant	1.000	.627

Extraction Method: Principal Component Analysis.

Total Variance Explained

Compone	Initial Eigenvalues			Extraction Sums of Squared Loadin			Rotation Sums of Squared Loadin		
	Total	of Varianc	umulative %	Total	of Varianc	umulative %	Total	of Varianc	umulative %
1	2.009	40.178	40.178	2.009	40.178	40.178	2.000	39.999	39.999
2	1.066	21.328	61.507	1.066	21.328	61.507	1.075	21.507	61.507
3	.810	16.192	77.699						
4	.652	13.049	90.747						
5	.463	9.253	100.000						

Extraction Method: Principal Component Analysis.

Component Matrix[a]

	Component	
	1	2
Delay	.810	-.065
Being ignorant	.725	-.317
Ignoring	.709	.064
Avoidance	.562	.286
Denial	.082	.936

Extraction Method: Principal Component Analysis.
a. 2 components extracted.

Rotated Component Matrix[a]

	Component	
	1	2
Delay	.813	.014
Being ignorant	.753	-.244
Ignoring	.700	.132
Avoidance	.532	.339
Denial	-.010	.940

Extraction Method: Principal Component Analysis.
Rotation Method: Varimax with Kaiser Normalization.
a. Rotation converged in 3 iterations.

Component Transformation Matrix

Component	1	2
1	.995	.097
2	-.097	.995

Extraction Method: Principal Component Analysis.
Rotation Method: Varimax with Kaiser Normalization.

Reliability analysis

Reliability of project outcome composite

Case Processing Summary

		N	%
Cases	Valid	101	99.0
	Excluded[a]	1	1.0
	Total	102	100.0

a. Listwise deletion based on all variables in the procedure.

Reliability Statistics

Cronbach's Alpha	N of Items
.899	6

Reliability of overestimation of uncertainty composite

Case Processing Summary

		N	%
Cases	Valid	79	77.5
	Excluded[a]	23	22.5
	Total	102	100.0

a. Listwise deletion based on all variables in the procedure.

Reliability Statistics

Cronbach's Alpha	N of Items
.647	3

Reliability of underestimation of uncertainty composite

Case Processing Summary

		N	%
Cases	Valid	78	76.5
	Excluded[a]	24	23.5
	Total	102	100.0

a. Listwise deletion based on all variables in the procedure.

Reliability Statistics

Cronbach's Alpha	N of Items
.524	3

Reliability of perceived effectiveness composite 1

Case Processing Summary

		N	%
Cases	Valid	80	78.4
	Excluded[a]	22	21.6
	Total	102	100.0

a. Listwise deletion based on all variables in the procedure.

Reliability Statistics

Cronbach's Alpha	N of Items
.875	7

Reliability of risk mediators composite

Case Processing Summary

		N	%
Cases	Valid	76	74.5
	Excluded[a]	26	25.5
	Total	102	100.0

a. Listwise deletion based on all variables in the procedure.

Reliability Statistics

Cronbach's Alpha	N of Items
.663	4

Multiple regressions

Variables Entered/Removed[b]

Model	Variables Entered	Variables Removed	Method
1	Risk mediators composite [a]	.	Enter

a. All requested variables entered.

b. Dependent Variable: Overestimation of uncertainty composite

Model Summary

					Change Statistics				
Model	R	R Square	Adjusted R Square	Std. Error of the Estimate	R Square Change	F Change	df1	df2	Sig. F Change
1	.111[a]	.012	-.001	.974	.012	.959	1	77	.330

a. Predictors: (Constant), Risk mediators composite

ANOVA[b]

Model		Sum of Squares	df	Mean Square	F	Sig.
1	Regression	.910	1	.910	.959	.330[a]
	Residual	73.031	77	.948		
	Total	73.941	78			

a. Predictors: (Constant), Risk mediators composite

b. Dependent Variable: Overestimation of uncertainty composite

Coefficients[a]

Model		Unstandardized Coefficients		Standardized Coefficients	t	Sig.
		B	Std. Error	Beta		
1	(Constant)	2.576	.401		6.428	.000
	Risk mediators composite	.127	.129	.111	.979	.330

a. Dependent Variable: Overestimation of uncertainty composite

Variables Entered/Removed[b]

Model	Variables Entered	Variables Removed	Method
1	Risk mediators composite [a]	.	Enter

a. All requested variables entered.

b. Dependent Variable: Underestimation of uncertainty composite

Model Summary

Model	R	R Square	Adjusted R Square	Std. Error of the Estimate	Change Statistics				
					R Square Change	F Change	df1	df2	Sig. F Change
1	.417[a]	.174	.164	.853	.174	16.252	1	77	.000

a. Predictors: (Constant), Risk mediators composite

ANOVA[b]

Model		Sum of Squares	df	Mean Square	F	Sig.
1	Regression	11.834	1	11.834	16.252	.000[a]
	Residual	56.065	77	.728		
	Total	67.899	78			

a. Predictors: (Constant), Risk mediators composite

b. Dependent Variable: Underestimation of uncertainty composite

Coefficients[a]

Model		Unstandardized Coefficients		Standardized Coefficients	t	Sig.
		B	Std. Error	Beta		
1	(Constant)	1.898	.351		5.407	.000
	Risk mediators composite	.456	.113	.417	4.031	.000

a. Dependent Variable: Underestimation of uncertainty composite

Variables Entered/Removed[b]

Model	Variables Entered	Variables Removed	Method
1	Risk mediators composite[a]	.	Enter

a. All requested variables entered.

b. Dependent Variable: Perceived effectiveness composite

Model Summary

Model	R	R Square	Adjusted R Square	Std. Error of the Estimate	R Square Change	F Change	df1	df2	Sig. F Change
					Change Statistics				
1	.556[a]	.309	.300	.702	.309	34.393	1	77	.000

a. Predictors: (Constant), Risk mediators composite

ANOVA[b]

Model		Sum of Squares	df	Mean Square	F	Sig.
1	Regression	16.927	1	16.927	34.393	.000[a]
	Residual	37.897	77	.492		
	Total	54.824	78			

a. Predictors: (Constant), Risk mediators composite

b. Dependent Variable: Perceived effectiveness composite

Coefficients[a]

Model		Unstandardized Coefficients		Standardized Coefficients	t	Sig.
		B	Std. Error	Beta		
1	(Constant)	5.109	.289		17.700	.000
	Risk mediators composite	-.546	.093	-.556	-5.865	.000

a. Dependent Variable: Perceived effectiveness composite

Variables Entered/Removed[b]

Model	Variables Entered	Variables Removed	Method
1	Perceived effectivene ss composite[a]	.	Enter

a. All requested variables entered.

b. Dependent Variable: Project outcome composite

Model Summary

Model	R	R Square	Adjusted R Square	Std. Error of the Estimate	Change Statistics				
					R Square Change	F Change	df1	df2	Sig. F Change
1	.596[a]	.355	.347	.722	.355	43.521	1	79	.000

a. Predictors: (Constant), Perceived effectiveness composite

ANOVA[b]

Model		Sum of Squares	df	Mean Square	F	Sig.
1	Regression	22.690	1	22.690	43.521	.000[a]
	Residual	41.187	79	.521		
	Total	63.878	80			

a. Predictors: (Constant), Perceived effectiveness composite

b. Dependent Variable: Project outcome composite

Coefficients[a]

Model		Unstandardized Coefficients		Standardized Coefficients	t	Sig.
		B	Std. Error	Beta		
1	(Constant)	1.623	.345		4.709	.000
	Perceived effectivenes composite	.635	.096	.596	6.597	.000

a. Dependent Variable: Project outcome composite

Variables Entered/Removed[b]

Model	Variables Entered	Variables Removed	Method
1	Overestim ation of uncertainty composite, Perceived effectivene ss composite[a]	.	Enter

a. All requested variables entered.

b. Dependent Variable: Project outcome composite

Model Summary

Model	R	R Square	Adjusted R Square	Std. Error of the Estimate	Change Statistics				
					R Square Change	F Change	df1	df2	Sig. F Change
1	.654[a]	.428	.413	.684	.428	28.467	2	76	.000

a. Predictors: (Constant), Overestimation of uncertainty composite, Perceived effectiveness composite

ANOVA[b]

Model		Sum of Squares	df	Mean Square	F	Sig.
1	Regression	26.674	2	13.337	28.467	.000[a]
	Residual	35.607	76	.469		
	Total	62.281	78			

a. Predictors: (Constant), Overestimation of uncertainty composite, Perceived effectiveness composite

b. Dependent Variable: Project outcome composite

Coefficients[a]

Model		Unstandardized Coefficients		Standardized Coefficients	t	Sig.
		B	Std. Error	Beta		
1	(Constant)	.869	.410		2.119	.037
	Perceived effectiveness composite	.641	.092	.602	6.937	.000
	Overestimation of uncertainty composite	.248	.080	.270	3.117	.003

a. Dependent Variable: Project outcome composite

Variables Entered/Removed[b]

Model	Variables Entered	Variables Removed	Method
1	Underesti mation of uncertainty composite, Perceived effectivene ss composite , Overestim ation of uncertainty[a] composite	.	Enter

a. All requested variables entered.

b. Dependent Variable: Project outcome composite

Model Summary

Model	R	R Square	Adjusted R Square	Std. Error of the Estimate	R Square Change	F Change	df1	df2	Sig. F Change
1	.706[a]	.498	.478	.646	.498	24.780	3	75	.000

a. Predictors: (Constant), Underestimation of uncertainty composite, Perceived effectiveness composi uncertainty composite

ANOVA[b]

Model		Sum of Squares	df	Mean Square	F	Sig.
1	Regression	31.003	3	10.334	24.780	.000[a]
	Residual	31.278	75	.417		
	Total	62.281	78			

a. Predictors: (Constant), Underestimation of uncertainty composite, Perceived effectiveness composite , Overestimation of uncertainty composite

b. Dependent Variable: Project outcome composite

Coefficients[a]

Model		Unstandardized Coefficients		Standardized Coefficients	t	Sig.
		B	Std. Error	Beta		
1	(Constant)	2.361	.603		3.913	.000
	Perceived effectiveness composite	.402	.115	.377	3.501	.001
	Overestimation of uncertainty composite	.486	.105	.530	4.614	.000
	Underestimation of uncertainty composite	-.417	.130	-.436	-3.222	.002

a. Dependent Variable: Project outcome composite

GLOSSARY

Terms which are used as part of a definition and which are defined in the glossary are shown in *italics*.

Case	System with boundaries or a relatively complete organisational unit.
Computer Service Provider (CSP)	Individuals or organisations commercially conducting an *IT project*.
Consequence	A result of *risks* to negatively effect *project performance*.
Constructionism	The philosophical assumptions which assert that the world is socially constructed and subjective; that the observer is part of what is observed; and that science is driven by human interest.
Data	Specific information, which may or may not be meaningful.
Effect Uncertainty	Incomplete knowledge about the effect of a future state of the environment.
Effect	See *consequence*.
Effectiveness	Successful in producing the desired *effect*. Outcome of expectations and actual result.
Epistemology	An inquiry into how it is possible for people to know things. It addresses the question: What is the nature of the relationship between the knower (the inquirer) and the known (or knowable)?
Estimate	An assessment of the likely result.
Experiment	*Research method* to gather *data* by observation of a tightly predefined range of variables under controlled conditions.

Explanatory Research	Research focusing on the relationships between variables.
Exploratory Research	Research focusing on discovery and a thorough examination of a phenomenon.
Extant Risk	Well specified and clarified uncertainty, not vague.
Fieldwork	The investigation in a "real" context as opposed to an investigation in a laboratory or virtual setting.
Generalisability	The extent to which findings can be applied in other research settings.
Grounded Theory	Process of analytic induction.
Historical Review	*Research method* to describe what happened in the past.
Impact	See *consequence.*
Information Technology Project (IT project)	The provision of a service to implement systems and solutions, including a variety of hardware and software products.
Likelihood	See *Probability.*
Methodology	The analysis of and rationale for using a particular *research method.*
Mitigation	See *Risk Response action.*
Modifying Factor	Factor to increase or decrease the *probability* of a *threat* becoming a reality or the probable consequence of such a reality.
Objective Risk	Quantifiable *risk* based on frequencies.
Odds	The ratio of probabilities of occurrence or non-occurrence (e.g.,

the odds of getting a 4 on the throw of a single die are 5 to 1).

Ontology An inquiry into what is the nature of "reality". It addresses the question: What is the nature of the "knowable"?

Overestimation of *Uncertainty* has been identified but has not actually
Risk materialised, or *probability* and/or *consequence* of identified *uncertainty* has been assessed as higher than its actual value.

Perceived Risk The outcome of *risk perception*.

Population A complete set of people, occurrences or objects from which a *sample* will be drawn.

Positivism The philosophical assumptions which underlie hypothetico-deductive method, which assert that this paradigm is the only rational way of knowing things; that the purpose of theory is application; that truth can always be distinguished from untruth; and that truth can be discerned either by deduction or by empirical support and by no other means.

Prime contractor An individual, partnership, corporation, or association that administers a subcontract to design, develop, and/or manufacture one or more products and services.

Probability The *likelihood* the risk will occur. The *risk assessment* of a probability may be expressed in Qualitative and Quantitative terms.

Process A set of activities performed for a given purpose.

Project Temporary undertaking to create a unique product or service.

Project Failure Excepted benefits such as of scope, cost and time are not met.

Project Management The application of knowledge, skills, tools, and techniques to *project* activities to meet the *project* requirements.

Project Manager	The individual who directs, controls, administers, and regulates a *project* acquiring software, a hardware/software system, or services. The *project manager* is the individual ultimately responsible for the *project*.
Project Risk	Anything that causes the actual *project* outcomes of cost, scope and time to deviate from their estimated value.
Project Risk Management	The systematic *process* of identifying, analysing, and responding to *project uncertainty* with the potential of an adverse *consequence* on a *project* objective.
Project Success	Excepted benefits of scope, cost and time are met.
Reliability	The precision of measurement, such that the same result would be obtained on re-measurement.
Research Method	A systematic and orderly approach towards the collection of *data* so that information can be obtained from those data. Not to be confused with *methodology*.
Research Technique	A step-by-step procedure for gathering and analysing *data*.
Residual Risk	Any *project risk*, which was not eliminated or transferred through a *risk response action*.
Resources	Components of a *project* such as budget, personal and material that could be affected by a *threat*.
Response Uncertainty	Incomplete knowledge about response alternatives and their possible *consequence*.
Risk	An uncertain event or condition which, if it occurs, has a negative effect on a *project*'s objectives. See *Uncertainty*
Risk Actors	Stakeholders directly or indirectly involved in the process of managing *risk*.

Risk Analysis	Measuring the *probability* and *consequence* of *risk* and assessing their implications for *project* objectives.
Risk Assessment	*Risk analysis* that includes estimating and evaluating *risk consequences*.
Risk Event	See *threat*.
Risk Identification	Determining which *risks* might affect the *project* and documenting their characteristics.
Risk Management Planning	Deciding how to approach and plan *project risk management* activities.
Risk Monitoring and Control	Monitoring residual *risk*, identifying new *risk*, executing *risk* reduction plans, and evaluating their *effectiveness* throughout the project.
Risk Perception	The combination of sensations related to *risk*.
Risk Register	A list of the *project risks*.
Risk Response Planning	Developing procedures and techniques to reduce *threats* to *project* objectives.
Risk Response Action	This is an activity which management may decide to implement with the intention of *mitigating* a *risk* (reducing *probability* and / or *impact*).
Sample	A set of people, occurrences or objects chosen from a larger *population*.
Stakeholder	Individuals and organisations that are indirectly or directly involved in the *project*, or whose interests may be positively or negatively affected as a result of *project* execution or *project* completion. They may also exert influence over the *project* and

its results.

Subjective Risk	Qualitative *risk* based on social construction and reconstruction.
State Uncertainty	Incomplete knowledge about the state of the environment.
Survey	*Research method* to establish people's views of what they think, believe, value or feel, in order to discover these views for their own sake, or to support an argument which is presented, *sampling* a *population* of potential respondents in order to generalise conclusions more widely.
Theory	Generally, a belief expressed in words and action.
Threat	Source of danger that may affect the outcome of a *project*.
Uncertainty	Condition characterised by incomplete knowledge.
Underestimation of Risk	*Uncertainty* with probable negative effects has not been identified but may actually materialise, or *probability* and/or *consequence* of identified *uncertainty* has been assessed as lower than their actual value.
Validity	The accuracy of measurement such that the process or event being measured is indeed properly measured.

State Uncertainty   Incomplete knowledge about the state of the environment.

Survey   *Research method* to establish people's views of what they think, believe, value or feel, in order to discover these views for their own sake, or to support an argument which is presented, *sampling* a *population* of potential respondents in order to generalise conclusions more widely.

Theory   Generally, a belief expressed in words and action.

Threat   Source of danger that may affect the outcome of a *project*.

Uncertainty   Condition characterised by incomplete knowledge.

Underestimation of Risk   *Uncertainty* with probable negative effects has not been identified but may actually materialise, or *probability* and/or *consequence* of identified *uncertainty* has been assessed as lower than their actual value.

Validity   The accuracy of measurement such that the process or event being measured is indeed properly measured.

www.ingramcontent.com/pod-product-compliance
Lightning Source LLC
Chambersburg PA
CBHW071355050326
40689CB00010B/1653